MAYA INTELLECTUAL RENAISSANCE

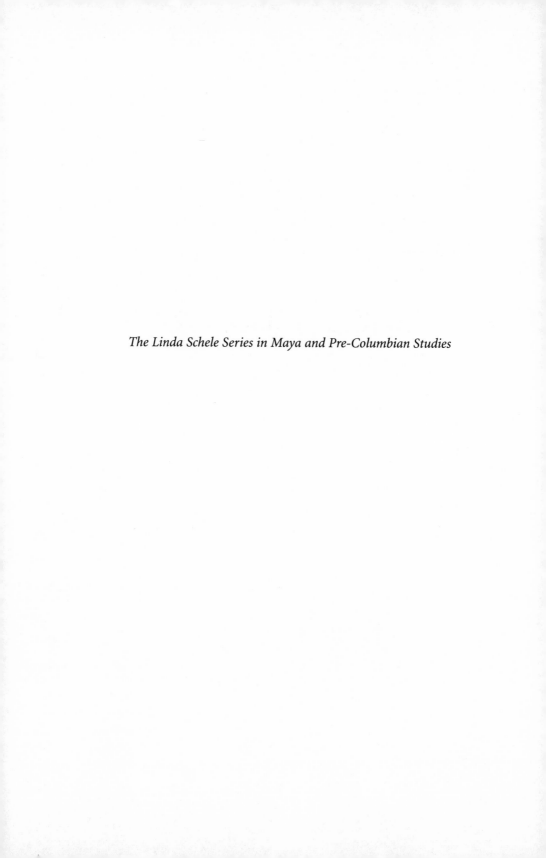

The Linda Schele Series in Maya and Pre-Columbian Studies

Maya Intellectual *Renaissance*

IDENTITY, REPRESENTATION, AND LEADERSHIP

Victor D. Montejo

UNIVERSITY OF TEXAS PRESS ▼ AUSTIN

Library of Congress Cataloging-in-Publication Data

Montejo, Victor, 1951-
Maya intellectual renaissance : identity, representation, and
leadership / Victor D. Montejo. — 1st ed.
p. cm. — (The Linda Schele series in Maya and pre-Columbian studies)
Includes bibliographical references and index.
ISBN 0-292-70684-7 (cloth : alk. paper) — ISBN 0-292-70939-0 (pbk. : alk. paper)
1. Mayas — Intellectual life. 2. Mayas — Ethnic identity. 3. Maya philosophy.
4. Latin America — Ethnic relations. 5. Latin America — Social life and customs.
I. Title. II. Series.
F1435.3.I57M65 2005
305.897′42 — dc22
2005001967

This book is dedicated to the Maya people who produce knowledge,
especially those unknown peasants and spiritual leaders
whose names cannot be registered and remembered
because they did not write their ideas on paper,
but simply lived them and uttered words of
advice and wisdom.
And it is dedicated to those young Maya scholars
who are now beginning to speak to the world about
the persistence of our Maya ways of life and culture.
Let us not forget the teachings of our forefathers,
but rather ignite the pitch-pine torches to illuminate our steps
as we walk together on the road to the future in this new millennium.

This book is also dedicated to the memory of my good friend
and colleague Patrick Morris, with whom I worked hard
for the establishment of the Commission for Human Rights
within the American Anthropological Association.
May he rest in peace,
knowing that this important work continues.

CONTENTS

ACKNOWLEDGMENTS

I would like to acknowledge my mentors and colleagues who have encouraged me to write and participate as a graduate student in national and international conferences and symposia. The short essays in this volume are my own critical views of the past and current situation of the Maya in Guatemala and my concerns for the future. As a Maya, I am involved in the debates concerning the future of Maya culture in the twenty-first century. As a Maya scholar and intellectual, I am responsible for my own statements and my critique of Maya culture and leadership from my own native perspective.

During my years as a graduate student at the State University of New York at Albany and at the University of Connecticut, I began work on several of the essays presented in this volume. I offer special recognition for the advice and influence received from James Farris, Scott Cook, Leigh Binford, Lyle Campbell, Robert Carmack and Gary H. Gossen, Mario Humberto Ruz, and Didier Boremanse. Similarly, I have received encouragement and support from other colleagues whose academic work has influenced me in writing these essays: Stefano Varese, Kay Warren, Mary Louise Pratt, Nora England, Christopher Lutz, Carol Smith, Charles Hale, Richard Adams, Victor Perera, Richard Millet, Ted Fischer, Quetzil Castañeda, and Arturo Arias, among many others.

I am indebted to my Maya friends and colleagues in Guatemala, to whom I have listened and talked about Maya culture and our hopes for a more democratic and peaceful Guatemalan nation. Among these are Luis Enrique Sam Colop, Irma Otzoy, Estuardo Zapeta, Alfredo Tay Coyoy, Rigoberto Quemé Chay, Narciso Cojtí, Rosalina Tuyuc, Manuel Camposeco, Gaspar P. González, Francisco Morales Santos, Maximo Ba', Elia Alvarado, Gamaliel Tevalán, Margarita López Raquec, Carlos Mendoza, Flavio Rojas Lima, Gustavo Porras, and many members of the Academy of Mayan Languages of Guatemala.

In addition, there are many other people to recognize: those who participated in the Maya-Ladino Dialogue workshops that Erick Bolaños and I organized and directed in Guatemala City and Quetzaltenango in 2000. Funding for those conferences came from Mary Deanne Conners and Peter Samson of the Cultural Affairs Office of the United States Embassy in Guatemala. I want to thank the Maya Commission for Peace and Reconciliation, an organization that I helped organize with the support of the nongovernmental organization

(NGO) Incidencia Democrática; Jeff Borns from the U.S. Agency for International Development, a very knowledgeable and caring man, for his useful advice; and Norman Shaifer, director of the Indigenous Media Network.

I am grateful for the financial support received from Dean Elizabeth Langland and Barry Klein, Provost for Academic Research of the University of California, Davis, for a publication award used for the editing and completion of this book. I am privileged to have outstanding colleagues in the Department of Native American Studies, Martha Macri, Inés Hernández-Avila, and Jack Forbes, and I am especially grateful to Stefano Varese who suggested the title for this book. For the editorial work, I am thankful to Fernando Peñalosa, president of the Yax Te' Foundation, to Christopher H. Lutz for financial support for editing services, and to Susan G. Rascón who helped me with translating and editing. Kerin Gould, my research assistant during Spring 2002, also translated parts of the text. Finally, I am deeply indebted to my wife, Mercedes Montejo, for many things, but for this volume she retyped the essays that were impossible to retrieve from old floppy disks used during graduate studies at the State University of New York, Albany, and the University of Connecticut.

Some of the chapters in this volume were presented as separate essays at major conferences in the United States and Guatemala. Four of them have previously been published, and I want to recognize the permission to reprint them here. The essay "Pan-Mayanism and the Multiplicity of Maya Culture" was originally published in a slightly different version in Spanish in the journal *Mesoamérica* (Publicación del Centro de Investigaciones Regionales de Mesoamérica y Plumsock Mesoamerican Studies, Antigua Guatemala y Vermont, No. 33, 1997: 93–123). "Truth, Human Rights, and Representation: The Case of Rigoberta Menchú" appeared in *The Rigoberta Menchú Controversy,* edited by Arturo Arias (University of Minnesota Press, 2001, 372–391). "The Multiplicity of Maya Voices: Maya Leadership and the Politics of Self-Representation" was included in *Indigenous Movements, Self-Representation, and the State in Latin America,* edited by Kay B. Warren and Jean Jackson (University of Texas Press, 2002). The chapter "Maya Ways of Knowing: Modern Maya and the Elders" appeared in a slightly different version in *A Will to Survive,* edited by Stephen Greymorning (McGraw-Hill Publishers, 2004).

I am particularly indebted to the reviewers for the University of Texas Press, Dr. Christopher H. Lutz of Plumsock Mesoamerican Studies and Dr. Kay B. Warren of Brown University, whose thoughtful comments and suggestions for a thorough manuscript revision greatly improved the organization and the readability of this volume. Although I talked with many people and asked for their comments and reactions to these essays, in the final outcome this book contains my personal viewpoints, my analyses, and my criticism. I take full responsibility for the strong opinions and comments expressed in this work.

INTRODUCTION

This book collects essays I have written over the last ten years. Some were contributions to collections of essays, others were presented at national and international conferences. Many of the ideas expressed in these essays first took form when I wrote a column for the Guatemalan newspaper *Siglo Veintiuno*. Taken together they present critical points of view about three issues facing Maya people in Guatemala today: issues of identity, representation, including the right to self-representation, and Maya leadership. Although the essays deal with cultural, political, or spiritual matters rather than the economic aspects of Maya culture, I believe that these themes are important because Mayas need to feel pride in their Maya culture in order to be secure in their personhood and in their nation.

The analyses and comments found here are strictly my own. As a Maya, I am part of the Maya movement, and many of these criticisms touch me as well. I am not free of the charges I have laid here against other people and groups. Throughout the book, I advocate an end to the racist treatment that Mayas experience and the construction of a new interethnic relationship as a means to achieve a more pluralistic Guatemalan nation.

The current process of revitalization of Maya culture serves as the foundation point of these essays and gives us hope for the future, creating new forms of identity beyond the old models of survival and victimization. Our pride in our own heritage and our link with our ancestral past has reconnected the fabric of Maya culture, worn by centuries of neglect.

The task before us is the elimination of racism and discrimination, a first step toward the goal of creating a Guatemala with respectful relationships between Mayas and ladinos and the elimination of economic barriers for the Maya. With economic self-sufficiency and appropriate higher education, indigenous people can shatter the ethnic tension and prejudice against them. Education is one major tool to move toward genuine ethnic reaffirmation and to obtain access to economic and political power in our country, but achieving this is difficult while the Maya majority remains mired in poverty in the most remote rural areas of the country. Past governments have not worried about indigenous people, and have kept them powerless as second-class citizens. And when Mayas criticize their oppressors, they are often accused of being racists or of promoting a reverse racism. Another important tool for us is autocriticism and ethnocriticism. Self-criticism and introspection are necessary to understand ourselves and others as we recognize our failures and achievements, not only as Maya, but as Guatemalans.

Anthropologists and foreign scholars have been closely following this process of revitalization of Maya culture in Guatemala and have written about it, hoping to be of service to the indigenous people they study and with whom they do research. Among the dozens of recent publications on the Maya, I will refer here to those having bearing on the issues of Maya leadership and the pan-Maya movement. These publications indicate much confusion among scholars on the definition of the pan-Maya movement and the delineation of its main actors.

One report on the revitalization of Maya culture written before the signing of the 1996 peace accords is *Unfinished Conquest: The Guatemalan Tragedy* by Victor Perera (1993). Perera wrote about the early (pan-Maya) relationship between Q'anjob'al refugees and Lacandón Maya in Mexico resulting from forced exile and refuge. During the armed conflict in Guatemala, thousands of Maya—Q'anjob'al, Jakaltek, Mam, Akatek and Chuj—came into contact with other Mayan linguistic communities in Chiapas: the Tzotzil, Tzeltal, Lacandon and Tojolabal Maya (Earle 1988, Gossen 1999, Montejo 1999a). These works give evidence that the Mayan linguistic communities across the Mayab', the area occupied by the Mayan-speaking people (past and present), have been in a process of cultural, political, economic, and religious revitalization since that time.

At present, it is impressive to see the literary and academic writings being produced by Maya in Guatemala. The collection of essays *Mayan Cultural Activism in Guatemala,* edited by Edward Fischer and Robert McKenna Brown (1996), presents samples of writings by a few prominent Maya scholars. Many are reprinted from older publications by Maya scholars and intellectuals, including Demetrio Cojtí, an early advocate for a Maya autonomy and nationalism. In its form, vision, and goals, the pan-Maya movement is very complex and multifaceted. Edward Fischer also argued that the pan-Maya movement has economic and sustainable development components with "its potential as an alternative to failed development projects of the past" (Fischer and Brown 1996:52).

The revitalization of Maya culture as a pan-Maya movement in Guatemala is well documented in the ethnographic work by Richard Wilson among the Q'eqchi' Maya of the Verapaces in northern Guatemala. In his book *Mayan*

Resurgence in Guatemala: Q'eqchi' Experiences (1995), Wilson chronicles the current process among the Q'eqchi' as they develop their identity as Maya by affirming a "shared past and a common future" (12). Wilson argues that the revitalization efforts among the Q'eqchi' are based on major symbols of identity, such as the symbolism of mountain spirits (*tzuultaq'a*), as an integral part of Maya religion and spirituality. The importance of religious tradition and Maya *costumbres* as providers of strength to the pan-Maya movement is also reported in Santiago Momostenango by Garrett Cook in his recent ethnography *Renewing the Maya World: Expressive Culture in a Highland Town* (2000).

The best-known work on the issue of Maya leadership and the pan-Maya movement is Kay B. Warren's *Indigenous Movements and Their Critics: Pan-Maya Activism in Guatemala* (1998). This book deals constructively with the current efforts of cultural, political, and intellectual revitalization of Maya culture in Guatemala. This text has been used widely as an authoritative ethnographic report on the current pan-Maya movement and its multiple expressions. Warren's work is an important contribution to Maya studies because it pays attention to the role of several Maya intellectual leaders, where previous works focused primarily on Rigoberta Menchú, one political Maya leader. As Warren suggests, the goal of pan-Maya intellectual leadership is "to undermine the authoritativeness of non-Maya, or *kaxhlan,* accounts—be they Guatemalan ladinos or foreigners—which, until the recent indigenous activism and resistance surfaced, monopolized the representation of Maya culture and national history" (37).

Scholarship about the Guatemalan army and their counter-revolutionary war against the guerrillas includes Jennifer Schirmer's *Guatemalan Military Project: A Violence Called Democracy* (1998). Schirmer argues that the Guatemalan army appropriated Maya symbols to combat the guerrillas and undermine Maya cultural beliefs and traditions. Thus, the army appropriated Maya ideas of pan-Maya unity stemming from the *Popol Vuh,* as if it were an army philosophy, including the following military call: "That you rise up everyone, that you call to everyone; that there is not a group, nor two among us. Everyone forward and no one stays behind" (114–115).

Anthropologist Diane Nelson has also contributed to the literature that deals with the Guatemalan armed conflict, and she too discusses the Maya role and activities in the current revitalization and pan-Maya movement, focusing especially on gender issues. As she interprets the role of Maya leaders, she refers to some of them as "Maya-hackers," a term that she may intend to use to impress readers with the sophistication of Mayas in the use of modern technology

(Nelson 1999b). But the term is not appropriate for the Maya who create and strengthen their identities as Maya producers with their own works and ideas and not by cracking computer codes and messing them up.

Another important work is Susanne Jonas's *Of Centaurs and Doves: Guatemala's Peace Process* (2000). In this volume, Jonas discusses in great detail the Guatemalan peace process and the peace accords. The positive role of Maya leadership is shown in this work, especially its participation in the Assembly of Civil Society (ASC) to establish priorities for the March 1995 discussions on the peace accords. The implementation of the specific accord on "Identity and Rights of Indigenous People" is perhaps the most important goal in the current Maya struggle for self-determination. This accord legally recognizes the different indigenous people living in Guatemala—the Maya, the Xinca, and the Garífuna—as well as the diversity of Maya culture itself. It calls for the protection of cultural rights and indigenous institutions, including the use of indigenous languages, traditional dress, ceremonial centers, sacred places, and Maya spirituality (Jonas 2000).

The Maya struggle for self-determination has persisted throughout the centuries. Different forms of Maya movements, and gender and leadership roles existed in the past. Historian Greg Grandin's book *The Blood of Guatemala: A History of Race and Nation* (2000) describes the role of local leaders in nineteenth-century municipalities and the issues they faced—land, community, politics, labor, and nationalism. Using the example of the K'iche' elite in Quetzaltenango, his book demonstrates that Maya have struggled at every level of society to maintain their distinctiveness and economic prosperity. Their short-term successes have been difficult to replicate for the majority of Maya because many obstacles block the way for their self-representation and self-empowerment.

The visibility of Maya leaders at a national level rose when they opposed the celebration of the quincentenary of the "discovery" of America (1492–1992). This was a period when the popular left organized international gatherings under the title "*Movimiento Nacional: 500 Años de Resistencia Indígena, Negra y Popular*" ("National Movement: 500 Years of Indigenous, Black and Popular Resistance"). Later, they dropped the word "black" from their list and stayed with "indígena y popular." Among the Maya cultural participants, primarily academics, some wrote poems, essays, and even letters to the king of Spain, denouncing the continuous destruction of the Maya people in Guatemala (Montejo and Akab' 1992).

At that time, Carol Smith wrote brief analyses of Maya cultural and political activism, offering insights into the movement on a more theoretical level. Smith rightly suggested that the Maya nationalist project of some Maya leaders during early 1990s started to become more radicalized. "As it takes on a more militant stance, the movement grows ever more apart from earlier forms of Maya resistance, which to date have guaranteed the strength and resilience of Maya culture" (Smith 1991:31). In a recent essay Smith has stated her current views:

> The Maya movement for indigenous revindication, like many such indigenous movements taking place today, has engaged many Maya who were not intellectual (or even literate), who did not leave written views or "archives," and thus did not leave a simple trail for us to trace. (Smith n.d.)

Her assertion is very important. We cannot forget those Maya who patiently work in their communities, telling stories and promoting the values of their cultures so that young Maya learn more about their histories and strengthen their identities. As Smith indicates, some may not leave traces of their knowledge or write about their views, but if we read the work of ethnographers, we see that elders and community leaders are constantly interviewed, and their voices are represented in these ethnographies. Smith is correct. There are thousands of unknown local leaders working for the revitalization of Maya culture who remain invisible to reporters and to those who write and produce written records for posterity. Unfortunately we cannot meet each individual. We can only see and document the contributions of those who have left indelible footprints during their lives, as they wrote, published, or promoted the revitalization of Maya culture.

Although *I, Rigoberta Menchú* (1984a), dictated to Elizabeth Burgos-Debray, has recently stirred up much turmoil in academia, it is also a contribution to the general pan-Maya movement of cultural reaffirmation and the survival of Maya people in Guatemala. In a similar way, my early works *Q'anil: The Man of Lightning* (Montejo 1984, 1999b) and *The Bird Who Cleans the World and Other Mayan Fables* (1991) represent an effort to maintain the creativity of the Maya and to rewrite Maya history. Later works such as *Testimony: Death of a Guatemalan Village* (Montejo 1987) and *Voices from Exile: Violence and Survival in Modern Maya History* (Montejo 1999a) are efforts to denounce the violence and massacres that were committed against the Maya, promote a pan-Maya consciousness, and stress the importance of self-representation.

Many scholars are also aware of the editorial and controversial journalistic works of anthropologist Estuardo Zapeta. In his collection of articles *Las Huellas de Balam* (The Jaguar's Footprints, 1999), Zapeta presents a critical analysis of the national situation in which the Maya play a weak role as a result of their internal divisions and the lack of real leadership. Another scholar and journalist engaged in the revitalization of Maya culture and in promoting the presence of Maya in the national arena is Enrique Sam Colop, whose poetic rendition of the *Popol Vuh* serves as a symbol for the Maya literary renaissance in Guatemala. The quincentenary of the "discovery" was described by Sam Colop in 1991 as the *500 Años de Encubrimiento* (500 Years of Cover-Up). Other academic works important to mention are *Cultura Maya y Políticas de Desarrollo* (Maya Culture and the Politics of Development, 1989) by Demetrio Rodríguez Guaján; *Universidad Maya de Guatemala: Diseño Curricular* (Maya University: Curricular Design, 1995) by Manuel de Jesús Salazar Tetzagüic et al.; *The Mayan Movement Today: Issues of Indigenous Culture and Development in Guatemala* (1997) by Alberto Esquit Choy and Víctor Gálvez Borrell; *Mayas y Ladinos en Cifras: El Caso de Guatemala* (Mayas and Ladinos in Numbers: The Case of Guatemala, 1994) by Leopoldo Tzián. Other poets and writers are equally important such as Humberto Ak'abal, José Mucía Batz, and particularly Gaspar Pedro González whose works are known nationally and internationally.

Recently, a number of works have been published by a Tz'ujuhil Maya using the name of Bizarro Ujpán. He keeps a diary and writes under the shadow of American anthropologist James Sexton. This mysterious writer has produced several books or diaries in which he describes daily life and events in local communities on the shore of Lake Atitlán. His recent book *Joseño: Another Maya Voice Speaks from Guatemala,* edited and translated by Sexton, describes the life of local leaders, prayer-makers, and traditionalists who struggled to maintain their cultures and beliefs despite military persecution in Santiago Atitlán during the years of *la violencia* (Ujpán and Sexton 2001).

Many other works by native authors and academics are now becoming widely read, but are not mentioned here. These works rely mostly on oral traditions as they strengthen and document storytelling and cultural transmission in rural Maya communities. Most are stories and folktales collected by local leaders in Maya communities in collaboration with anthropologists or NGO personnel interested in documenting indigenous beliefs and traditions. As an example, the organization Casa de Estudios de los Pueblos del Lago de Atitlán has produced several documents including *Literatura Oral de los Pueblos del Lago de Atitlán* (Petrich 1998). There are many more unknown Maya writers, poets, and historians who work locally with schoolteachers to produce text-book materials for Maya schools and bilingual education.

The most important theme in this book is that of Maya leadership. From historical, cultural, and political points of view, Maya leadership in Guatemala is very complex. To understand the complexities of the current Maya move-ment, which is linked to the past history of the Maya, we must ask the following questions: What is Maya leadership? What roles have Maya leaders played in the processes of historical and political changes in Guatemala? Who are these Maya leaders who have developed resistance against the complete assimilation of Maya culture? What are their objectives and goals? What ideologies have they acquired and applied in their struggle for cultural reaffirmation? What is their relationship with the non-Maya population and the dominant elite? How have their roles and strategies changed in the past and present? Which factors forced or motivated these changes? These and other questions can be partially answered when we study the important roles that Maya leaders have played in the past and present. I do not pretend to have all of the answers here, but this work suggests directions for further research so that we may know the tal-ent, courage, creativity, and vision of Maya leaders. By respecting and valuing Maya leadership we will be able to create a better future for the generations of Maya and non-Maya yet to come.

I present these themes in the hope that we may continue an informed de-bate about the effectiveness and contributions of the Maya leadership. Know-ing about the dreams, achievements, and failures of Maya leaders in the past and in modern times, we may find ways to contribute more seriously to the education of young Maya leaders for the future. I hope that they will have more and better options and strategies for their struggles and that they can contrib-ute to the construction of a multiethnic nationality in Guatemala. I think that the Maya are aware of how important these times are and of how their pres-ence is necessary for advancing the needed changes to improve the conditions of marginalized indigenous communities. Maya leaders must make themselves heard above the murmur of confused voices in search of social justice. It is to be hoped that one day we will all hear those voices in unison, searching for consensus and approval of those common goals that will make Guatemala a great nation. Insofar as the people remain strongly united, the more power can be generated for action. The people of Santiago Atitlán showed us this when they, with unified force, expelled the army from their community in December 1990, even though such courageous action cost the lives of many Maya (Carlsen 1997; Ujpán and Sexton 2001).

The first two chapters of this book discuss Maya identity and interethnic relations in Guatemala. Chapter 2 appeared in a slightly different version in Spanish in the journal *Mesoamérica*. Current processes of self-representation are enabling the Maya to emerge from under centuries of denigrating images as "Indians" and second-class citizens. The shared Maya base culture draws upon the values and creative knowledge of the ancestors, and the new and powerful pan-Maya identity arising from the ancient Maya culture can shatter the stereotypes imposed in 1524.

Chapters 3, 4, and 5 discuss the representation of the Maya by themselves and others. Chapter 3 shows how the Maya are depicted in a third-grade social studies textbook and deconstructs the hidden ideology behind the educational system as it promotes the views of the dominant class and its links to Western thought and values. Chapter 4 was first published in Kay B. Warren and Jean E. Jackson's *Indigenous Movements, Self-Representation, and the State in Latin America* (2002). It delineates the multiple nature of Maya voices and Maya participation in Guatemalan political parties. There is an urgent need for the Maya to reorient their political work and participation in order to insist on the implementation of the peace accords. Chapter 5 discusses the controversy over the testimonial book *Me Llamo Rigoberta Menchú* (Burgos-Debray 1983) generated by David Stoll's *Rigoberta Menchú and the Story of All Poor Guatemalans* (1999). This chapter originally appeared in Arturo Arias's edited volume of disputatious arguments from scholars and activists, *The Rigoberta Menchú Controversy* (2001). The bitter debate between those who elevated Menchú to iconic status and Stoll's assessment of her conflicting statements and misrepresentations raged briefly, but cannot detract from her role as an international figure promoting human rights and supporting the prosecution of those involved in massacres and genocide in Guatemala.

Chapters 6 through 9 examine issues of Maya leadership. Chapter 6 briefly discusses the ethnohistory of Maya leadership, beginning with the symbols of power and leadership represented in the stelae and Maya codices of antiquity. In the period of contact and conquest, it includes the great Maya leaders Tecún Umán and Kaib'il B'alam, who fought bravely against the invaders for the freedom of their people, and toward the end of the colonial period, Atanasio Tzul and Lucas Aguilar. Maya leaders during the conservative and liberal periods under the governments of Rafael Carrera and Justo Rufino Barrios are largely unknown. Some of the better-known leaders of the late twentieth century, from both the popular and culturalist movements in Guatemala, are included in the discussion. Chapter 7 presents a theoretical and strategic basis for understanding the Maya movements and the role that their major exponents and leaders have played. My hypothesis is that Maya leaders have always worked within a larger framework of repression and disintegration, and their role has been to find ways to advance the survival and self-determination of their people. The current revitalization of Maya culture is seen as occurring in a prophetic cycle of time, *oxlanh b'aktun*. Chapter 8 examines Maya ways of knowing and of producing knowledge as well as the role of the elders in accommodating and continuing Maya culture within the modern world system. Despite economic limitations and political and religious repression, elders have been, and continue to be, teachers and promoters of indigenous knowledge and Maya worldviews, perpetuating Maya ways of knowing through the oral transmission of fables, stories, and parables. Chapter 9 looks at the role of Maya leaders and intellectuals and the problems of transparency, charisma, and the manipulation of some leaders by ladinos. In spite of the different ideologies in play, especially during the armed conflict, Maya intellectuals, activists, and revolutionaries were influential in forcing the Guatemalan government to end the counterinsurgency war and negotiate the cease-fire and the peace accords. All this is presented in an effort to understand, revise, and refine the political, cultural, and economic strategies for a better future for the Maya.

Chapter 10 and 11 provide some concluding notes. An earlier version of Chapter 10 was originally presented as a lecture in the panel "Indigenous Rights and Security Issues in the Americas" at the conference "Security in the Post-Summit Americas" in Washington, D.C., in 1995. The material has been updated for this book. It presents the argument that national security begins with respect for and protection of the cultures and peoples that compose the nation. And finally, Chapter 11 presents my hopes for the future of the Maya people and for all Guatemalans. The current preoccupation with the endemic corruption and violence in Guatemala often obscures the view of a more hopeful tomorrow. All Guatemalans must focus on the reconstruction of the country and the development of a true interethnic dialogue that can lead to a nonviolent political culture of peace.

It is my hope that this book will serve as a foundation for future studies of Maya leadership, with the ultimate goal of improving social relationships between Maya and non-Maya in Guatemala. By knowing and valuing the contribution of each sector or ethnic community, we will realize that we have done much to separate or divide ourselves and little to unify ourselves. The emphasis must be on cultural diversity and not on assimilation, a national policy that has violated the rights of the Maya for self-determination. Self-determination is the moral and political authority of the Maya to decide their own future, free of the discrimination and control to which we have been subjected for centuries. We need to be able to call ourselves Maya and Guatemalan at the same time, without fear of repression or discrimination. This book does not promote separatism, but rather advocates for the rights of indigenous people to exist and to be a living part of the nation-states where they coexist with other citizens.

To achieve this, we need good Maya spiritual, political, and intellectual leaders. All people and nations need leaders to open new paths and to serve as guides for their people. The Maya have many leaders on all levels of society, known and unknown men and women who are engaged in the revitalization of Maya culture; leaders in all regions and linguistic communities; and those leaders who stood up for the Maya people and lost their lives during the armed conflict: catechists, schoolteachers, diviners, healers, artists, and simple farmers who were killed or who disappeared during those terrible years. Their example and vision should help motivate us to better understand our histories and our dynamic Maya cultures, which are so in need of a dignified space in our country. We need a leadership that proposes alternatives, with viable strategies that can help us start a true nation-building project based on social justice, democracy, and respect for human rights.

MAYA INTELLECTUAL RENAISSANCE

CHAPTER 1

Maya Identity and Interethnic Relations

The atmosphere of stability hoped for as a result of the signing of the peace accords in 1996 seemed to offer an opportune moment for relations between Mayas and ladinos to become more harmonious and mutually respectful. But in actuality, ethnic relations have not improved, and have even deteriorated into a climate of violence and political stalemate. Our attention is currently focused on the unjust, discriminatory, and racist relations that have long characterized ethnic relations in Guatemala. Historically and on all levels, discrimination has always existed between the Maya and ladinos, and the latter group has promoted this as something that is normal or natural.

The systematic discrimination against the Maya by some ladinos has been an ideological instrument codified in the concept of "the Indian." In this concept, indigenous people are represented as backward beings condemned to disappear or assimilate into the ladino and hegemonic Guatemalan culture. The anti-Maya, racist attitudes of many ladinos toward indigenous people is really a polemic against what is considered "Indian" and not against what is Maya. The dominant class and its servant, the Guatemalan army, have always been disgusted by current "Indians," while at the same time they have used the classic Maya culture to promote their nationalism.

Racism in Guatemala

Racism in Guatemala is best understood by examining the problems that originated in the inequality established by the Spanish conquest. The Spanish view of the indigenous people was that of barbarians who needed to be controlled and civilized, and the need for *encomienda* labor motivated the Spaniards to enslave them in the European feudal system they replicated in the New World. Tzvetan Todorov (1987:148) says of this process:

> The Indians are posited as inferiors from the start, for it is the Spaniards who determine the rules of the game. The superiority of those who promulgated the *Requerimiento,* one might say, is already contained in the

fact that it is they who are speaking, while the Indians listen. We know that the conquistadors had no scruple in applying the royal instructions as it suited them and in punishing the Indians in cases of resistance.

The term *indio* was initially used by Christopher Columbus on his first voyage in 1492 when he thought he had arrived at the Indies or the land of Cathay. "To the first island which I found, I gave the name San Salvador . . . the Indians call it 'Guanahani' " (Columbus in Jane 1988:2). In his journals, this is the first use of the term. Despite the recognition that he had his geography wrong, the term continued to be used, and its meaning changed through time, becoming transformed into a pejorative term meaning naked, wild, and vicious. The natives of this continent were thus both placed in an inferior position and labeled "indios." During the colonial period, the label became even more derogatory, acquiring the connotations of being lazy, dirty, opposed to progress, and, in sum, an inferior person (Asturias 1977).

In addition to importing slaves from Africa, the Spaniards enslaved the indigenous people and used their labor in the mines and on the encomiendas so that these new lords could accumulate their great wealth and distinguish themselves as powerful masters. Their prideful sensibilities produced in the Spanish colonial world a caste society of stratified classes and races. On top were the pure-blood Spaniards born in Spain, called *gachupines;* on a slightly lower level were the Spaniards born in the New World, called *criollos.* The conquerors were expected to go home to marry and produce offspring; to have children born here, even to Spanish women, denoted lesser rank. But expectations and social reality were quite different, and indigenous and African women bore children sired by the Spanish conquerors. Many lower-level Spaniards, the soldiers, sailors, craftsmen and workingmen, could not return home to procreate, and they made use of indigenous and African slave women, with and without their consent, producing mixed race (*mestizo*) children. The children of African mothers were called mulattos. For the Maya women, if the mothers were raped and abandoned, the children were usually brought up as indigenous, but if a woman entered into a consensual relationship with a man, the children were raised to speak Spanish and were inculcated with European values. These mestizos or ladinos, as they are known in Guatemala, were taught to value their European background and denigrate their indigenous or African roots. They became useful adjuncts to the European elites in managing and controlling the indigenous population, serving as intermediaries, overseers, police, and soldiers, and freeing the elite from any necessary contact with the despised indios. Ladinos never gained equal status to the European elite, but, like poor Southern whites in the United States, could take pride and comfort in their non-Indian standing. The colonial order of social standing was always: Spanish-born elite, Spaniards born in the New World, lower-class Spaniards and ladinos (a term that came to encompass the mestizos of mulatto and Maya descent), and the Maya, the "indios" on the bottom.

For centuries, the Maya people served the European elite, which expanded in the nineteenth century in Guatemala to include Germans and Italians, generation after generation, always on the bottom of the economic and political structure of the nation. Guatemala's racial discrimination infiltrates all aspects of society and reflects this history of unequal social relations, the closed doors to a better life, and the exploitation of the Maya people by the non-Maya. It is not mitigated by other social institutions. As noted by Marta Casaus Arzú (1992:9), "those who have obtained a higher education are the ones who show the most intolerance and racist or ethnocentric opinions."

At present, the interplay of class and ethnicity in Guatemala is somewhat ambivalent. There are class differences among the elite and the ladinos. The oligarchy is composed primarily of twenty-two families of European background, mentioned by Casaus Arzú, who have political and economic hegemony in Guatemala. The ladinos range from very rich to very poor. The indigenous population also has class differences, with the richer Maya families engaged in commerce and textile production in Quetzaltenango, Totonicapán, and El Quiché. Other Maya families are extremely poor. Land shortages combined with periodic droughts and depressed world prices for basic crops have brought more Maya families into immiseration. Some recent poverty statistics for Guatemala put the percentage of poor families in Guatemala at 80 percent; 90 percent of all Maya families are poor, and 50 percent of those suffer from extreme poverty (www.minorityrights.org; accessed August 11, 2001). The internal conflict forced many Maya to flee, and some found refuge in the United States. Between this asylum migration and the succeeding waves of economically motivated, illegal migration, some indigenous people have acquired a higher status through remittances or through transferring funds back to Guatemala to build good houses, capitalize a small business, or buy land to increase their standard of living. Now some Maya can compete with middle-class ladinos for jobs, political positions, and prestige. At present Guatemala's second greatest source of income (behind agricultural exports) is the remittances sent back by immigrants in the United States, the majority of whom are Maya (Loucky and Moors, 2000).

The stereotypes that characterized the social relations between ladinos and indigenous people have been maintained because of prejudice, ostracism, and the belief that whoever is an Indian is inferior (Adams 1990; Casaus Arzú 1992; Cojtí Cuxil 1996; Montejo 1999a). Indigenous people have been rejected as active participants in the social, economic, and political life of the country. A hegemonic nationalism has been created in which the ancient Maya are glorified and the present Maya are disdained and discriminated against (Riding 1985). Ancient Maya art has been elevated to the status of "classical art," while contemporary Maya art and Maya crafts are considered only primitivist folk art. Maya art and artisanry have been commodified, and their current producers are viewed as "Indians" rather than as Maya. Accordingly, ancient Maya are seen as extraordinary beings, and today's Maya, if they are thought of as Maya at all, are just a hazy reflection of their ancestors and are therefore considered merely "Indians" (Otzoy 1996).

We Maya have no reason to view ourselves in the mirror of ladino stereotypes. But is it possible to free ourselves from these stereotypes if we continue to replicate the valuation of the individual, the "Indian," that the dominant class has imposed? This valuation has always been negative and racist. In the past, Mayas have absorbed the ladino insult of the inferior Indian and have acted with submissiveness, fear, and self-denigration. They have internalized the oppression and accepted those pejorative terms, still in use as weapons of ideological oppression in the pursuit of economic and political hegemony. During the 1960s and 1970s, some Maya undertook the process of assimilation and ladino-style accommodation. Some people changed their Maya names to ladino or gringo ones. Xunik became Juan or "Yonni." Others bleached their hair with peroxide to become *canches* or blondes. Although there is freedom to do whatever one wants with one's own persona, these actions were really aimed at masking all that was Maya or indigenous in these individuals.

Discrimination against the Maya is so obvious and persistent that it seems as if it were natural (Casaus Arzú 1992). Justice has been denied the Maya in the past, and that injustice continues into the present. The thousands of Maya murdered or disappeared during the internal conflict have simply been forgotten by ladino Guatemala. The administration of justice in Guatemala is not equitable. For the ladino and the well-to-do, courts are more attentive and active, as in the case of the kidnapping and murder of Señora Bonfassi de Botrán, a wealthy old lady of Guatemala City in January 1997. The prosecution of those responsible for this crime was immediate, and the government and the Unidad Revolucionaria Nacional Guatemalteca (URNG; Guatemalan National Revolutionary Unity) had to negotiate to erase evidence that could have compromised the dialogue and the signing of the peace agreement that had just concluded. In the case of the guerrilla fighter Everardo, his American wife, lawyer Jennifer Harbury, used the help of international organizations and extraordinary tactics to pressure the government, the army, and even the State Department of the United States to find answers and take action. By obtaining court orders for exhumations and opening up previously restricted documents, she established precedents in the United States, if not in Guatemala, and these precedents are encouraging for the struggles of the Maya to bring to light the crimes committed against them during the armed conflict.

But for the thousands of dead indigenous people, many of whom had no contact with the guerrillas, little concern has been shown about identifying or bringing to justice the perpetrators of the crimes that cut off their lives. The organization of Guatemalan widows, Coordinadora Nacional de Viudas de Guatemala (CONAVIGUA), led by Rosalina Tuyuc, and other Maya organizations have not had the resources or the support necessary to have their demands heard. Finally, Rigoberta Menchú has now appealed to the International Court of Justice in the Hague to seek the justice that has been so elusive. Just recently, twenty-two Maya communities formed the Association for Justice and Reconciliation (AJR), and with the help of the Centro para la Acción Legal en Derechos Humanos (CALDH; Center for Human Rights Legal Action), it has brought charges of genocide, crimes against humanity, and war crimes against former presidents Ríos Montt and Lucas García and their staffs in the Guatemalan courts. The charges, however, are stalled in the court system. In Guatemala, justice and human rights are sometimes very selective, and that selectivity is based on ethnic identity.

The Tasks for Maya Leadership

The ideological conversion to Maya identity and Maya ways is a process of self-reflection for urban Maya who have reached higher economic levels than those found in villages. The feeling of being Maya should lead them to mingle with simple folks from the villages and not just with their employers (*patrones*) or with international advisors. Maya leaders from the capital are caught between two worlds, the Maya and the non-Maya. As a consequence, urban Maya have developed a type of fluctuating identity. Racial competition makes no sense for the Maya people who are seeking unity and solidarity with all of the peoples of Guatemala. One hopes that Maya leaders, together with ladino leaders, will be able to lift the social and economic status of all Guatemalans in order to construct a country that is just and respectful of diversity. We need a society of social justice that benefits all Guatemalans and not a racial and egotistical competition between Mayas and ladinos that will perpetuate the ethnic conflict.

To avoid the separation of Maya middle-class people and leaders from the less fortunate Maya and the people in the rural villages, I propose a total acceptance or conversion to this key Maya identity. This generative term for our identity has millennia-old historical roots and unifies us through space and time: the ancient Maya, the contemporary Maya, and the Maya of the future. For this reason, the implementation of the "Agreement on the Identity and Rights of the Indigenous People of Guatemala" in the peace accords is of vital importance in reaffirming our identities and breathing life into this national, multicultural, and pluriethnic project of our dreams.

In addition, Maya leaders must extend themselves beyond their anticolonialist arguments and look forward in search of a better future for our people. We must change our own mentality of seeing ourselves as oppressed and dominated Maya into one of creative and supportive Maya. It is time to liberate ourselves from this frame of mind, so long used as a bulwark against discrimination. We need generations of Mayas who perceive themselves in positive ways. The struggles and the efforts of the current Maya leaders have opened up this path toward mental liberation against the syndrome of victimization.

It is possible that a Maya nationalist sentiment in favor of Maya unification may develop. Today, Maya intellectuals and politicians recognize that their strength can play a leading role in this unified Maya nationalism. But before this can occur, Mayas must reinforce feelings of pride in being Maya and must project the Maya image according to our vision of ourselves. This Maya-centrism, however, does not have to be antagonistic to or separate from the genuine efforts of the many Maya and non-Maya working to create a multicultural, pluriethnic Guatemala.

From Indian to Maya

We must pay attention to the Maya culture because it is the primordial source of our identity and because that which is Maya should be the focus of our attention rather than that which has been termed "Indian," the category historically used for our control and domination. The term "Maya" must be used by all Guatemalans, since it is a generator of identity for both Mayas and ladinos.

Maya-centrism can be negative if we don't admit that the ladinos themselves, as "Guatemaltecos" (a Nahuatl-derived name for our nationality), also have a part of their blood that is Maya and that they share this identity. What the ladinos must do is to activate this part of their identity and generate positive relationships of solidarity between the ladino and Maya populations of Guatemala.

The use of the term "Maya" is a great advance, and all indigenous people should feel proud of being Maya. Reaffirming identity is an excellent form of breaking away from the stereotypes that have held us mentally captive. If we do not strengthen our identity, we accept the ladino supremacy that has controlled the destiny of our people. In this dominated, oppressed, and victimized mental encapsulation, we cannot make the true value of self-determination understood. Fortunately, the peace accords include the rights of Maya to freely use their own languages, cosmovision, and spirituality. These fundamental guarantees give the Maya the possibility of deciding their future within a multicultural nation. But in order to lift up the dignity of the Maya people, we need charismatic leaders who will be the visionaries of the future and who will not lead our people down a path of chaos and violence, as occurred during the years of armed conflict.

Mestizaje *or Hybridity?*

While the Maya try to redefine themselves by using the term "Maya," the ladinos must also redefine themselves within their mestizaje (mixed-blood population) or ladino-ness. Some ladino intellectuals are already redefining themselves by using the concept of mestizaje as a cultural hybridity. Mario Roberto Morales (1998:20), following Nestor Garcia Canclini (1984), has focused on the cultural aspect of mestizaje and hybridity as a process for democratizing interethnic relationships in Guatemala.

> The intent is to democratize the disglosia, hybridization, and the migrant discourse through the democratization of the spaces where differences are articulated, so that such articulation takes place under democratic conditions. In all, mestizaje is democratized, relativized, converting it into a mestizaje which is based on respect for differences and not its dissolution in a chimeric "national" harmony. The notion of an (inter)cultural and democratic mestizaje . . . does not refer to a happy fusion, or a "cosmic race" destined to rule the world and not to the disappearance of cultural differences.

I prefer not to use the term hybrid or hybridity, since it has a connotation of the forced and monitored crossbreeding practiced on animals to produce a certain desired type. This is not the case here, because we are speaking of human beings and not about biological experiments. Morally speaking, it is preferable to use the term *mestizo* to avoid discussions with a racist tinge. In the case of Guatemala and Latin America, the issue of identity is founded more on a cultural base than a biological one. There are ladinos who have indigenous blood and deny it. There are Maya who have ladino blood and also reject it, preferring to identify with that which is Maya as defined by its cultural aspects. In this ethnic and cultural diversity in our country, we cannot say that we are all mestizos or that we are all Maya.

Some ladinos say that the indigenous people of Guatemala are not Maya, since the Maya do not exist and are all mixed as well. This argument is used by those who do not want to accept a world that is confused and without clear roots and who must attack others in order to accept their own roots, roots that are uncomfortable to bear. These ladinos fear that the Maya seek a separate society and must be reminded that they are also mestizos. This same fear of a racial division of power has motivated many to reject recognition of the particularity or unique characteristics of the current Maya culture. Thus, when the Maya speak of the cultural and historic essence that gives their identity a foundation, they are accused of being essentialists, as if it were a sin to affirm that the Maya culture has millennia-old roots and that the current Maya speak languages that descend from this ancient Maya culture (Watanabe and Fischer 2004).

Those who insist on the argument for the hybridism of the Maya want to see the Maya recognize themselves as their own oppressors. Their reasoning can be summed up this way: if historically the ladinos (who have assumed power) have been spoken of as the oppressors of the Maya, and now the Maya are also ladinos, then they have oppressed themselves. We return to the same problem of blaming the victims as responsible for their situation of domination, poverty, and repression. If we all call ourselves mestizos, before long we will all be calling ourselves "white" or elite ladinos, and then we will pass for being our own colonizers. As one can see, this is a facile and clever way to avoid the responsibilities of a just relationship and the recognition of cultural diversity in our country.

I recognize that the debate about identity and the argument for hybridity are made in the hopes of promoting a type of national unity, homogeneity, or "Guatemalan-ness" (Hale 1999). But this national unity cannot exist unless we all contribute to its just and equitable construction. We need to put our cards on the table in order to discuss as equals what our contributions will be to this nonelitist, democratic, and multicultural nationality that we dream of constructing. This debate should not take place at the opposite ends of the frequent accusations where we question one another's identity. One can often hear people say, "You are not what you say you are" or "You are not true Maya." We must keep our eyes on ethnic diversity in our country and recognize our ethnic or cultural differences. We must start from this multiethnic affirmation in order to construct a free, just, and democratic Guatemala. Haven't we spoken and even bragged about having a pluricultural, multiethnic country in our discussions? Now it is time to construct it and live it as Guatemalans.

We must recognize that the immense majority of Maya and ladinos are not enemies. There has always been an inclination toward nationalism and unity or solidarity among indigenous people and ladinos. If we strengthen these bonds of friendship between Maya and non-Maya, we can then prevent the tyranny of an elite minority from wielding power over the Maya majority that has been reduced to a "minority" due to its exclusion from the country's historic, democratic process. We Maya must understand that not all ladinos or mestizos are bad or racist, that non-Maya can also recognize that the humanity of the Maya has been trampled for centuries, and that it is necessary for all to appreciate the dignity of our people and our historic, millennia-old roots in Guatemala.

Toward a Maya Guatemala

The reconsideration of the Maya identity, or the affirmation of Guatemalan indigenous people as Maya, can give us the sense of belonging to a powerful culture or civilization. Our sense of belonging to a unique place containing the roots of our being, our culture, and civilization can be broadened through relationships of brotherhood and friendship at the local, community, and national levels. The recognition and promotion of our identity can be carried out if we develop a feeling of acceptance toward our cultural patrimony that can serve as the basis for an ethnic alliance in the construction of our truncated nationality. This national unity project will not be easy, since it always will be subject to the critiques and interpretations of those who don't want to see that which is Maya, but rather only that which is white and European, as the foundation for Guatemalan nationality.

What would happen if we began to recognize the cultural and linguistic identity of the Maya peoples according to the way the Constitution and the peace accords read? Or at least complied with what Guatemala has ratified concerning the international legal instrument known as the International Labor Organization's Convention 169? Let us remember that it is not sufficient to recognize that Maya identity is unique and has internationally recognized values. What is needed are compliance with the peace accords and a new revision of the Constitution, this time with the participation of all Guatemalan people, so that it becomes inclusive in its laws and articles. Our current Magna Carta is, in large part, the vision of powerful ladino people and excludes in practice the cultural, political, and religious rights of the Maya people. We need to truly think of the advancement of the country and to lift all of its citizens up to a more dignified standard of living. We cannot speak of a just nation while the majority of the Guatemalan people continue to suffer from the marginalization in which they have been functioning for centuries.

We must frankly recognize the true humanity of the Maya. They are human beings with spirit, life, and dignity, and the human rights that Bartolomé de Las Casas advocated on behalf of indigenous people in the courts of Valladolid in 1550. Everyone must understand that, as true human beings, the Maya are both Guatemalans and the native population of the *Mayab'* here in the heart of the Americas.

Can the human sentiment of solidarity be developed among all Guatemalans, so that we can live together in lasting peace and in a place where human rights and the fundamental right to life are truly respected? Why has Guatemala been buried in chaos and violence during the last two decades? The immediate answer is that we are not united, that we do not know one another or support one another. Those who manage the country have never experienced the suffering and poverty that the majority of Guatemalans have experienced. And since they do not know their people or their country, they do not realize that they cause the country's backwardness by failing to give opportunities to the less fortunate. The massacres during the 1970s and 1980s remind us of this insult to our lives, when the hegemonic power of the army and government decided to eliminate thousands of Guatemalans. And we are all silent, as if nothing had happened. The exception is Rigoberta Menchú and a few Maya who have continued to insist that Guatemala be not only a nation of law but also a nation of justice.

Healing the Wounds of the Present

The Frente Republicano Guatemalteco (FRG; Guatemalan Republican Front), which governed during the period 2000–2003, promoted injustice and corruption. Its legacy was a country infested with crime, fraud, corruption, drug trafficking, and all manner of white-collar and violent crime. To combat this, all Guatemalans must act in unity and solidarity. We are called upon to develop respectable and just social relations between Mayas and non-Mayas. The custom of insulting people by using the term "Indian" should end, because in a civilized nation, discrimination and racism should be punishable crimes. To participate in the democratization of the country and to free ourselves from our racial prejudices is the duty of all. Our differences are great in terms of ethnicity, race, and culture, but after nearly five centuries of living together in the same territory, one would hope that some bond of solidarity should tie us together. Unfortunately, our ethnic differences deepen even more when the Maya are considered people who are good only for hard and poorly paid work or people without any leadership abilities. South Africa is a good example for us. South Africa had and has many factions, as we do in Guatemala, but blacks and whites have managed to unify their efforts to govern together and end apartheid.

When those who murdered and massacred their own people receive medals and promotions to positions of honor, we are far from achieving peace and justice in Guatemala. The widespread armed assaults, kidnappings, and drug trafficking in Guatemala show us that it is not indigenous people who run these mafias. Indigenous people know how to live in peace, respect life, and love their country, since they are not the ones who are driving the country into misfortune. There is impoverishment of the spirit, increased immorality, and disdain for life in Guatemala. This legacy of violence now punishing the country was made possible by the "peace without justice" of the unrealized peace accords. The abuse of human beings is compounded by the bribery and corruption that lets criminals go free. We hope that these abuses will cease with the implementation of the peace accords and that the fever that sickens those who consider themselves to be above the law and continue to act with impunity will also stop. The political parties play a big role in this. To be elected, each successive government offers the public what it does not want to and cannot give. The parties fill all positions, not with people who are capable and prepared, but with party faithful or opportunists who have contributed to the electoral campaign, as exemplified by the nepotism practiced by the FRG government. The

Maya should give thought to a biethnic Maya and ladino party for the next or future elections. We need a centrist party that includes members of the Maya and non-Maya populations, a true national party that overlaps ethnic frontiers. Its top priority should be the national good and not the private interests of the few. Only in this way will we be able to talk about a national unification that has representation in the upper echelons of politics and government.

I believe that the racist attacks in Guatemala are against "Indians" and not against the Maya. In 1991, with the help of several Maya leaders, I proposed to the congress of the American Anthropological Association in Chicago that it was time to take a step forward in the redefinition of our identity and begin to call ourselves Maya. At that time, the term "Maya" was not used in indigenous discourse, but only the term "indio." It was necessary to analyze the use of various pejorative terms and destroy the intragroup and interethnic racism among Mayas. One issue is that of skin color. Some light-skinned Maya act like ladinos and mistreat their own neighbors who have dark skin or a Maya phenotype. These Maya individuals play along with ladino racism and call other Maya by disparaging terms because of the color of their skin. Light-skinned Maya often direct insults such as *k'ej sinhso lej* (black and disgusting) at those who are darker in color.

These insults are the internalized result of racism, exacerbated by media promotion of "blond is beautiful" and by Maya who see light-colored skin as superior. But racism and the anti-Indian attitudes of racist ladinos (and not all ladinos are racist) are deeper than the racist insults of some Mayas. Since the Spanish invasion, the Maya and the ladino people have not lived together in peace and equality for one moment. The Maya have faced misfortune and discrimination ever since they were generically named "Indians"; the Spanish conquerors didn't care that there were many peoples and cultures on this continent. By globalizing the term "Indian," they erased the cultural and linguistic diversity of thousands of indigenous peoples in existence before European contact.

To understand this situation of racist and degrading treatment toward an entire people such as the Maya, we must analyze the reasons that reinforce or sustain this racist vision. In reality, very few ladinos have thought seriously about the historic depth of the rejection and humiliation that the indigenous people have suffered through the centuries. The holocaust that the Maya suffered as a result of wars, epidemics, and slavery during and after the Spanish invasion has been repeated through the centuries. The fear of massacres and genocide and the danger of violent elimination have always been latent, if not

present. The hatred and racist attitudes of certain elements in the army over-
flowed again during the armed conflict, when thousands of indigenous people
were massacred and villages were completely wiped out. The Maya have always
commented on the racist attitude of the ladinos with whom they rub elbows
within the national territory. One Jakaltek elder commented in regard to a
ladino who lived in the community, "*Ah, wal ya' ich tu, kochnhe kaw chonh sya
ya'jilni*" (Ah, this gentleman, you can really see that he is disgusted by indigenous people).

Today the Maya are not hated and discriminated against because of their
religion, as were the Jewish people for example, but for their race and ethnicity—that is, for the very fact of being called "Indian." It has been the colonialist identity that has justified the racist treatment toward indigenous populations. Indigenous people have been seen as inferior beings and as incapable
of assimilating modern technology and adapting to today's capitalist world.
Fortunately, the Maya have millennia-old roots in the land where they live, and
they cannot be forced out or shut away in ecological preserves or restricted
territories. The Maya are numerous, and their presence is totally visible in the
national arena. The Maya have a millennia-old culture that gives them their
identity and helps them survive, even in periods of intense repression and
genocidal war. What has helped them survive has been their ability to resist
the constant suffering and to subsist on very little. Their poverty, developed
out of five hundred years of alienation from their land and servitude to their
conquerors, was not relieved by any program of government social services.
In Maya communities, older people, especially those without living children,
struggle to subsist. The extended family has helped many poor families to get
by. And in spite of their extreme poverty, these people were accused of being
communists and were the object of massacres and of "scorched earth" military
strategies.

Understanding and respect for the dignity of all the ethnic peoples of Guatemala can be the beginning of interethnic unification and solidarity. The analysis of the failure of ethnic relations in Guatemala must begin in the heart of
each ethnic group. Only when the ladino population is self-critical and recognizes the monsters of racism and discrimination it has hidden for centuries and
becomes free of them will it be able to treat the indigenous people on equal
terms. The Maya must also be self-critical in order to establish the basis for an
identity that can promote them as dynamic agents of their own history and
constructors of their own future. In this way we will see the failures that have
occurred because we have not managed our social relations in the light of the

moral laws of justice and respect for the lives of humans and the other beings with whom we inhabit the earth. Only by knowing and valuing our common history can we rise above the ladino ethnocentrism that now dominates the ethnic relations in Guatemala. Perhaps some day the ladinos who look down on indigenous people will free themselves from this corrosive chauvinism and see the country through a more global, plurinational lens. And so, in the process of Maya revitalization and the action of its leaders, we must be careful not to promote hostile attitudes or reverse racism toward the ladinos and mestizos.

Guatemala needs the support, solidarity, consensus, and collaboration of all indigenous and nonindigenous sectors of the country in order to leave behind this postwar chaos. It is true that the Maya have their own revitalization projects concerning identity, spirituality, Mayan languages, and education, and it is necessary to educate the non-Maya population about our advances and results. A paranoid public can see or confuse positive work toward the revitalization of the Maya culture as a threat toward those that are in control.

Another issue to be clarified, mainly for those on the revolutionary left, is the idea that indigenous people and poor ladinos are natural allies, since they suffer equally from poverty and discrimination. This argument is not realistic in the sense that Mayas and ladinos are different and move within different conceptions of the world. In reality, this construction was only a rhetorical form used by the leftists in order to accelerate the unity of the sectors and lower social classes into the revolutionary movement. The casting of Maya culture and identity as irrelevant in this process did not produce the results the guerrillas expected. Not even the poor ladinos knew exactly what they wanted within the revolutionary movement. Leaders were created and put forth to represent Maya and non-Maya alike, and in the end these leaders lost popularity because neither group of people could identify with them.

For this very reason, we insist that cultural differences and political identities exist and cannot be conglomerated into one network in order to tell people what to do. This is even truer now that there are Maya critics who see and disapprove of the use to which other Maya are put by some power-hungry ladinos. Mayas have suffered from racial discrimination, not only from the elite that excluded them from national projects, but even from the small-town ladinos with whom they are constantly rubbing elbows. One cannot speak of a true Guatemalan apartheid like that of South Africa, but our pervasive racial discrimination is only softened by the visibility of the Maya and the sentiments of compassion expressed at times by ladinos. The vibrant culture of today's Maya has at least filed down the cutting edge of the brutal discrimination of the past.

Although poor Mayas are considered inferior and not equal to ladinos, their crafts and artistic production are prized and consumed by some ladinos and tourists, thus giving some recognition to the value of modern Mayas as creative and productive people.

Maya people cannot remain silent. The paternalistic good intentions of non-Mayas in leading pro-Maya causes, without the participation of the Maya, must change. That paternalism was seen in those Maya organizations that participated in the popular movement and in the pan-Maya revitalization movement during the peace negotiations. Not many Maya represented their communities, even on commissions or institutions of the utmost importance to the Maya. The Commission for Historic Clarification, for example, had only one Maya representative, Otilia Lux de Coti.

Maya people have not forgotten the violence experienced in the past. Fear, insecurity, and violence are still alive in this country and circumscribe those Maya voices in the national arena willing to speak openly about those memories. When the peace accords were signed, both common and organized criminality were unleashed, and corruption at high levels of government opened up like a pus-filled wound, infecting all the regions of the country. In this situation, Maya spirituality, respect for life, and the Maya cosmovision of solidarity and compassion should be promoted in order to rescue the country from so much crime.

My main argument is that the contribution of the Maya culture now in the process of revitalizing itself can serve as a bandage on the wound of racism and human-rights abuses in Guatemala. It can recover that which is good, the cultural values of this country, and little by little close the abyss of indifference and abuse that has existed in Guatemala, so that the signing and the implementation of the peace accords will be a real project that makes us seriously think and act within the parameters of justice, liberty, and human rights. The first step is to set aside the prejudices against indigenous people, since these unfounded prejudices have given rise to racist treatment toward the Maya by some of the ladinos. If we look at the resources we have, without partisanship or reductionism, we will see that we are in a country that is rich in human and natural resources. What we have been lacking is the genuine interest in walking shoulder to shoulder, Mayas and ladinos, toward true progress for this country, with the efforts and contributions of all of us applied to generating a new nationalist vision of unity and solidarity among the Guatemalan people.

CHAPTER 2

Pan-Mayanism

The Complexity of Maya Culture and the Process of Self-Representation

Introduction

Understanding the dynamics of change and continuity in Maya culture is of great interest in current Maya studies research. This research, however, has centered mainly on the ancient Maya and has paid relatively little attention to the struggle of contemporary Maya to redefine themselves in the modern, capitalist world system. Although interest in the modern Maya is secondary to interest in their ancestors, Maya scholars insist that the modern and ancient Maya are equally relevant if one wants to understand the dynamics of their culture and its strategies for survival (Montejo 1993a; Cojti Cuxil 1994). Over the last five hundred years, Maya culture has demonstrated its capacity to absorb external aggression, attenuating it at the same time with the Maya philosophy of pacific coexistence with people, nature, and the universe. The current process of revitalization of the Maya culture in Guatemala is an example of this powerful will to survive even in a climate of extreme political violence (Smith 1991; Warren 1994). Applying Eric Wolf's (1982) concept of culture, we can say that Maya culture as we know it today has passed through different phases of construction, dismantling, and reconstruction as seen, for example, in the preclassic, classic, postclassic, historic, and modern Maya periods. Once again a resurgence of Maya culture is taking place, this time in response to the extreme pressure imposed on the indigenous cultures during the last decades, when massacres provoked ruptures in Maya worldviews and traditions.

The current revitalization of Maya culture reflects also the continental mobilization of indigenous people seeking self-determination on the American continent. On many different levels—cultural, linguistic, political, and religious—Maya are participating in the process of unifying the different native Maya peoples into a pan-Maya movement for cultural revitalization and resurgence in the *Mayab'*, the Mayan-speaking region.

To understand the importance of this process, we must examine the underlying foundation of the Maya culture (the macrolevel) and the present adoption of the term "Maya." I am proposing the existence of a unique, base Maya culture, shared within the Maya region. This supposition is grounded in the idea that the cultural history of the region has produced a culture that we can consider a totality, but one that is also unique and has become varied in space and in time (Carmack 1988). We recognize that different Maya cultures share this basic culture, one that was possibly hegemonic in the classic era. Maya culture is, then, pluralist and tends to diversify over time (Worsley 1984). By considering the plurality of the Maya culture (diversity within unity), the pan-Maya movement for cultural reaffirmation will express itself as a cultural strategy developed by the Maya to assure the survival and continuity of their culture in future *katunes* (twenty-year cycles of the Maya calendar). Only then will we be better able to understand Maya civilization, past and present, and its current struggle for self-determination. More importantly, I intend to demonstrate the multiform nature of Maya cultural tradition and the current process of construction of a pan-Maya ethnic identity and tradition, emphasizing the continuity of Maya culture and the dynamic force that has carried it through to the present with all of its consequent transformations.

The Underlying or Base Maya Culture—The Ancient Past

My focus on the pan-Maya cultural renaissance movement now taking place in the Maya region is predicated on the idea that there is a shared or base Maya culture on a macrocultural level. We find material remains throughout the Maya region supporting the argument for a shared macro-Maya culture that may have been elitist and hegemonic in the classic era (300 BC–AD 900). According to linguists, there was a unique proto-Mayan language from which the offspring languages that are now spoken in the Maya region are derived. Mayan languages are related. Linguists have not found a genetic relationship beyond the thirty-one known languages in the contemporary Mayan language family (Campbell and Kaufman 1985). The cultural patterns that contemporary Maya share converge in one great Maya tradition, and thus, geographically, we can speak of a distinct Maya culture in this Mesoamerican cultural area.

As a consequence of current critical thought, our knowledge of Maya development grows clearer as the ancient, mythologized Maya become less mythical and more humanized. We know from archeology that during an early period, Maya civilization received strong influences from other preclassic, non-Maya cultures, including the Olmecs of Mexico and the Izapa cultures of the Pacific coast. It was in this era—the formative period (1200–300 BC)—and in the late preclassic period (200 BC–AD 250) that followed, that Maya culture developed (Willey 1982). The art and iconography of Izapa, bearing the Olmec legacy, influenced the development of Maya art and writing (Campbell and Kaufman 1985). David Friedel has argued that the culture of Izapa, along with that of Kaminaljuyu, gives evidence of the early development of hieroglyphics, but hieroglyphic writing reached its peak in the lowlands, demonstrating common Maya cultural development in different geographic regions (Friedel 1986; Justeson 1985).

Leventhal has suggested that the late preclassic period showed a uniformity of Maya culture in material objects, again giving evidence of a shared Maya culture (Leventhal 1987, personal communication). Maya ideology, especially religion and cosmology, motivated the development of this civilization, which in turn created elite classes in the preclassic and classic periods that continued into the postclassic (Schele and Miller 1986; Schele, Friedel, and Parker 1993). The construction of the Maya world continued and was recreated or reconstructed in the lowlands, where it flourished in the classic era. Important innovations caused the elite to become more powerful. The religious and cosmological order became essential for elite domination, and its maintenance was required by the governors to reaffirm their divine origin (Schele and Miller 1986). Maya ideology is, therefore, a powerful, unifying force that explains why Maya culture has "persisted as a distinctive entity for the last 3,000 years" (Gossen 1986:25).

In Vogt's genetic model (1964), we can also find arguments in favor of a unique Maya culture. He affirms that the physical, linguistic, and systemic patterns converge rather than diverge as we go back in time to the common origins of the Maya. The social and historic cohesion that existed in the preclassic period began to diversify, especially during the period between 700 and 300 BC. In this era, the process of mixing, remaking, borrowing, and inventing was intense and provoked a great deal of diversification. This is, therefore, the most explicit, decisive time in the diversification of Maya culture.

Despite this diversification, Maya culture continued on a macrolevel within which cotraditions developed. It is difficult to authenticate this macrolevel of cultural cohesion, but it has persisted, and one can enumerate cultural traits that are currently shared among the modern Mayan language groups, and although different from one another, all of these linguistic families are part of the great Maya culture. There are specific differences that distinguish one from the other, but they share the same base Maya identity and culture. The Jakaltek Maya are different from the Mames, the K'iche', or the Lacandons, but all belong to the great Maya culture. They call themselves Maya. They are different ethnic communities, each with their own specific cultural characteristics within a great tradition of shared culture. Thus, the Maya culture is pluralist at the microlevel while maintaining its unity in its macrolevel manifestation.

In addition to the archeological and linguistic data presented here to support the macro-Maya level, the ethnographic and ethnological data reinforce my arguments for the existence of a shared Maya culture. For example, Maya cosmology is a powerful unifying element for this culture, as it is expressed in Maya mythology, rituals, and oral tradition. "By working back and forth from the ancient cosmology to the modern, we are becoming increasingly convinced of the integrity and continuity that Maya thought displays over thousands of years of history" (Schele, Friedel, and Parker 1993:43). The Maya world duplicates a cosmological order, and religious and political functions were fused together under the guidance of the sacred calendar. Maya cosmology recounts the sacred forces that direct lives, the *skanh stxukut,* the four corners of the earth, and the four *bakab'* that hold up the universe. According to the ethno-historic document, the *Popol Vuh:*

> Great was the description and the story of how all of the sky and the earth were formed and divided into four parts, as it was indicated, and the sky was measured, and the measuring cord was brought and was laid out in the sky and on the earth, in the four angles, the four corners, as was told by the Creator, the Maker, who is both mother and father of life. (Recinos, Goetz, and Morley 1983)

These stories, recorded by the Quiché Maya of the *altiplano* (high plateau) of Guatemala, are similar to those recorded by Yukatek Maya in the *Chilam Balam* (Makemson 1951). In the Yucatán, these pillars of the four corners of the earth are the bacabs who also appear in the ancient codices, the folded books of hieroglyphic writing of the postclassic period. Diego de Landa tells us that the Maya prayed to the four bacabs or Year Bearers. "People said that there were four brothers that God (*Hunab'k'u*), when creating the world, placed at the four corners to hold up the sky" (Landa 1982). The four bacabs are central figures in the Maya cosmology and also function as the Year Bearers in the ancient Maya calendar, still in use today. The bacabs correspond to the Year Bearers among the Ki'che' (Carmack 1979), the *Ijom Hab'il* (Year Bearers) among the Jakaltek Maya of the Guatemalan altiplano (La Farge and Byers 1931), and the Year

Bearers among the Tzotziles of the highlands of Chiapas (Vogt 1969). These figures are also found among the Mopán speakers of San Antonio in Belize, who, according to Thompson, were descended from the immigrants from the Maya village of San Luís Petén. "Today's indigenous people in San Antonio associate certain colors with the world's directions, but they don't know the color that is associated with the different points on the compass any more" (Thompson 1930:80).

The knowledge of the four cosmological directions and the colors associated with them was essential in Maya rituals and ceremonies. This is, then, a pan-Maya belief still existing among the modern Maya of different regions. This supports our argument for a macro-Maya culture derived from the past and recreated in current Maya communities. In addition, leading scholars of Maya civilization in the last hundred years have assumed the existence of a unique Maya culture (Thompson 1954; La Farge and Byers 1931), arguing that all Maya groups shared a Maya tradition, that hieroglyphs could be deciphered using any of the currently spoken Mayan languages, and that the knowledge of hieroglyphic writing could still exist among the different Maya cultures of the Mayab'. Their efforts were directed toward the study of what they called the "vestiges" of this great Maya culture now disseminated among living Maya. This was the motivation for the first expedition organized by Tulane University in 1924 and the subsequent expeditions carried out under the auspices of the Carnegie Institute of Washington and the Peabody Museum of Harvard University. From these expeditions, North American scholars recognized that

> the indigenous people of the Mayan linguistic trunk who live in the South of Mexico, the Yucatan and Guatemala are generally considered to be the ethnic and cultural descendants of the people who constructed the great temples and created the inscriptions in the now-deserted cities, around which the modern Mayan villages are distributed. (La Farge and Byers 1931)

Contemporary Maya communities continue to adhere to many of their ancient, sacred patterns and rituals. The increasingly common celebration of the Maya New Year, *Waxaqib'b'atz,* in the majority of Maya communities and the continuity of the ancient Maya calendar promoted by the *ahb'eh* or the *aj-k'ij,* Maya priests, show the continuous connection of modern Maya culture to the past, present, and future.[1] Maya culture continues its dynamic process of re-

Jakaltek Maya spiritual leader at a ceremony for the repatriation of *The Year Bearer's People* by Oliver La Farge, Jacaltenango, 1997 (author's photo)

construction and resurgence in spite of the internal and external forces that have strongly affected it over the last five hundred years.

As members of a macro-Maya cultural base, each linguistic community shares a collective, pan-Maya identity that gives it strength and certain elements for the process of redefining its future. All Maya peoples of the region can retrace their lineage to ancient Maya culture. In Guatemala, "The approximately 4 million indigenous people are Mayan: they speak Mayan languages [and] they are cultural heirs to the pre-Hispanic Mayan societies of the past" (Carmack 1979:2). Referring to the continuity of Maya culture, Barbara Tedlock (1993:154–155) has stated:

> Few regions of the world show as clear concordance between language and culture as the Mayan region. If we trace a circle around the habitat of the current speakers of the twenty-nine Mayan languages, this will also include the archaeological sites belonging to the Mayan civilization. . . . The continual distribution of their languages, and the relatively small variations among these languages, shows that these speakers of the Mayan language have inhabited this region for millennia.

This recognition of a shared Maya culture is shown in the practice of Maya ceremonial institutions that are pan-Maya, which persist among nearly all of the current Maya peoples. Some Maya have expressed this nexus between the ancient Maya culture and the modern in a very simple way by saying that "the Maya culture lives on, because we, its descendants, live on."

The Diversity of the Maya Culture — The Recent Past

Research on other civilizations has suggested that cultures exist and develop as they adapt to their environment. Thus, the construction of early Maya culture, or the origin of Maya civilization according to Sanders and Price, is symbiotic. Different ecological niches create the need for societies to develop different strategies for survival. In the case of the Maya, their diverse ecological environment has been an important factor in producing great variability. A distinction is usually made between the geographically different lowland and highland Maya groups. Contemporary researchers observe that the lowlands region presents more ecological uniformity than the highlands region, which holds greater ecological and cultural diversity (Sanders and Price 1968).

Archeological data suggest that around AD 300 there was a common Maya cultural tradition, but that after that time, the remaking of the material and ideological culture was so strong that it created great diversity during the classic and postclassic periods. Referring to the Maya material culture, Willey (1982:265) states that

> the Mayans continued to receive foreign or external influences. During the Early Classic it seems probable (evidence of stylistic similarities) that Tikal had the leadership, a hegemony over the greater part of the Mayan lowlands, or at least the southern regions, Quiriguá and Copán, through marrying the daughters of royalty to the governors of other cities.

In spite of Tikal's hegemony over other cities, these same larger cities, such as Copán and Quiriguá, began to develop their own cultural identity during the classic period. Emblematic glyphs and distinctive art styles were developed in different centers. By the end of the classic period, centers were more diverse, and it was more difficult for a single center to maintain hegemony over the others. The development of competitive centers led to the creation of alliances, coalitions, and the attainment of power by different states (Friedel 1986). Perhaps the diversity of the different Mayan cultures can be more clearly observed in the postclassic period, when groups dispersed and differences grew as their interaction became less important. In a similar way, "the contemporary Mayan groups continue to be isolated and alienated from each other by poverty, by politics that discourage unification and communication, and by national borders" (Schele, Freidel, and Parker 1993:41).

Ethnohistoric records like the *Popol Vuh, Annals of the Cakchiquels,* and *Title Deeds of the Lords of Totonicapán,* among others, tell that the forebears of the inhabitants of the altiplano region of Guatemala came from a single place, Tula in Mexico, and that afterward they differentiated more and more. According to the *Popol Vuh,* each tribe of Vukamag took possession of a different ecological niche where it developed ethnic variations. At this time, even if they had shared the same traditions when they arrived in the Guatemalan altiplano, they began to practice different ceremonies that reorganized their vision of the world, based strongly on their religion. According to the *Popol Vuh,* not long after their arrival, the K'iche's began to cause their neighbors suffering in order to satisfy the wishes of their governors and of *Tohil.* "It was not little what they did, neither were few, the tribes which they conquered. Many branches of the tribes came to pay tribute to the Quiché; full of sorrow, they came to give it over" (Recinos, Goetz, and Morley 1983:228).

The historic accounts also tell that the Maya of the Yucatán, Petén, and Tabasco had conflicts during the postclassic period. Bishop Diego de Landa stated in his sixteenth-century work, *Relación de las cosas de Yucatán,* that the Kokomes allied with the Tutul Xiues, but later ended their friendship in an internal civil war; the groups separated and established their lineages in different ecological zones. The Cheles, who live on the Yucatán coast, did not allow the foreign Kokomes to extract salt and fish from their territories. In the same way, the Kokomes, who lived in the heart of the jungle, did not permit the Cheles to hunt or collect fruit in their territory (Landa 1982). These conflicts contributed to each Maya group's emphasizing its own unique or distinctive character, and these differences became heightened after the Spanish invasion in the sixteenth century. The results of these historic, geographic, and cultural adjustments are reflected in the variations of language, social organization, technology, artistic life, and traditional dress. Despite this distinctiveness, these characteristics remain interrelated on a macrolevel of cultural identity. Thus, all Maya cultures can be configured within a basic Maya pattern that continues to be strong and persistent as a result of this diversity.

Maya culture has survived because distinct ethnic communities adapted in different ways to their ecological environments and developed different survival strategies with which to face five hundred years of subjugation. The diversity within Mayan culture is the result of many parts — thirty-one linguistic communities in the Maya region (Guatemala, Mexico, Belize, and Honduras) — adapting and changing in varying capacities. Surely some passed more quickly through processes of change and acculturation, while others maintained greater continuity with their ancient and recent past.

The concept of culture in Wolf (1982) — a group of ideas and processes in constant change leading to the formation of an ideology — is relevant to the Maya case. It is in their religious system that we can more clearly observe the process of forming an ideology. Different Maya cultures have reelaborated the Maya religion in a syncretic process, retaining the use of religious symbols of continuing importance, such as the cross. To illustrate this, the *ceiba,* or kapok tree, is the "cosmological tree of life" and bears much symbolic application (Morley and Brainerd 1983). Long before the conquest, the ceiba was the tree of life to the Maya, and they believed that it held up the skies. In the Yucatán,

in the Postclassic, the Mayan paradise was described as a place of delights, where there was no suffering and where food and drink abounded.

> Growing there was a *yaxche,* sacred tree of the Mayans [the ceiba], in the
> shadow of which one could always rest from one's labors. (Morley and
> Brainerd 1983:468)

With the imposition of Christianity, the Maya adopted the Christian cross,
seeing the similarity between it and Maya crosses like those seen at Palenque.
Since then, the cross has expressed diverse ritual functions. Maud Oakes, for
example, observed that in the *Todos Santos* (All Saints' Day or the Day of the
Dead) celebration in the Guatemalan altiplano, the cross is a special element in
witchcraft. "In order to provoke sickness in a *brujo* (sorcerer, shaman) that has
caused you damage, make three crosses from old, red pitch pine and put them
into a bottle" (Oakes 1951:167). Among the Chamulas of the Chiapas highlands,
the cross can protect the traveler's path. On a path going to Tuxtla, there was a
demon who was killing and devouring travelers, until two Chamulas decided
to kill him. "When he appeared, they made a cross in the ground with their
sticks. This forced the demon to drive his sword into the ground rather than
into them. They beat him to death right on the place of the cross" (Gossen
1984:292). The cross can also be related to very ancient Maya ceremonies similar to the erection of stelae every twenty years, as is done among the Jakalteks of
the Cuchumatan Mountains. Every so often, large crosses were erected in front
of the churches. "These crosses see, think, hear, and even talk to the Mayan
priests that know how to get in touch with them" (La Farge and Byers 1931:186).
The cross is also an important symbol in the ceremonies related to the planting
of *milpa* (cornfields). For example, among the Q'eqchi' Maya and the Mopanes
of Petén and Belize,

> the night before sowing the corn, those that are going to help assemble in
> the home of the milpa's owner to keep watch through the night. A cross
> is placed at one end of the hut and before it, on a table or on a piece of
> bark, they place the sacks of corn that will be used as seeds. (Thompson
> 1930:48)

Finally, among the Maya of the Yucatán the transformation of the role of
the cross is evident. According to Farriss (1984:315), "The Speaking Cross of
the Maya Caste War is a prime example of the divergence between form and
meaning."

The remaking of Maya culture has led it to become divergent and pluralistic, as evidenced in the distinct Maya areas of the Guatemalan altiplano, the

Chiapan highlands, the Yucatán, Petén, and Belize. The cultural similarities are derived from the great Maya macroculture. Cultural actions and identification with the underlying Maya culture have given modern Mayas their identity or Mayaness. The recognition of a great, shared Maya culture is expressed in a variety of rituals, both secret and public, including the use of the ancient, sacred calendar and the public tradition of the system of *cargos* (offices or responsibilities) that has been maintained in the Maya region as a politico-religious system of mutual, community work and leadership. Its current manifestation retains the ascent through a series of positions and duties, and also serves as an equalizing mechanism in Maya communities (Farriss 1984).

As each group has developed different strategies for maintaining and preserving its part of the (macrolevel) ancient Maya culture, some changes have resulted in transforming the meaning of the original cultural traditions. The Maya culture is not static; even as it has gone through many processes in the distant past, it is going through others now in the forms of revitalization and pan-Mayanism, and it will continue to go through changes in the future. Currently, we must take into account the internal and external forces that provoke changes or that sustain continuities among modern Mayas. One external force, a source of much pressure to change, is Protestant fundamentalism. Here the change is especially oriented toward a new ideology and social organization and the eradication of ancient religious practices. In Sacapulas, for example,

> the missionaries win converts; part of the process seems to include a distancing of these converts from participation in broader community issues. From the point of view of practical evangelism, it is necessary to remove the converts from the traditional organization of the *cofradía* [religious brotherhood] and from the religious beliefs associated with it. (Hill and Monaghan 1987:146)

The impact of Western economies, including feudalism and capitalism, in the entire Maya region has been another such external force. The conflict between different modes of production, as Wolf (1982) suggests, has brought cultural transformation. As traditional Maya economic systems have been replaced or modified, the impact of capitalism can be noticed everywhere. The new economic models have provoked ruptures in traditional lifestyles. Different modes of expropriation and exploitation of native land, from *encomiendas* and *haciendas* to plantations, submerged indigenous people into dependent economic positions. The colonial reorganization of towns and settlements encapsulated Maya populations as they tried to resist the invasion and control of ladinos (Lutz and Lovell 1990). Capitalist transitions created constant ruptures among the different groups, further accentuating the isolation of Maya communities.

Among recent factors working against the continuity of traditional Maya culture, and perhaps the most threatening, has been the armed conflict between the Guatemalan army and the Guatemalan National Revolutionary Unity (URNG). In this conflict, thousands of Maya have been killed, and their culture has been undervalued by the forces involved in this conflict. Both sides have used the indigenous people for their own political, military, and ideological objectives. In the same way, the existence of civil patrols in the Maya communities contributed to the destruction of Maya traditions, such as the respect for elders and communal solidarity.

Maya resistance and continuity can be strongly distinguished as a mechanism for cultural survival that gives a new form to modern Maya identity or Mayaness. The current process of constructing a coordinated effort toward subsistence and cultural reaffirmation among these Mayan linguistic communities, or pan-Mayanism, is the result of the violent history experienced during the last four decades. Maya culture was most dramatically affected during the military confrontation between the army and the guerrillas from 1982 to 1992. The Maya people have responded by organizing for their own reaffirmation. This cultural resurgence requires the Maya to be able to express themselves freely and contribute their own systems of knowledge, ideology, and community politics to the construction of a new multicultural Guatemalan nation-state.

The Construction of a Pan-Maya Ethnic Identity — The Present

Panindigenous movements have always existed when the indigenous cultures in question have been under external pressure and thus in danger of total extinction. In North America, panindigenous movements developed at the end of the colonial era as a result of the continuous dismantling of indigenous cultures and their confinement on reservations and as an alternative to extinction. The policy of the government of the United States at the end of the 1840s sought

> to impede indigenous interference in the activities of the "civilized" race
> at the same time as it exercised a benevolent paternalism to assure the

survival of at least part of the native population, even if under controlled conditions. (Trennert 1975)

Panindigenous movements developed as a response to the needs of the cultures to survive and as organized resistance to brutal domination and expropriation. Indigenous uprisings were attempted in an effort to rid themselves of the oppressors and resuscitate their cultural traditions, reactivating indigenous religious symbols and beliefs. An example is the Ghost Dance among the Plains Indians of North America in the 1890s (Mooney 1965). Unfortunately, these indigenous movements were considered irrational uprisings of "savages" against the civilized people (European Americans), and this supposed irrationality justified the destruction of the Indians and their movements at the hands of government troops, as happened at the massacre at Wounded Knee, South Dakota in 1890. Other examples of these panindigenous movements include the revolt of Tupac Amarú in South America in the 1780s, the Caste Wars in the Yucatán in 1850 (Reed 1964), and the Kikuyo revolt in Africa in 1870, from which pan-African movements derived with even more radical agendas (Nwafor 1973). Historically, then, the efforts of indigenous leaders to attain their peaceful dreams of retaking and reviving their traditional ways of life have run into the armed violence of the nation-state controlling their destiny.

In Latin America during the past decade, multinational, panindigenous organizations have arisen "from their fragmented histories of oppression, marginalization, and war" (Messer 1993:231). In recent years, the indigenous movements for self-determination have developed within a global framework of human rights, mutual respect, and valuation of cultural diversity. Efforts have been oriented toward the attainment of "unity in the practices of basic human rights without destroying cultural diversity" (Messer 1993:232). And like many other indigenous groups struggling to survive and make themselves visible to the world, the Maya of the Mayab' region have encountered great interference from their own governments. In Guatemala and in Mexico, the Maya are struggling to maintain their Mayaness in spite of the tremendous impact of militarism and other forms of political, religious, and academic intrusion into their cultures. In this situation, Tedlock (1993:169) states that

new communal cultures are arising today in the context of the Mayan diaspora to resist Western domination and control. Languages, myths, traditional Mayan dress, sacred lands, and the ancient 260-day calendar have become key cultural values and symbols for the construction of a transnational, pan-Mayan identity.

Among the Maya exiled in Mexico between 1982 and 1996 there developed a consciousness of belonging to and sharing the same base Mayan culture: "since the mid-1980s, pan-Mayan groups have taken on more importance, although, due to linguistic diversity, they have adopted Spanish as their *lingua franca*" (Warren 1993:26). Similarly, when referring to the process of construction of an identity and pan-Maya ethnic relations among the Maya, Carol Smith (1990:279) has stated that

> the primary goal appears to be the creation of a new and stronger, *general* Maya identity, one that maintains the values of the past while dealing with development issues in the present—a goal they recognize to be highly charged in political terms. (emphasis in original)

The idea of belonging to a larger Maya civilization has strengthened the different communities in their struggle for cultural survival. In the refugee camps in Chiapas, Mexico, some Maya participated in reviving and promoting their culture as a means of relieving the anguish of exile. Different ethnic groups, such as the Q'anjob'ales, the Chujes, the Mames, the Jakalteks, the Huistecs, and impoverished ladinos, shared the same refugee camps. They were all survivors and victims of the same violent repression of 1982. In this common suffering, they unified their efforts to remain in exile and denounce with their presence the continuing violations of human rights in Guatemala. Their remaining in the refugee camps in the face of pressures from both the Mexican and Guatemalan governments to return was a powerful and effective response to the antisocial and anticultural strategies of the government of Guatemala.[2]

The refugee camps made it possible for Maya groups to learn different survival strategies from one another. Out of the painful experience of exile, the Maya built a broad ethnic solidarity. The positive ethnic relationships in the refugee camps also extended to the Mexican Maya with whom the refugees had contact. The solidarity among the Maya groups across these national borders was applicable and unique to that setting.

> Despite regional and historical diversity, this common identity of exiles and "hosts," of Indian refugees and Indian protectors, is quite specific to the Mexican-Guatemalan situation. (Pellizzi 1988:160)

In the refugee camps, Maya culture was reborn and flourished. An interesting case is that of the Tzotzil-Tzeltal-speaking villagers of Las Maravillas, Tenejapa, who hosted Maya refugees in their community. Beyond humanitarian reasons, the Tzotzil Maya welcomed the Guatemalan Q'anjob'al and Chuj Maya for the help they could provide in improving the local economy. The refugees worked picking coffee for the Tzotzil villagers, and in return the Guatemalans had access to community resources.

> In addition to land-use rights and employment, benefits include a school for their children, access to the Mexican medical personnel who visit the collective, and a community that cares for them as equals, as Mayans. (Earle 1988:261)

This encounter between Mexican and Guatemalan Maya in Mexican territory gave meaning to the pan-Maya ethnic identity, a new political and cultural development. The stereotypes and previous images that one Maya linguistic group had of another remote Maya community lessened as Maya of different regions came into direct contact with one another. The refugee camps were a fertile field for the different groups to share their culture. The Mexican Maya gave help and expressed solidarity with their brothers and sisters who were living in miserable conditions in the camps, thus developing a broad consciousness and a better understanding of the ethnic barriers and linguistic differences that exist.[3]

The contact between Guatemalan and Mexican Maya opened a strong relationship beneficial to the continuity and survival of the great Maya tradition. For example, some Q'anjob'al Maya women who had long ago forgotten the art of weaving relearned it from Tzeltal and Jakaltek weavers, sharing their knowledge to strengthen and enrich life in the camps and open ethnic borders and cultural barriers that in the past had kept them isolated.

A similar situation of sharing and increasing consciousness has been occurring among the Maya immigrants to Florida in the United States. According to Allan Burns, the original Maya settlers in Indiantown (in southern Florida) were mostly Q'anjob'al Maya from San Miguel Acatán, but by the 1990s they had been joined by people from other Maya communities. "The people from San Miguel Acatán continued to be the majority, but a growing number of people joined them from Todos Santos, El Quiché and other areas of the Guatemalan altiplano. Many community leaders began to forge a pan-Mayan identity" (Burns 1993:14). The mobilization of the indigenous people across international borders has increased during the last decade, and "this process of pan-indigenism is also a result of the current mobilization and forced redefinition within the capitalist world system" (Varese 1988:14). The immigrants arriving in the United States (Florida, Southern California, the Southwest) tend to keep their unity as ethnic groups through common symbols such as the patron saint (in Indiantown it is San Miguel) and the marimba, although the marimba is being replaced by *norteño* music, such as that played by the Mexican artistic group Los Tigres del Norte.

In these healthy transcultural relationships, Maya of many origins openly learned and shared each other's cultural conditions. There developed a better understanding of cultural differences and similarities, intensifying common cultural roots.

The Present Situation in Guatemala

In Guatemala, it is important that Maya reaffirm their cultural identity within the politics, epistemology, and ideology of Maya culture (Montejo 1993a). Pan-Mayanism is a cultural movement of self-understanding and valuation of the Maya heritage without including the advocacy of the nonviable, perhaps even dangerous, concepts of an encapsulated Maya nation-state or an ambiguous Maya nationalism, as has been proposed by others (Smith 1991). Many Maya prefer to direct their efforts to redefine their identity within a process of self-determination and self-representation that will help to create a pluralist Guatemalan nation-state. Pan-Mayanism is a fundamental phase for the attainment of future objectives because, first, we should feel proud of our Maya culture in order to understand its dynamic history, and, second, the stereotypes and the ideological constructions or images that are rooted in the minds of non-Maya people within the national state must undergo a radical change into positive images through an appreciation of Maya history and culture, past and present. It is not enough to idealize history and use the rhetoric of Mayaness if we do not create a Maya knowledge that will go into the construction of a multiethnic and multicultural Guatemalan nation, built with the commitment of both Maya and non-Maya. If Guatemala wants to continue proclaiming its unique character as a nation by using Maya elements and symbols, then it must recognize the active role of Maya people and culture as integral to the construction of the nation-state.

One officially recognized Maya institution of national and international status, the Academia de las Lenguas Mayas de Guatemala (ALMG; Academy of

Mayan Languages of Guatemala), is a strong vehicle for promoting Maya culture. The role of the ALMG has been fundamental in the recovery, maintenance, and promotion of Maya culture and Mayan languages. It has reached different Mayan linguistic regions of the entire Guatemalan territory to stimulate

> the use of native tongues in state schools and other institutions and promote the use of a unified alphabet to write the 21 Mayan languages. It was granted official recognition in 1999 as an "autonomous state entity" with the mandate to "promote the knowledge and use of Maya languages and to research, plan, program and implement relevant linguistic, literary, educational and cultural materials." (Smith 1991:30)

The ALMG pursues Maya objectives by putting its programs into practice in different Mayan linguistic regions, with the understanding that all Maya belong to the basic Maya culture, the macro-Maya cultural tradition. After all, the ALMG must maintain its condition as an "autonomous state entity" in order to continue its work. To assimilate into a government bureaucracy or to be manipulated into adopting political programs promoted only by the state can only change or alter the original objective of having Maya people recognize their part and their place in the overall Maya culture.

Another important organization is the Consejo de Organizaciones Mayas de Guatemala (COMG; Council of Maya Organizations of Guatemala), an umbrella organization that played a more political role by channeling indigenous demands for autonomy and self-determination and strong Maya participation in the peace negotiations in Guatemala.

> COMG even brings up the taboo subject of army repression, and specifically requests participation *as Maya* in the dialogue currently taking place between the government and the Guatemalan National Revolutionary Union (URNG) guerrillas. As they see it, the ladino state and ladino guerrilla commanders should not decide the fate of the Maya traumatized by the actions of each. (Smith 1991:30; emphasis in original)

In the construction of a pan-Maya ethnic identity, the role of the Maya media is fundamental. Among the institutions dedicated to the diffusion of Maya ideas and information are the Cholsamaj publishing company *Rutzijol* and the multilingual newspaper *El Regional*. Cholsamaj publishes books and booklets on Maya issues; *Rutzijol* is a bimonthly news magazine that presents a selection of articles about Maya people; and *El Regional* is a weekly newspaper containing articles in Mayan languages as well as in Spanish for Maya readers in western Guatemala.

The work of a wide variety of Maya leaders on national and international levels advances recognition for the Maya people. There are many Maya men and women quietly working at local and national levels for the improvement of Maya communities. Some are more visible and are heard on a larger stage. One is Nobel Prize winner Rigoberta Menchú, whose efforts have put indigenous issues at the forefront of discussions in Guatemala and the Americas. The role of the *ajq'ij* or Maya priests has become a symbol of rebirth and unification of the Maya culture on a national level.

The very complex Maya culture is the expression of several levels of understanding. Different visions of the world are being reworked by each of the linguistic communities in the Maya region, which also contain the expression of different sectors of the Maya population: intellectuals, small farmers, and traditional religious leaders, both men and women. We must listen to all of these voices to avoid radicalizing our actions, which would in turn limit the access and expression of each Guatemalan Maya sector. We must understand the political environment, not only on a local level but also on national and international levels. The world is changing dramatically, and we must reinforce our national sentiments through the recognition of other ways of thinking. As a result, pan-Mayanism must bring to light the value and the creativity of the whole Maya culture. We want our culture to be seen, not just as a relic from the past (the classical Maya), but also in the present, as Maya who are creating and recreating our culture, even in the aftermath of war and violence.

The distinctive character and the cultural manifestation of each Maya community are recognized and valued within the pan-Maya understanding of the Maya cultural identity. Pan-Mayanism is the recognition of the different ways in which the Mayan linguistic groups have contributed to the maintenance and continuous transformation of Maya culture. Maya cultural diversity should be seen as an advantage for the continuity of the basic Maya culture and not as an obstacle. As Smith (1991:31) has argued,

> while the fragmentation of Maya identity is usually seen as a weakness by both leftists and Maya nationalists, it is actually a source of cultural resilience, which allows for a variety of adept responses to changed circumstances, and prevents the state from assaulting all Maya communities at once.

Pan-Mayanism: Basic Objectives, Looking toward the Future

In Guatemala, the rebirth of Maya ethnic identities has gained much strength in the face of the systematic destruction of native communities, and interethnic movements are recreating and redefining pan-Maya identity. This effort to deepen and promote the Maya legacy and reaffirm Maya identity is a political act. Its occurrence is thus inevitably successful, despite the barriers encountered by modern Maya when practicing their sacred beliefs and traditional knowledge. From pre-Hispanic times through the Spanish conquest, colonial domination, and into the modern era, Maya culture has flourished and constantly diversified, even in the restricted spaces available for its development. Maya cultural diversity has developed different resistance strategies over a period of five hundred years, unique and sophisticated strategies for survival. The recognition and valuation of the distinctive cultural character of each Mayan linguistic group make the pan-Maya identity strong and complex. Pan-Mayanism advocates for a common Maya identity, one that shares a base Maya culture and also values and recognizes the diversity that empowers the Maya culture to continue into the future. This movement of mutual recognition does not impose a specific role on each Maya group, but rather values the part each plays in the Maya culture. Pan-Maya ethnic identity validates the role that the culture has had for centuries. Although modern Maya have not erected temples as our ancestors did, we, too, are Maya fighting for our space in this century and in the millennium just begun.

The importance of the development of a pan-Maya cultural identity can be summed up in the following way:

1. By reaffirming that we are Maya like our ancestors, because we have inherited the millennia-old traditions that we are still recreating in the present;
2. By recognizing that Maya culture is not a monopoly of a single Maya group, the Yukatek Maya or K'iche', as some anthropological research has led us to believe, but rather that the different Maya groups share a basic, common culture that gives them their pan-Maya identity;
3. By making the diversity of Maya cultures visible, to reaffirm our presence as Maya in this twenty-first century;
4. By making pan-Mayanism an interethnic movement that values and recognizes the importance of diversity within the unity of Maya culture;

5. By considering any violence that affects any particular Mayan linguistic group as an attack on Maya culture in a broader sense;

6. By recognizing that the existing stereotypes among Maya ethnic groups are a result of the isolation forced on them by other groups. All Maya should understand and recognize that there are different ways of being Maya;

7. By seeing the defense of the cultural patrimony of the Maya as a concern for all Mayan linguistic groups;

8. By developing communication and relations, not in such a way that homogenizes Maya culture by imposing ideas of any Maya cultural elite, but rather through discussing the diversity of Maya culture as a value and a strategy for maintaining the culture's strength and vitality for the future;

9. Most importantly, by Mayan linguistic groups unifying their efforts to defend this pluralism in their rights and cultural patrimonies;

10. By Maya seeking this pan-Maya identity for legitimizing their cultural revitalization projects both within and outside of the nation-state;

11. By acknowledging that pan-Mayanism is a process of overcoming the restrictions of the so-called "closed corporate community" favored by the colonial system.

Thus, the culture shared with other Maya ethnic communities should be progressively recognized, maintaining equality and respect for differences and cultural particularities. With a greater understanding of their role as Maya, the Maya can reach a better consensus, one that will allow them to participate directly in negotiations and discussions that affect their lives. An indigenous perspective is needed to find solutions to the problems remaining in postconflict Guatemala, and this will be achieved through integrating into society the Maya philosophy of esteeming a harmonious life, respect, and coexistence with people, nature, and the universe.

Pan-Mayanism gains relevance when there are forums in which the different Mayan linguistic regions and groups meet to promote their voices and their creativity. A pan-Maya culture will lay the foundation for the construction of a Guatemalan nationalism that is multicultural, where Maya and non-Maya are treated equally as Guatemalans. This cooperation can provide the basis for more permanent peace and security, rejecting the current nationalist project of the ladino elite. Maya do not want to isolate themselves in small nation-states. Historical factors of uneven development have given some Maya groups advantages over others. Maya who do not belong to an advantaged group would face the double pressure of domination by the ladino or mestizo elite and by Maya from these more privileged groups.[4] We need to recognize the presence, contributions, and leadership of other nonmajority Maya peoples such as the Chujes, the Mames, the Jakalteks, and the Ixiles. We do not need to create another Yugoslavia or to produce ethnic wars and tribal conflicts such as those that occur in Africa. All Guatemalans, Maya and non-Maya, must coordinate their efforts to contribute to peace and solidarity as a basis for the construction of a pluralist Guatemalan nation-state.

Conclusion

As we have seen, Maya culture is a very complex system, a group of subsystems partially interrelated and partially distinct. Clearly, more comprehensive regional studies should be undertaken by Maya scholars, ethnographically within each ethnic group and ethnologically using comparative methods for the region as a whole. In this way we can begin to understand the dimensions and the depth of the macro-Maya culture that we share.

These attempts to unify Maya tradition are undertaken in a most violent time, when aggression against indigenous people has reached the category of genocide or ethnocide in both Guatemala and Chiapas. It is possible that the process of Maya unification could awaken a radical change in Guatemala that would benefit Maya and non-Maya alike. In this process, all ethnic groups must be taken into account, since there is currently no hegemonic Maya group which can speak for all and since many individual actors seem to be jealously guarding their identities and particular ways of life. A recognition and appreciation of other forms of Maya ethnicity as a part of a broader Maya culture will contribute to promoting pan-Maya culture, that is, diversity of Maya culture within its unity, and will be valuable for the construction of a multicultural nation-state in Guatemala. I am hopeful that the current demands of the indigenous people for self-determination and the support of the United Nations of those demands will help the Maya coordinate efforts to know and value their own unique character and so to contribute to the greatness of the Guatemalan nation.

CHAPTER 3

Representation via Ethnography

Mapping the Maya Image in a Guatemalan Primary-School Social-Studies Textbook

Introduction

Following the current debates and new developments in the field of anthropology, postmodern ethnography has become an influential and useful tool for native intellectual critics of older anthropological studies. In *Writing Culture* (1986), Clifford and Marcus call this an experimental moment in ethnography. Marcus and Fisher argue that in the postmodern world we must deal with postmodern everything. But "the part of these conditions in which we are more interested is what we call a crisis of representation" (Marcus and Fisher 1988:8). James Clifford (1988:23), speaking of postmodern ethnography, says:

> It is more than ever crucial for different peoples to form complex concrete images of one another, as well as of the relationships of knowledge and power that connect them; but no sovereign scientific method or ethical stance can guarantee the truth of such images. They are constituted — the critique of colonial modes of representation has shown at least this much in specific historical relations of dominance and dialogue.

Attracted by the openness of this experimental moment in ethnography, I would like to identify some aspects of this crisis in the representation of the Maya image in Guatemala. While critical anthropologists advance their political discourse on decolonization, the images of the Maya portrayed in some earlier ethnographies persist and continue to exert their negative influence on the life of the subjects studied. This chapter attempts to come to grips with the colonialist effect of anthropology on historical social relations (Asad 1988).

In general, the continuous distortion in the representation of non-Western people is based on the assumption that these people "needed" to be spoken for.

Assuming that awkward native peoples are silent and passive subjects, anthropologists have in fact participated in the implementation of national agendas
that have legalized and continued the economic, political, and sociocultural
domination of natives. Marcus and Fisher (1988:1–2) argue that anthropologists have employed many artifices to minimize the non-Western cultures they
have studied:

> Among these rhetorical devices [used by anthropologists] are devalua-
> tions of contemporary Arabs, Greeks, Egyptians, or Mayans relative to
> their ancient forebears. . . . Still today, the search is too often for survivals
> of this glorious heritage in decayed and corrupt form among descen-
> dants, while denying any intrinsic value to their contemporary cultures.

The Maya of Guatemala are marginalized despite their being the majority (60
percent) of the Guatemalan population. Their case is complex: the issues involved are colonialism, power relations, ethnicity, nationhood, and class formation. But my focus in this chapter is the creation and maintenance of a distorted image of the Maya, the result of which has been the loss or blurring of
their ethnic identity. The goal of this process for the dominant class has always
been the complete assimilation of Maya communities into the nation-state, a
goal that has eluded them for the past century.

This analysis borrows from Canclini's theoretical approach to the study of
cultures as a contested arena for hegemonies (1984). Canclini suggests that one
approach to the study of popular culture is the one that considers culture as an
instrument to comprehend, reproduce, and transform the social system. Canclini asks us to consider cultures as the "spontaneous creation of the people,
their memories transformed into merchandise or an exotic spectacle of backwardness that the industry translates into a curiosity for tourists" (Canclini
1984:15).

This approach bears considerable relevance in the case of the Maya of Guatemala. Obviously, the Maya constantly create and recreate their worldview, but
this Maya cultural "creation" is only valued by the dominant sector of society
when it can be used as merchandise or for its curiosity value in attracting
tourists. Canclini (1984:17) sees this as a vital, if contradictory, link between
dominant and dominated groups because it sets up a constant and conflictive
interaction between the different hegemonic sectors in an expanding capitalist world.

Capitalism, above all that which is dependent with strong indigenous roots, does not always advance by eliminating cultural traditions but rather also by appropriating them, restructuring them, reorganizing the meaning and the function of their objects, beliefs, and practices. Their preferred resources . . . are the reordering of production and consumption in the country and in the city, the expansion of tourism and state politics of ideological refunctionalization.

In the case of Guatemala, a dependent country with strong indigenous roots, the dominant white and ladino population does what Canclini describes. Maya culture is appropriated, although governmental actions have also aimed at eliminating the bearers of that same culture through ethnocide and assimilation. This cultural domination has occurred mainly through the expansion of tourism and state political ideologies, particularly the sale of the image of the Maya through tourism promotion and exotic souvenirs ranging from postcards to textiles, while promoting that "fossilized" image of the Maya through the state educational system and curricula. In Guatemala, the persistent colonial and neocolonial representation of the Maya as Indians is found in elementary social-studies textbooks. This mode of representation can be traced to the early ethnographies on the Maya. I argue that this scientific knowledge produced by early North American anthropologists studying the Maya has been taken at full face value and placed in primary-school textbooks in order to fulfill racist and classist national agendas that perpetuate social control and intellectual domination.

This chapter puts forth three major hypotheses. First, that some early scholars of the Maya have constructed histories that distorted Maya images and that this scientific knowledge has been taken as true to construct Guatemalan primary-school social-studies textbooks. Second, that these textbooks have supported an agenda of social control and domination by presenting the Maya (the "Indians") as a defeated race, thus providing ideological constructs that serve the dominant class interests by locating the Maya in a timeless past without connection to the living people of today. Third, that textbooks are themselves polysemic constructs (documents with multiple meanings) that can be broken apart or deconstructed for the purpose of revealing some elements of that dominant ideology.[1] This analysis will also take a comparative perspective, drawing upon similarities and differences between the Guatemalan Maya and the Maya of the Yucatán in Mexico. Particular attention is given to the representation of the Maya "image" as described by some early writers and ethnographers, including the work of Bishop Diego de Landa and other early scholars of the Maya like Sylvanus G. Morely and J. E. S. Thompson.

Early "Authorities" on the Maya

One early account described as a masterpiece of Maya representation and endowed with an overwhelming authority is the *Relación de las Cosas de Yucatán* by Bishop Diego de Landa, written in 1560. After burning the Maya codices in the Yucatán as part of his missionary activities, and possibly repenting of the devastation he caused, Landa decided to "rewrite" the Maya history he was so instrumental in destroying. To do so, he interviewed two young Maya leaders, Nachi Cocom and Antonio Chi, and constructed his own history on the nature of the Indians and their beliefs.

This work holds great value for understanding ancient and pre-Hispanic Maya culture, but it is not without its limitations, containing as it does many distorted images that persist to the present and that are still quoted and reproduced in early-twentieth-century ethnographies. The most influential stories are those related to the cultural destruction of the Maya. Diego de Landa was among the first clergy to categorize Maya intellectual achievements and religious rituals as the teachings of the devil. His power and destructive authority are illustrated in his comments on the burning of Maya books, which were written in a hieroglyphic system:

> These people also used certain characters or letters, with which they wrote in their books about the antiquities and their sciences; with these, and with figures, and certain signs in the figures, they understood their matters, made them known, and taught them. We found a great number of books in these letters, and since they contained nothing but superstitions and falsehood of the devil we burned them all, which they took most grievously, and which gave them great pain. (Landa, in Gates 1978:82)

Landa's writings represented the Maya as people with no reasonable control over themselves, but directed and manipulated by evil powers that had to be destroyed. Because Landa was compelled to deny the values of Maya tradition, he perpetuated the image of the Maya as pagans and savages who did not want to become civilized or embrace Christianity.

Landa's ethnocidal action in devaluing Maya tradition has been reenacted time and time again by the dominant elite in both Mexico and Guatemala. As a missionary who came from Spain expressly to save the Indians' souls, Landa saw the presence of the devil everywhere; in every Maya ritual there was a practice of paganism and an adoration of multiple gods. By means of the Inquisition, Landa fiercely persecuted the Maya priests who tried to maintain the practice of their ancient religion.[2] Since then, Landa's authority has been used in the construction and maintenance of the image of the Maya, and these same images have been borrowed and reinforced in modern ethnographies about the present Maya. Proceeding from Landa's assumption that Maya culture, and in particular Maya religious tradition, is the expression of the devil, the dominant class has justified the continuous destruction of Maya culture, calling it a "degenerate" culture that must be assimilated or destroyed.

Other important sources for understanding the image of the Maya prevalent during the twentieth century are nineteenth-century travelers' accounts. During the first part of the twentieth century, a growing number of scholars became interested in unraveling the "mystery" of the Maya, and their interest was fueled by the travel accounts of Stephens and Catherwood in their *Incidents of Travel in Central America, Chiapas, and the Yucatán* (1841). Stephens and Catherwood compiled much of their information about the Maya from the ladinos, politicians, and missionaries whom they met in their journey. Their images of the Maya are greatly distorted in these accounts because their representation of the Maya is not based on actual contact or conversations with them. On their way to visit the Maya ruins of Palenque, Stephens and Catherwood talked with the parish priest of Santa Cruz del Quiché in northern Guatemala. The priest told them the story of a great living Maya city in the Ixil region that nobody had been able to enter.[3] Interested, Stephens and Catherwood tried to change their original plans in order to "discover" this mysterious Maya city (possibly the Maya ruins of Yaxchilán). Stephens (1841:197) seriously considered a plan in which

> five hundred men could probably march directly to the city, and the invasion would be more justifiable than any ever made by the Spaniards; but the government is too much occupied with its own wars, and the knowledge could not be procured except at the price of blood.

Fortunately, Stephens abandoned this adventure, one in which the priest also wanted to participate, as if to revive the adventures of the Spanish conquest of the sixteenth century. This is an example of how the Spanish priest and the ladino authorities represented the Maya as savages and fierce people whose land should be invaded by army troops, even if the price was bloodshed, and all to satisfy the curiosity of two travelers. As the travelers continued on their originally planned route, they were constantly provided with Indian carriers forced by the *justicias* (ladino authorities) to transport the travelers' baggage on their backs from village to village. Written by Stephens and illustrated by Catherwood, *Incidents of Travel* was a major document that opened the unknown Maya to Europeans and North Americans.

It was not until the first part of the twentieth century that systematic studies of Maya culture were sponsored by major educational institutions. Harvard, Tulane, and the University of Pennsylvania, among others, established field schools and archaeological institutes to salvage whatever was possible of this "decaying" Maya civilization. The focus of attention was the past, as if the modern Maya were somehow completely severed from their ancient roots and heritage. In this way, the stereotype of the Indians, created and reproduced since the conquest, was perpetuated in the work of scholars who insisted on the greatness of the past but showed disappointment of the present Maya. None of these researchers spoke Mayan, and whatever they learned about the contemporary Maya was obtained through a Spanish-speaking intermediary, either ladino or Maya. Although some scholars were aware of the unjust social relations seen in the treatment of Maya peasants by rich ladinos and white landowners, they were reluctant to make any political statements against these injustices because they considered these men their hosts. And in many ways their own research was supported and facilitated by the same ruling elite, a common practice in the early days of anthropology.[4] Since research was supposed to be scientific and apolitical, the separation of the anthropologist from the realities lived by the people they studied was taken for granted.

Twentieth-Century Maya Misrepresentation

The dominant representation of the Maya until the beginning of the twentieth century was that of the "primitive," savage, dirty Indian. Although the artistic expressions of this culture (weavings, ancient Mayan murals, and archaeological sites) were appreciated and appropriated, the contemporary Maya were thought to be incapable of human feelings and indifferent to their subjugation and the direct destruction of their culture by civilized white men. Thus, the distorted religious and cultural myths created by Landa and other early missionaries continued to be repeated by early-twentieth-century scholars, thereby receiving the mantle of scientific "truth," which would be echoed by later specialists in Maya studies.

Meanwhile, this erroneously produced knowledge about the Maya was appropriated by the dominant class and is still used as a marker of social differentiation and class stratification today. The Maya were placed on the bottom of the scale at the time of the Spanish conquest, and since then they have been seen as inferior, condemned to hard work and exploitation, often "for their own good." Throughout the centuries, the images and misrepresentation of the Maya have been reinforced and manipulated by members of the dominant class, perpetuating these persistent misconceptions about the Maya.

While traveling and studying Maya life during the 1930s, Erna Fergusson (1949) interviewed several landlords who shared with her their view of the Maya, as in this statement by a Guatemalan *finquero* (plantation owner).

> You can't deal with the Indian, either, on any human basis. Don't get a lot of sentimental ideas about him. He is an animal, that's all. There is no decency or gratitude in him. You can take care of a man and his wife for years, lend him money, get him out of jail, give him work in hard times, patch up his wife when he beats her, and the first chance he gets he walks out and leaves you. They lack the human instinct, I tell you. (Fergusson 1949:290)

This landlord's rationalization takes the form of a racist argument based on biological premises. Landlords have justified their oppressive and exploitative plantation system in numerous ways that permit them to comment on the impoverished lives of the Maya as a "natural" way of life. The *finca* planters believe that the Maya are happy with their miserable existence. Maya needs are denied or reduced to nothing, as explained by another plantation owner:

> All an Indian really needs is a handful of beans, a couple of tortillas, and chile. Chile, you know, contains a wonderful vitamin. Just see how strong they are, how they can carry their quintal (100 pounds) a day and never feel it. Look how rosy the women and children are! They are perfectly happy and well off. Nothing to worry about. (Fergusson 1949:287)

This cruel representation of the Maya has not only persisted since the Spanish invasion, but was popularized by the Guatemalan author Miguel Angel

Asturias, winner of the Nobel Prize for Literature in 1967, who caricatured the Maya as having a "wide nose and mouth, thick lips with turned-down corners, sharp cheekbones, slanted eyes, a straight forehead and large and simple ears often with adhered lobes, [which] give the Indian a physiognomy ugly in itself" (Asturias 1977:77). Since the people who own and control the media (newspapers, magazines, books, comics, and textbooks) have the means to reproduce these negative images, these representations become set in the national consciousness and take on the aura of natural hereditary traits.

During the first fifty years of the twentieth century, interest in the Maya as "exotic" creatures intensified. Scholars of the Maya (particularly archaeologists), tourists, travelers, looters, and vagabonds visited Maya sites and villages, collecting objects for European or North American museums. The Maya became a source of curiosity and speculation, and they were exhibited in national fairs. Guatemala, as a developing nation, wanted to advertise to the world that it still had "savages" in its territories who could be enjoyed by tourists and visitors from the "civilized" world.

One instance of this humiliating treatment and exhibition of "Indians" was organized by Guatemala's president Jorge Ubico in 1938 to celebrate the seventh anniversary of his dictatorship. He resolved to have the most exotic arrangements possible for his national fair. When some of his advisors thought that a group of "savage" Indians would enhance the show, several Lacandon Maya were kidnapped from the northwestern Guatemalan border with Mexico and taken as captives in a small plane to Guatemala City to be exhibited. According to Víctor Perera and Robert Bruce (1982:36),

> the most interesting place in all the fair was a large area encircled by a tall bamboo fence. At one end sat several women who wove on looms. . . . In the middle of this enclosure behind a barbed wire fence guarded by soldiers, a group of five Lacandon Indians was housed in a small hut of bamboo and palm thatch intended to duplicate their jungle home. They wore long white tunics and had shoulder-length, matted hair . . . The look of sadness and confusion in their eyes will stay with me forever.

The dominant class has tried to restructure Maya culture for its own purposes and interests, but the Maya have also presented a constant and subtle resistance against complete assimilation, an annihilation of their Maya identity. The persistence of Mayan languages serves as an example of this resistance. In primary school, Maya children are taught Spanish, beginning in a preprimary program known as *castellanización,* as a strategy to attenuate their culture at an early age, but at home and in the community, the Mayan languages are used to carry out almost all activities of daily life. Maya children learn Spanish, but they also retain their Mayan language, thereby maintaining the hegemony of Maya culture over Spanish within Maya communities.[5] By the 1990s a small program of bilingual education (Mayan and Spanish) was allowed by the Ministry of Education in experimental schools run by the Programa Nacional de Educación Bilingüe Intercultural (PRONEBI; National Program of Bilingual Intercultural Education), the first such deviation from strictly enforced education in Spanish. This program has been extended to become the Programa Nacional de Educación Bilingüe (PRONADE).

Writing Histories for the Maya:
The Role of Non-Maya Scholars of the Maya

In the process of representing Maya culture, or in creating a distorted image of the Maya, we can recognize the roles played by missionaries, tourists, anthropologists, and by the government through the Instituto Guatemalteco de Turismo (INGUAT; National Institute for Guatemalan Tourism), a major agency for the social and cultural appropriation and commercialization of Maya culture. Anthropologists have been key in the creation of Maya images. The scientific knowledge produced by anthropologists has been appropriated by the dominant elite and used in primary-school textbooks in Guatemala as the sole "truth" about the Maya. This has been possible because ethnographers have had the power and the authority, through their interpretations and deciphering, to make pronouncements about what is or is not legitimately Maya.

One of the most influential of the early scholars, Sylvanus G. Morley began writing about Maya culture in 1910. The cultural image and history that Morley created, working in the Yukatek Maya area, have become influential in the construction of the prototype or general image of all Maya, extending beyond the Yucatán and encompassing all thirty-one modern Mayan linguistic communities in the region.[6] From his work in the Yucatán, Morley assigned names to the "Maya gods" from the Yukatek-Mayan language. Morley did not distinguish between different Mayan languages, and his references to "the Mayans" really refer only to the Yukatek Maya and their language.

Morley, like many subsequent scholars, relied heavily upon information provided by Diego de Landa. In accepting literally Landa's information about the Yukatek Maya, however, Morley affirmed the infallibility of the *Relación de las cosas de Yucatán,* which became the most important source of "correct" information about the ancient Maya. Ironically, and certainly inappropriately, what was said about the ancient Maya was applied to modern Maya cultures, thus legitimizing the authority of scholars of the Maya who have just to mention Landa's work to prove the authenticity of their arguments.

In the preface of the first edition of *The Ancient Maya* (1946), Morley insisted that among the sixteenth-century missionaries' reports, the most important work, without a doubt, was

> the contemporary narrative by Fray Diego de Landa, the second Bishop of Yucatan. His *Relación de las cosas de Yucatán,* written in 1566 and extensively quoted in the following pages, is *and remains today indisputably our leading authority on the ancient Maya.* (Morley 1983:v; emphasis added)

Using Landa's ethnographic authority and borrowing from subsequent ethnographic research, successive waves of scholars constructed Maya history, so, "as we will see, there were many hands involved in the preparation of the 'Mayan soup' that we have today" (Morley 1983:12). True to the image of the Maya established by the early missionaries and colonial administrators, Morley (1983:53) commented that "the Maya had a fatalistic mind which may be the product of their ancestral times, in which to die sacrificed was something common and their gods were more hostile than benevolent."

Landa's influence on Morley's concept of Maya religious life can be seen here. Morley did not witness those events (nor had Landa), and yet he states this information as "fact." By creating this speculative image of the ancient Maya and then establishing it as "historic fact" in ethnographies, scholars have helped to distort not only the image of the ancient Maya but that of the present Maya as well. Thus Morley, a dedicated scholar who acknowledged the greatness of the ancient Maya culture, also called into question the intellectual capacity of the present Maya. On this issue he wrote:

> No foreigner has considered them as really stupid although they lack inventiveness and they are happy to follow the same kind of life as their ancestors. It is believed that they have a good memory and good obser-

vational abilities; especially in the cornfields, they are excellent. (Morley 1983:53)

Morley's comment raises doubts about the "human nature" of the Maya. The prototype image is repeated here as elsewhere in the literature. No foreigners consider the Maya as "really stupid." With this statement, Morley suggests that the Maya are indeed stupid, an image clearly held by some Guatemalans, which foreign scholars have reinforced. Like the Guatemalan elite, Morley also insists that the Maya lack any type of initiative and are very reluctant or opposed to change. This justification absolves those who oppress the Maya, a people who have to be "directed" or civilized because they do not know how to conduct their lives. Furthermore, Morley's statement about their capacity as field hands is an old one used by the landlords for their own benefit. It is the classic argument about the tireless Indians who can work like animals or machines without ever complaining or getting tired. The images given credence by anthropologists have thus helped the exploiters by providing convenient images of the Indian as an object to be used, whose place is in the field where he can be productive, especially in the plantations at the service of the powerful landlords.

Most relevant in this Maya "soup" is the creation of many gods for the Maya. In accepting Landa's earlier account, the emphasis on Maya culture as "the work of the devil" or the practice of paganism is expressed again in Morley's work and is followed by his later colleagues.[7]

The K'iche' Maya of Guatemala have articulated the importance of corn in the life of the Maya people in the *Popol Vuh,* which contains a Maya creation myth of the first grandmother making four men and four women from corn dough. Corn also is present as an important Maya element in the Yukatek Mayan ethnohistorical document the *Chilam Balam.* In neither of these documents, however, do the Maya call corn a "god." Rather corn is the gift of God, containing the spirit of creation. Nevertheless, Morley appears to accept the early missionaries' understanding of the place of corn in Maya culture, quoting from the *Crónica de la S. Provincia del Santísimo Nombre de Jesús de Guatemala,* (ch. VII, XVI century ms.) the following: "As we realize, everything that they [the Indians] did and said was related to corn, which to them was *almost as a God*" (Morley 1983:15; emphasis added).

This quotation from early chronicles states that corn was not a Maya god, but that the Maya love for corn was so intense that corn came to symbolize life itself. We in fact learn more about this early chronicler's approach to the concept of God when he notes that corn was prized and loved "almost" as a God. But Morley goes one step further and boldly tells us that corn is a god and that it is represented in Maya iconography.

> God E, as patron of husbandry, is shown engaged in a variety of agricultural pursuits. Rulers impersonating God E are occasionally depicted in Classic period sculpture scattering grains of maize (or drops of blood). Like the maize he typified, he had many enemies, and his destiny was controlled by the gods of rain, wind, drought, famine, and death. (Morley and Brainerd 1983:474)

Thus Maya gods were established through the authority of the scholars of the Maya. Moreover, since archaeologists had already "identified" the image of the Maya god of corn, it was not a problem for Morley to add it to Landa's extensive list of Maya gods, although he also acknowledged the Maya concept of Hun-Hab-K'u (The-Only-One-God) of the Yukatek Maya, known as "The Heart of Heaven" among the K'iche' Maya of Guatemala, stating that "Inasmuch as all Mayan deities were aspects of the same power, the Mayan supernatural realm can be viewed as monotheistic" (Morley 1983:468). He nonetheless chose to follow Landa's authorial statement that "among the multitude of gods which these people adored . . ." (Morley and Brainerd 1983:465).[8] Morley goes on to note:

> A series of studies, made to classify and describe these deities, used the Mayan codices, where the portraits and associated glyphs representing particular anthropomorphic deities are most clearly represented. But although there is a general consensus about the identity of a dozen or so of these deities, there is confusion about the remainder and even disagreement over the total number of separate deities. (Morley and Brainerd 1983:468)

Morley has given us an inordinate number of "gods," such as the four gods or *bacabs* (Year Bearers), the thirteen gods of the Upperworld, and the nine gods of the Underworld, all of which are the commonly seen among other scholars of the Maya. From the codices he has identified the following:

a) Itzamna, the primary deity (God D); b) Chac, a rain deity (God B); c) Bolon Tzacab, a ruling lineage deity (God K); d) Yum Kaax, a maize deity (God E); e) Yum Cimil, a death deity (God A); f) Ah Chicum Ek, a North Star deity (God C); g) Ek Chuah, a merchant deity (God M); h) Buluc Chabtan, a war and human sacrifice deity (God F); i) Ix Chel, a rainbow deity (Goddess I); j) Ixtab, a suicide deity. (Morley and Brainerd 1983:471)

Morley's roster continued, listing gods for almost everything: thirteen deities of the *katuns* (Maya calendric periods of twenty years); nineteen month deities of the year (the deities of the Maya months of twenty days), and gods of the numerals zero through thirteen. Another series of gods included the patrons of the fourteen head variants of Maya numerals, giving us a partial list of gods and goddesses (Morley 1983). The creation of this mythological history for the Maya has had an impact on the way the image of modern Maya has been represented. The true religiosity of the Maya has been converted into a myriad of misunderstandings, from Landa's accusations of the Maya as devil worshipers, to later ethnographers' and authorities' representations of the Maya as worshiping all sorts of bugs and objects.[9] By focusing on archaeological facts and insisting that the "true" Maya have disappeared, these scholars have obscured present Maya consciousness and identity. The Maya consider corn sacred because it contains the spirit of creation that sustains humanity and because it has its own guardian or spirit protector, but they do not call it "God." But even more damaging, this "scientific" knowledge of the Maya has also been placed in the social-studies textbooks used by Guatemalan children, both Maya and non-Maya, in the elementary school educational programs.

From Ethnographies to the Textbook

Morley's personal interest was in resolving the "mystery" of the Maya. His ethnographic work, however, has been appropriated by the Guatemalan educational system and placed in social-studies textbooks. No other work has been used as extensively in the construction of these textbooks as Morley's *Ancient Maya,* an indication of how obsolete these textbooks are. What is the link between the early scholars and the national project of the Guatemalan government from which the "acceptable" image of the Maya has been constructed? How has it been possible for the dominant group to appropriate the knowledge produced by scholars in order to control and dominate the Maya population? How is scientific knowledge used to confirm and promote the hegemony of the dominant elite? This knowledge about the Maya is inculcated in Guatemalan children, both Maya and non-Maya, perpetuating a preferred Maya image used by textbook constructors at the behest and service of the dominant class. Two important aspects of Morley's work are important here: the linguistic mixture of Mayan languages and the persistent idea that Maya worship all sorts of objects as gods.

When writing many of the Maya names, Landa distorted their meaning and form, thereby initiating the distortion of the Maya cultural tradition. Yukatek-Mayan terms were generalized and applied to the entire Mayan-speaking area without distinguishing any language differences. For example, although each Maya linguistic community has specific names for the days of the Maya calendar, scholars of the Maya have insisted on using solely the Yukatek-Mayan terms, thereby giving priority to one Maya ethnic group over other Mayan linguistic communities. The same Yukatek-Mayan names coming from Landa and reworked by Morley have been transplanted into Guatemalan textbooks, even though the day names for the Maya of Guatemala are different from the Yukatek ones.

To illustrate how such ethnographic information is utilized in the Guatemalan education system, consider the following statement in a third-grade social-studies textbook (Cortés 1990:5): "*Se les dice Mayas, a los pobladores se la península de Yucatán y Quichés a los que habitaron la región del Usumacinta y del Petén*" (They call the inhabitants of the Yucatán peninsula Maya, and Quichés those that inhabit the region of Usumacinta and the Petén). (All translations from this textbook are my own.) This short statement presents many contradictions. First, the Maya inhabited and still inhabit the whole Mayan-speaking region, not just the Yucatán. Second, the K'iche' Maya still inhabit the Guatemalan central highlands, but there are other Maya groups there besides the K'iche'. But the use of the past tense *habitaron* (they lived) implies that they all died long ago and that the Indians living now do not have any relationship or historical link to the ancient Maya.

On Maya religious life, the textbook provides the following information:

> The Maya were polytheistic, that is, they worshiped many gods; however, they believed in a supreme God, Hunab-Ku, . . . Other gods: Kinich-ahua Itzamna: symbolizes the sun, his wife Ixchel, the goddess of maternity and medicine. Yum Kaak: the god of corn and abundance. Kaman Elk: god of wind and thunder . . . Ah Puch: god of death. Chac: god of rain. Ek Chaual: god of war. There were other gods such as Yum Chac, god of water. (Cortés 1990:3)

This quotation shows how the misinformation of the scholars has become the true knowledge to be learned about the Maya. Information, obsolete in the light of modern research on the Maya, is put forth in the primary-school social-studies textbooks as the truth to be learned by Maya and non-Maya children throughout the country.

Guatemalan Primary Education and the Maya

Since the 1920s, the Guatemalan government has made efforts to bring schools to Maya communities, however inadequate and culturally inappropriate those schools might be. In 1965 Nathan Whetten (1965:268) noted that

> many of the educational efforts of the past in Guatemala have been poorly adapted to the situation of the rural Indian living in culturally isolated areas. The Indian probably educates his children to the values, needs and goals of his culture, and to the means of attaining them as effectively as do his ladino compatriots. Formal education is a new factor that is alien to the cultural tradition of the Indian. Formal is taken to mean the standardized information imparted to the child in subject matter not directly related to everyday life experience.

Forty years later, the same basic educational system, with all its deficiencies, still prevails.[10] The educational process, institutionalized by the Guatemalan government, exerts subtle social control over Maya children by subjecting them to textbooks that emphasize the elite ideology and by denying them a broader education or one that offers any respect for their culture. These textbooks play a particular role in dispossessing contemporary Maya from most facets of the national culture. Following Belsey (1980), I consider the textbook not an innocent construct, but a way to hide the ideology of a dominant group and convey information that children must absorb and internalize. For the primary-school teacher and for elementary-school children without the intellectual training to decode the hidden ideologies within the text, the messages become the natural and obvious truth.[11] This is the "false obviousness" or "naturalness" that Barthes (1989) rejects as the bourgeois project of confusing history with nature. In this context, the schoolteacher follows an established national program or agenda; it is his or her role to repeat and make children memorize information thought to be relevant for promotion to the next grade, an operation that Althusser called the Ideological State Apparatus (ISA):

The central ISA in contemporary capitalism is the educational system, which prepares children to act consistently with the values of society by inculcating in them the dominant versions of appropriate behavior as well as history, social studies, and, of course, literature. Among the allies of the education ISA are the family, the law, the media, and the arts, all helping to represent and reproduce the myths and beliefs necessary to enable people to work within the existing social formation. (quoted in Belsey 1980:58)

In a class-structured country like Guatemala, the elites have managed to retain and impose their ideology in part by denying the values and the expression of Maya culture. What has been included in the official textbooks is information that distorts or obscures Maya identity. By using some Maya cultural elements (the quetzal, Atanasio Tzul, Maya ruins), the dominant class appears to be negotiating and compromising with the threatening and contesting Maya hegemony.[12] This coming to terms, however, is mostly fictional because the dominant class has the power to decide any national issue without Maya participation, as is evident in the composition of national primary-school textbooks, by which the dominant class decides which information is relevant or "authentic," and therefore is to be taught.[13]

It would not be to the benefit of the Guatemalan dominant class to let the Maya know that they actually have a powerful, living Maya culture; this information would weaken the traditional image repeated *ad nauseam* to the Maya that they are dirty and lazy. The elite discourage the expansion of Maya political consciousness because they see it as a threat to the status quo. As Canclini (1984:158) states,

the bourgeoisie not only has appropriated nature and privatized it via technical domination and not only has it appropriated economic surplus via social exploitation, but it has also appropriated the past, the past of social groups that it oppresses and that it puts at the service of its needs for distinction.

This appropriation is observable in primary-school textbooks that are essential in providing the mythical version of the Maya "reality"—a great Maya civilization collapsed and disappeared—and obscuring both the presence of the modern Maya component of Guatemalan society and the reality and identities of different modern Maya ethnic communities. Maya and non-Maya children re-

Historical sequence inside the front cover of a third-grade social-studies textbook (Cortés 1990)

ceive the same version, containing images and information about the Maya that seem very exotic and distant, giving official sanction to the distorted images of the Maya that persist today.

Deconstructing a Social-Studies Textbook: An Example

The elementary-school textbook *Estudios Sociales, 3er Grado* by Elsy de Cortés is full of contradictions and misrepresentations of the Maya. The textbook begins on the first page with an impressive collection of pictures, presumably as a way of telling children what is relevant in this world.

In order, the images depict a dinosaur, a caveman, an Egyptian, a Roman hero on a gold coin, Joan of Arc, George Washington, Thomas Jefferson, Adolf Hitler, Albert Einstein (the largest figure of all), a DC-27 [*sic*], an astronaut, the numbers 9 . . . 8 . . . 7 . . . 6 . . . , as if counting for the blastoff of a space rocket, and, finally, the moon.

At first reading, these images tell of the "evolution" of the world from dinosaurs to spaceships, but among all these figures, there is no place for or presence of the Maya at all. Instead, we have Egyptian and Roman faces to remind readers of their Western heritage. This omission of Maya culture implies that since it is not part of the Western tradition, it is presumably inferior. To in-

Textbook illustration of Pedro de Alvarado and the conquest of Guatemala, 1524
(Cortés 1990)

clude the Maya in this parade of Western traditions would be to tell the world
that the Maya have important values too. For this reason, the gap is consciously
maintained by the textbook writers as they mythologize the Western world's
achievements. This first visual contact with "history" as constructed in the textbook has an ideological purpose: to tell schoolchildren that astronauts and
space rockets are essential and the products of civilization, but the Maya do
not count at all in this historical process because "they don't have science" as
Western cultures do. These alienating images force Maya children to think of
the world outside their culture as something "superior," a world to which they
must assimilate.

The Conquest of Guatemala

The Spanish Conquest is greatly emphasized in the teaching of Guatemalan
history in elementary schools. This section of the text, *"Conquista de Guatemala,"* begins with the following statement: "As we have already said, when the
Spanish came to Guatemala, they found that it was inhabited *only* by indigenous people divided into kingdoms" (Cortés 1990:18; emphasis added). This
sentence apparently intends to emphasize that the land was not inhabited ex-

cept for some Indians who did not constitute a unified nation. That this land was inhabited "only" by Indians is like dismissing the humanity and the rights of the Indians as real people.

In another paragraph, the following is carefully worded. "The Spanish *were not many,* but they were armed; they brought firearms and steel that the Indians did not know, as well as horses that were also unknown to them" (Cortés 1990:18; emphasis added). "*Los Españoles no eran muchos,*" but those courageous few were able to impose their power over the numerous Indians. In this way the child is taught that the (many) Indians were technologically inferior and unable, or not smart enough, to defend themselves against a few Spaniards during the conquest. Since this is the version of history written by the conquerors themselves, the other side of the story is hidden. The myth of the "few invincible Spaniards" may be accepted without criticism, but fortunately

Conquest of Guatemala by the indigenous allies of Alvarado, depicted in the Lienzos de Tlaxcala (Acuña 1985)

the natives themselves have also written ethnohistorical documents and drawn pictures that depict the Spanish invasion.

The Spaniards were not alone in the conquest. First, they were preceded by waves of diseases brought from Europe by the first explorers. These diseases, remnants of the European plagues, rapidly spread from group to group throughout the Americas, leaving weakened populations to protect themselves against the invaders. The Maya ethnohistorical document *The Annals of Cakchiquels* contains a description of these illnesses. And second, even in the destruction of Tenochtitlán, the Aztec capital, by Pedro de Alvarado (in the absence of Cortés), some twenty thousand Tlaxcaltecas, a Mexican group in conflict with the Aztecs, joined the Spaniards (Prescott 1934). Tlaxcaltecas and other Mexican allies accompanied Alvarado on the invasion of Guatemala in 1524. They were at the front of every battle as the principal allies of the Spaniards during every war of conquest in this region.[14] In this way the dominant class portrays their ancestors with the images that fit their interests. The many actual battles between Spaniards and Maya are consolidated in the text and illustrated by one mythical encounter.

> Tecún Umán killed the horse that Don Pedro was riding and the latter, red with rage, mortally wounded the brave Tecún Umán, and when the Indian chief fell dead, *our* beautiful quetzal also fell at his feet, signifying that with the death of the chief of the Indians *the freedom of his race would also die*. (Cortés 1990:20; emphasis added)

The destiny of all Indians is hereby sealed in the death of Tecún Umán, and children learn that freedom for Maya people was forever denied them at that fatal moment.

The emphasis on Tecún Umán killing Alvarado's horse gives the impression that Tecún could not distinguish between the man and the horse. Tecún (and by extension all Maya) is thus portrayed as ignorant. The "superior" Alvarado kills Tecún Umán, and the legend says that "when the Indian chief fell dead, *our* beautiful quetzal . . ." Although Tecún Umán is identified with the Maya people (with whom white society does not identify itself), the Maya symbol of the quetzal is appropriated by claiming it to be "*nuestro bello quetzal*" (our beautiful quetzal), confiscating one element of Maya culture while clearly denying any link to the defeated "indios" as they are pictured in the history books.

During the invasion of the K'iche' Maya on April 4, 1524, Alvarado showed his inhumanity when he burned the rulers of the K'iche' alive. This criminal

Burning of the Quiché rulers as traitors (Cortés 1990)

act is justified in the official textbook history by the argument that the K'iche' rulers planned to kill the Spaniards when they arrived at the K'iche' capital, Utatlán. Don Pedro realized, however, that

> the city was very strong, the streets narrow, and they only had two entrances, and he felt misgivings about going out with his soldiers to sleep in the field, and later he *knew through an Indian traitor* what they wanted to do with him. When the kings arrived to visit him, he took them prisoners and burned them alive. (Cortés 1990:20; emphasis added)

This passage emphasizes the stereotype of the Indian traitor. Alvarado and the textbook author suggest that burning the K'iche' rulers alive was not really Alvarado's fault, but their own fault because they rebelled against him. Or it was the Indian traitor who condemned the rulers to death. The text thus condemns the *Maya* for opposing the will of the conquerors.

Occasionally the textbook mentions some of the abuses that the Spaniards and colonizers committed against the Maya. "The Spaniards who conquered these lands committed many abuses against the Indians, and these, defenseless, *fled to the mountains where it was difficult to civilize them*" (Cortés 1990:24; emphasis added). This apparent acknowledgment of Spanish atrocities is weakened by the subsequent insinuation that the Spaniards had come to save the Indians' souls and to civilize them. When this was not possible — that is, when Indians were not killed or converted — they "fled to the mountains where it was difficult to civilize them." The clear implication here is that the Indians who fled (and all their descendants) were savages or uncivilized. Thus, the Spaniards and their descendants have always denied that the Maya had any kind of civilization beyond the "teachings of the devil" (Landa 1983). Even today, the modern Maya are considered by many Guatemalans to be a people without feelings, devoid of any type of understanding or knowledge. In his proposal for saving the Indians from this disgrace, Miguel Angel Asturias (1977:98) suggested: "Let us educate the Indian in the ideas of solidarity and cooperation, let us nourish faith and hope in his creed of life and awaken in him a sympathy for his fellow man, for his animals and for his land."

Representing the Maya as people without human feelings, the dominant class gives itself credit for teaching them about cooperation, solidarity, and sympathy for the land. In fact, the Maya have always lived and survived with cooperation, mutual support, and communal solidarity. The land also has given them the basis for their deep-rooted historical identity. It has been their homeland, and they respect the land as a gift from their ancestors. By asserting that Indians do not appreciate the land, the ruling elites have justified their expropriation of it, another devaluation of the Maya to maintain the economic dominance and control by the elite, forcing the Maya to become wage laborers on elite plantations.

At the conclusion of the section on the Spanish conquest in the textbook, there is a full-page picture of Alvarado as he fell from his horse, defeated in Guadalajara, Mexico. The textbook provides this explanation of his death:

> Alvarado attacked the Indians, but these overthrew him and, in the retreat a rider named Baltazar Montoya was running with such fury that his horse threw him to the ground as they were coming around the cliff. In his fall, he took Don Pedro with him, who died as a consequence of the injuries in Guadalajara the fifth of July, 1541. (Cortés 1990:26)

The most vicious of the Spanish conquistadors, Pedro de Alvarado died in one of the battles of resistance waged by the Mexicans. The chroniclers are careful in their explanation of the death of this most mythologized conqueror of the

New World. First, we are told that Alvarado was defeated by the Indians, but then a soldier named Montoya, who "was running with such fury," crashed into Alvarado, who fell with his horse into a deep ravine, dying later as a result of this accident. This construction of history serves to perpetuate the myth of Alvarado as the invincible Spanish captain. He was killed, but not by an Indian. He died through a "mistake" of one of his soldiers who ran over him while running for his life, an example, perhaps of Spanish cowardice, or in modern warfare terminology, "friendly fire."

Conclusion

Despite some minor changes in the Guatemalan educational system since 1996 as a result of the implementation of the peace accords, the educational program is still obsolete and inappropriate for Maya people, and it needs revision to include Maya values and knowledge. The continued use of Landa's Yukatek Maya names indiscriminately throughout the Maya region denies the existence and relevance of thirty-one distinctive Mayan linguistic communities. The distorted image of the Maya in history books and other documents promotes the interests of the dominant elite, and the present reality of the Maya is denied or minimized. The elite appropriation of Maya symbols maintains their power and hegemony. Thus the quetzal becomes the national currency as well as the national symbol of freedom, and Maya ruins are used by INGUAT to attract tourists in such a way that, as Canclini has stated, "The past is mixed with the present, for people as well as for stones: a ceremony for the Day of the Dead and a Mayan pyramid are both scenery to be photographed" (Canclini 1984:16).

The dominant group also appropriated some of the most important moral values of the Maya: respect, community solidarity, and "respect for the land." Arguing that the Maya are lacking in these values, the elites present themselves as the "civilizers" of the Maya who teach them how to be humans.

In this process of appropriation, ancient Maya civilization is glorified while the present Maya are condemned as responsible for the backwardness of the nation. In this entire process, the agenda of the educational system in Guatemala has been to present the Maya as a people opposed to national unity, a people who need to be civilized. Because Guatemalan children often receive their first understanding of national life from the information in textbooks, the distorted image of the Maya is internalized at an early age. For non-Maya, this distorted image becomes the basis for their persistent prejudice and discrimination against the Maya. For the Maya themselves, this distorted image erodes

First Congress on Maya Education, Quetzaltenango, August 1994; *left to right:*
Rigoberto Quemé Chay, Otilia Lux, Victor Montejo, and Camilo Chan Ajché
(author's photo)

Maya identity, causing some Maya to abandon their Mayaness and adopt a
ladino identity. The Maya ethnic identity is then consequently questioned by
both non-Maya and some Maya themselves, those who believe that the indigenous people living now in Guatemala are not Maya, but just indios.

For five centuries, the Maya have been forcibly kept under various systems
of socioeconomic and political control. And although conditioned by imposed
cultural amnesia, many Maya have managed to retain, transform, and continue
their traditional Maya culture, presenting a constant challenge and resistance
to the dominant hegemony of the Guatemalan elite. From the armed rebellions of the past to more subtle forms of resistance in the present, the Maya
have maintained thirty-one different Mayan languages and distinctive cultural
traditions. The current revitalization of Maya culture can add Maya voices to
the struggle to reconstruct Guatemala into a more just and more democratic
nation-state. Educational reform is a tool to that end. By updating the texts
and curriculum with positive images of the Maya, with corrected history, and
with the inclusion of Maya knowledge and worldviews, education in Guatemala can be truly inclusive and multicultural, forming the basis for developing
understanding, respect, and cooperation among all Guatemalans.

CHAPTER 4

The Multiplicity of Maya Voices

Maya Leadership and the Politics of Self-Representation

Mach xhjiloj stzoti' heb'ya' komam komi' yinh janma.
Hatik'a sb'elen heb'ya' ha' b'ay xhkawxi ko k'ul.

(Don't forget the teachings of the ancestors.
In their paths we will find hope for the future.)

— A MAYA ELDER

Introduction

The promise of anthropologists to understand themselves more critically while portraying and representing non-Western cultures (Marcus and Fisher 1986) has not been fulfilled. In most parts of the Americas, anthropologists have continued to represent indigenous people as "primitives" and as objects of study (Tierney 2000), although their rhetoric and academic terms have shifted to more relativistic modes (e.g., from informants to collaborators).[1] Most talk about the postcolonial and postmodern eras, but from a local or regional perspective we can see that most indigenous people are still living in a colonized world. Others with more resources live in a neo-colonized world (economically and intellectually), but most of them cannot call their world postmodern. The rhetoric used in anthropology is a powerful device for maintaining the indigenous worlds as intellectually colonized (Said 1979).

I am not saying that all anthropologists have created works that are designed to colonize the minds of indigenous people, since ethnographies are unlikely to be read by the people themselves, except by a few intellectuals from those cultures. Some anthropologists are writing ethnographic descriptions and analyses that value the current contributions of indigenous people to their communities in the search for ways to promote the process of self-representation (Warren 1998a). In the case of Guatemala, the role of anthropologists should be focused not only on working with indigenous people, but also on starting a process of dismantling the stereotypes and images created by early anthropologists, which have fossilized the image of the classic Maya and covered over the contemporary Maya. To represent themselves, the Maya must now focus their attention on the construction of texts (autohistory) that could destroy the negative images that are embedded in the minds of the ladino (non-Maya) population of Guatemala. Contemporary Maya are living in the present, and the Maya writers of today are telling the world that they, too, carry the creative power of their ancestors (Montejo 1991, 1999a).

As a Maya anthropologist and writer, I am contributing to the present Maya renewal. I believe that anthropologists must contribute to the self-determination of the indigenous people whom they study. This may be a more difficult task for foreign anthropologists, but in my case, being a Maya, I can see the multiple ways in which I can contribute to the autorepresentation of my people. I have been writing testimonial literature to denounce the injustices perpetrated against the Maya. I have also engaged in creative writing, including the writing of children's books, because the negative stereotypes about the Maya must be destroyed at an early age. The multiple voices of the contemporary Maya should be heard because they are no longer silent or sunken in centuries-old amnesia. We remember who we are and where we come from as we fashion our hopes for the future. We are active subjects of our histories and Guatemalan history, too, which was written during the past two k'atuns (twenty-year periods) with Maya blood. We are alive, and we (at least the Maya intellectuals) are now using print capitalism to manifest the persistence of Maya roots going into the next century (Anderson 1990). This time, I insist, we have to listen to the multiplicity of Maya voices because in the past the international solidarity community, mostly leftist, has created pictures that purported to represent Maya or Indian America as a homogeneous whole: for example, the portrayal created for Rigoberta Menchú as the only voice of Indian America.

The Maya must be critical in the construction of their images and Mayaness through a process of ethnocriticism. This ethnocriticism should be placed at the juncture of epistemic roads, Maya truths and Western truths. In other words, a Maya ethnocriticism should position itself in between discourses, at the contested frontier, in order to be an interactionist discourse.

As proposed by Arnold Krupat, ethnocriticism "is concerned with differences rather than oppositions, and so seeks to replace oppositional with dialogical models" (Krupat 1992:15). This dialogical model must be used by Maya to carry out autocriticism of their own Maya culture in relation to foreign, discursive, and ideological control. It is sometimes said that Maya should not criticize some major Maya figure because the "solidarity internationalists" would say that it is anti-Maya. I am willing to criticize my own culture because, like any other civilization, it has its own problems and little hidden monsters and demons.

I would like to open this dialogue by referring to the multiplicity of Maya voices in Guatemala within the current process of self-representation. As a part of the implementation of the peace accords, there is an urgent need for Maya to revise and reorient their current politics and projects for self-representation. In this context, the two prevailing forms of Maya leadership, the popular movement and the pan-Maya movement described below, need to be reoriented. Their previous roles have already been bypassed and taken over by non-Maya politicians, who are now negotiating the future of the Maya population with the formation of new political parties. Also, the problems of leadership among the Maya *are* visible; there is a need for an organized effort to step beyond sectarian-reductionist ideas in order to reconstruct a new Mayan political front that would make Maya voices and knowledge relevant to the current process of national reconstruction. There is a sense of voicelessness, which is unfortunate at this historical moment when the implementation of the peace accords requires strong and effective Maya leadership. In order to achieve stronger expression and reaffirmation of Maya identity, Maya need to redefine their goals and use their ancestral heritage, both material and spiritual, as major symbols for their self-representation. This recharging of Maya identity will dispel the political amnesia of the majority of Maya and ignite a stronger desire to empower ourselves and promote our identities for the future.

This chapter focuses on the current problem of leadership among the Maya and suggests the political avenues possible for articulating this intercommunity effort to reaffirm their Mayaness. One of these avenues is the pan-Maya movement (Warren 1998a), which is developing a bridge between Maya traditionalists and Maya activists, who together would then coalesce into a more viable political entity or regenerationist movement of self-representation. The data that inform this essay are based on regional politics and cultural identity in Guatemala. They focus on national efforts to revitalize Maya culture and the search for ways to achieve political power at the national and international level. But the major issue is to eliminate the stereotypes created about the Maya and other indigenous people of the Americas. Scott Vickers has noted that "the Indians of the Western hemisphere have suffered not only the denigration of their own tribal religions, but also the brutalization of being stereotyped as less-than-human entities, unworthy of basic human decency" (Vickers 1998:27).

Maya and the Self-Representation Projects

I believe that the Maya revitalization movement going on in Guatemala has not yet seriously focused its attention on strategies for self-representation. Until now, political struggles have tried to take power away from the dominant elite through the popular movement's protests and uprisings or by emphasizing the division between two major ethnic communities making up the Guatemalan nation, Maya and ladino. That is why the proposals for the construction of a unified Guatemalan nation-state have always been antagonistic. The most radical representatives of pan-Mayanism argue that Maya and non-Maya cannot develop a united nation-state, but that Maya must have a nation separate from the ladino nation-state. The rhetoric focuses heavily on the issue of internal and external colonialism (Cojtí Cuxil 1996), but offers no clear proposal for achieving such autonomy. In reality, some Maya ideologists are busy thinking about ways of creating a multicultural and multiethnic nation-state, while the majority of the Maya population, which is rural, is living in a state of political amnesia. The reason is that there is still a high rate of illiteracy among the Maya, and their participation in national politics is minimal. It is hoped that, as Guatemalan citizens, they will fully exercise their right to vote. One factor is that literate Maya, like most Guatemalans, do not have the habit of reading, and the few who want to write in national newspapers are not given the space by those who control the media. In other words, print capitalism is not yet fully available to the Maya. The production of knowledge is important; as we can see in the case of Guatemala, those who write and voice their concerns are more likely to be recognized as leaders of the Maya movement (Warren 1998a).

Unfortunately, most of these intellectual leaders are not very effective at convincing other intellectuals and the majority of the Maya population to follow their leadership. Their projects are mostly individual and do not respond to the necessity of bringing changes and prosperity to the Maya. Also, those Maya leaders who talk about decolonization and autonomy are mainly immersed in the political and international patronage of institutions like UNESCO (United Nations Educational, Scientific, and Cultural Organization), USAID (United States Agency for International Development), and the World Bank that maintain the neocolonialist system in Guatemala.

So-called Maya leaders are now competing individually against the rich ladinos, and their attention is focused mostly on economic advantages. Maya leaders in Guatemala are always asking or inquiring if such and such an individual is already *nivelado,* that is, enjoying the status and perks of the affluent dominant class. In other words, to be nivelado is to own and drive an expensive car; have a house in Guatemala City; have a well-paying job with the government or with an international organization such as UNICEF (United Nations International Children's Emergency Fund), USAID, or a powerful international NGO. However, those leaders who claim to be progressive are not free to act unless the Unidad Revolucionaria Nacional Guatemalteca (URNG; Guatemalan National Revolutionary Unity), the former guerrilla leadership, allows them to. When Maya leaders respond to the dictates of political groups run by non-Maya, the movement is impaired and channeled to sectarian interests. This is where the popular Maya movement and, to a lesser degree, the cultural movement stand now. Obviously, this situation has its own reasons for being and presents a difficult historical background to understand and interpret.

From 1960 to 1996, Guatemala was immersed in an internal war that claimed the lives of tens of thousands of Maya and drove thousands of others into exile (Montejo 1987; Carmack 1988; Manz 1988). Finally, on December 29, 1996, the government, the army, and the URNG signed the peace accords that put an end to the armed conflict. Maya are now hopeful that the agreements will be implemented, especially those concerning Maya identity, education, land, and spirituality. Even as the legacy of terror—in the form of thousands of war widows, orphans, and displaced persons—persists, the Maya have clearly survived, and so has their culture. This survival is expressed through the current pan-Maya movement, which is presently restructuring its projects and visions for the future.

The prophetic words of those elders who were concerned about survival are now obviously relevant. In 1982, during the height of the military violence, the elders reminded Jakaltek youth, *"Mach xhqiloq stzoti' heb' ya' komam komi' yinh qanma. Hatik'a sb'elen heb'ya' ha' b'ay xhkawxi ko k'ul"* (Don't forget the teachings of the ancestors. In their paths we will find hope for the future.) These prophetic and hopeful words are now being listened to. Maya believe that when their culture is under attack, the younger generation will pass on the torch and reconstruct Maya culture for following generations. The revitalization of Maya culture responds to this faith and the hope for a better future. The Maya movement has developed little by little, and it needs the support of all Guatemalans and the international community in order to be effective in its contribution to the economic development projects and positive historical changes that must stem from community bases.

The Maya have struggled for centuries against marginalization and the lack of educational and economic opportunities. Besides the long internal warfare,

Maya have had to cope with forced indoctrination, fear, and death as a result of guerrilla warfare, the army's scorched-earth policies, and paramilitary organizations such as the civil patrols. It is important to be aware of the current struggles of the Maya people and their efforts to make their presence visible in this historic moment of national reconstruction. There are several ways in which the revitalization of Maya culture is taking shape. Most importantly, it is an effective and nonviolent form of reconstruction and a peaceful alternative to conflict. For example, the revitalization of Maya culture is the main goal of the pan-Maya movement, which has taken enormous pride in the Maya cultural heritage. The revitalization of Mayan languages, religion and spirituality, native knowledge, Mayan schools, and political consciousness is among the most expressive forms of this pan-Maya movement of self-representation and cultural resurgence (Montejo 1997; Warren 1998a).

The Rise of Maya Activism

As mentioned above, contemporary Maya activism resulted from the chronic violence that enveloped Maya life and history. Little by little, contemporary Maya began voicing their concerns and increasing their activism. At the same time, they were also being studied by anthropologists. Foreign scholars have followed the rise of Maya activism very closely and have either collaborated with or ignored it. Anthropologists working in Guatemala since the 1950s have written extensively about Maya politicization and have tried to explain this phenomenon according to their own outsider perspectives. The early investigators considered themselves pure scientists who went to the field and wrote about Maya culture. In their works, the modern Maya were seen as objects of study and the Maya region as a place to collect artifacts for museums and private collections (Castañeda 1996).

Some ladino scholars and literary critics who work on the periphery of the Maya movement have been examining this process from a vaguer and less accurate, if not cynical, position. For example, Mario Roberto Morales has characterized the Maya revitalization movement as a regressive or fundamentalist movement (Morales 1996). Others believe that this is a movement devoted only to reviving ancient patterns of Maya culture as essential relics to be worshiped (Fisher and Brown 1996).

I personally believe that the agenda of Maya scholars and activists is not to embellish ourselves with a romantic past or to wrap ourselves in ancient Maya garb, but to revitalize our Maya identity and weave back in the sections worn away by centuries of neglect. Contemporary Maya are constantly creating and recreating their Maya culture and redefining themselves. I have argued elsewhere that the Maya culture of the future will be conceptually different from the classic and postclassic Maya. Many minds are engaged in building our future, thinking about it, and recreating it. The idea is to use the powerful symbols of the past to reconstruct the present and build the future, as we retrace the footprints of our ancestors on the ancient bridge that links the past to the present. From those building blocks we want to create the Maya culture of the future. It is not, then, a bad thing to have the essential parts of our culture, such as language and respect for land and the elders, as the foundation of this dynamic process of self-representation we are promoting for ourselves. This will be possible only if we understand the prophetic time in which we are living and contribute to the writing of our own histories within the cyclical patterns of our worldviews.

Another issue raised to explain the process of revitalization of Maya culture is the concept of invented traditions, "the use of ancient materials to construct invented traditions of a novel type for quite novel purposes" (Hobsbawm 1988:6). The concept of invented traditions applies to Maya culture, of course, but not to the same degree as in Western cultures. And as stated by Eric Hobsbawm (1988:13):

> The element of invention is particularly clear here, since the history which became part of the fund of knowledge, or the ideology of nation, state or movement, is not what has actually been preserved in popular memory, but what has been selected, written, pictured, popularized and institutionalized by those whose function it is to do so.

What has been preserved in popular memory may not be important to colonizers and nonindigenous ideologues who interpret and invent traditions to accommodate themselves among established and historically deeply rooted indigenous cultures and communities. For us, the Maya cultural heritage is clearly visible, and its roots are still strong and firmly embedded in Maya soil. The fund of knowledge that Hobsbawm mentions is what has been preserved in Maya memory, such as the ceremonies performed at sacred sites by Maya priests and the use of the Maya calendar. For example, when I reaffirm my Mayaness, I don't need to go into a time machine and travel back in time to visit imaginary worlds in order to see my ancestors, as Westerners do through films and science fiction. Instead, I just have to visit the sanctuary of the Jakaltek hero Xhuwan Q'anil and recharge my identity by participating in the Maya ceremonies and prayers carried out in my native Mayan language, Popb'alti'. This is to belong to a tradition with roots still strong and deeply embedded in the land, its sacred places, and geography (Montejo 2001). Also, we Maya can go to Tikal, to Palenque, or to other sacred sites in our own communities and see, touch, and feel all around us the presence and power of the ancestors. Maya spirituality helps us in this way, and that is why the role of the Maya spiritual leader is also essential in this project of Maya reconstruction and representation. The land is essential for Maya survival, and perhaps during this new century we will be playing a role that will definitely go beyond survival. I am not saying that Maya culture is static; it changes, but not like Western culture, which invents and creates nationalism in new postcolonial settings. Maya have been struggling to express their Mayaness through the centuries and even millennia, but their culture is substantially and essentially based on Mayan languages and worldviews.

There are several reasons why Maya leaders and scholars use an essentialist approach in the revitalization of Maya culture. First, they are descendants of the magnificent ancient Maya. The persistence of Mayan languages and the visibility of Maya monumental architecture make them proud of their heritage. Unfortunately, those who are in positions of power in Guatemala may continue to deny this ancient heritage and invalidate the Maya land claims and struggles for self-determination. The reaffirmation of their Mayaness is important at this time of implementation of the peace accords. We could say that we are living in much the same kind of political environment as when the *Popol Vuh,* the *Anales de los Kaqchikeles,* and the *Título de Totonicapán* were written in the early colonial period.[2] After the Spanish invasion, the Maya had to rely on the power of their own traditions, especially the origin myths. They insisted on their roots and origins while they claimed communal ownership of the land that was taken from them after the Spanish conquest.

Another reason for Maya to insist on their links to the ancient Maya culture is because they are interested in writing their own histories and representing themselves from their own indigenous perspectives. They want to be called Maya, and their link to the ancient Maya legitimizes this desire. In other words, not all of them are interested in theorizing about what they are doing or how they are doing this or that. I believe this is where the role and contributions of anthropologists will be important. Nevertheless, I would caution anthropologists to be careful with their analyses and interpretations of the process as well as the methods they use for gathering their data. Foreign anthropologists are very visible, and their role is definitely very important. Now, in the postwar period in Guatemala, more young anthropologists from around the world are arriving "to study the Maya." Another reason why Maya are drawing strength from their heritage is that some ladinos continue to insist that what we have or what we are is not Maya. This is an issue where foreign scholars of the Maya can help people understand why Maya are using this name to create and recreate their culture. Maya know that what we have now is not classic Maya, because identity changes in time and space, but we call ourselves Maya because we have clear links to the pre-Hispanic Maya culture. In other words, we are aware that the classic Maya were not the same as the preclassic or the postclassic and are, of course, different from the contemporary Maya. But because of these links, we consciously call ourselves Maya, and this makes our identity historically powerful.

The Maya Movement of Self-Representation

The tremendous hiatus in Maya writing and self-representation during the colonial and postcolonial periods (1600–1900) is truly painful for us to remember. The Maya during this time were unable to express pride in their heritage. Instead, they were placed under colonial domination, including forced labor, and obliged to pay tribute. They were labeled "Indians" and therefore considered inferior. Under such extreme exploitation, the Maya had to find ways to send letters to the king of Spain asking him to stop the abuses against them. Those who exploited the indigenous population were military leaders, *encomenderos,* and clergy, including some bishops who became known as protectors of the Indians, such as Bishop Francisco Marroquín.[3] The Indians from the central valley of Guatemala complained to the king of Spain, denouncing the abuses of their rights as human beings. From a recent publication, *Nuestro pesar, nuestra aflicción* (Lutz and Dakin 1996), we have become aware of the extent of Maya suffering under colonial rule. The oppressed Maya leaders wrote letters asking for the intervention of the king of Spain to ease their pain. "Help us, you, who are our King, Philip the II, King of Castile. We the *macehuales* [common people] are suffering excessively. The *macehuales* go about naked, without clothing. The people suffer too much, having to keep paying the tribute ordered by Pedro de Alvarado and Bishop Francisco Marroquín" (Lutz and Dakin 1996:79).

Despite the continuous resistance by indigenous people in Guatemala, Maya produced no texts in Mayan languages during this period; the just-mentioned letters were written in Náhuatl. The lack of written histories of this Maya suffering means that non-Maya have forgotten how their forefathers perpetuated this suffering of the Maya. This atrocious enslavement was, of course, responsible for weakening the roots of Maya culture during the colonial period. As a Maya writer, I believe that the greatest loss of all was the loss of the knowledge of reading and writing the Maya hieroglyphs. Modern Maya greatly lament that knowledge of the glyphs was not passed down through the generations. The colonial Maya did realize this great loss of knowledge, and complained:

> We complain in great sorrow, in loud voices and death. Our grief is torment. We are pierced with a great longing to read the books of wood and the writings on stone, now in ruins. They contain the seven wellsprings of life! They were burned before our eyes at the well. At noonday we lament our perpetual burdens. (Makemson 1951:5)

The voices of the Maya were not heard again until the early decades of the twentieth century, but then only in the writings of ethnographers. That much of the culture had survived was documented systematically by early ethnographers such as Robert Redfield (1950), Ruth Bunzel (1981 [1952]), Oliver La Farge and Douglas Byers (1931), and many others. After the Jacobo Arbenz reforms of the 1950s, Guatemala's indigenous people began to talk and express themselves in writing. Contrary to the belief that the Maya would disappear or be totally assimilated, they began to organize themselves, and some began to pursue higher education. Guatemalans and people of other nationalities realized that the days of submission and silence imposed on the Maya were over. The pioneering works of the K'iche' educator Adrián Inés Chávez promoted self-expression and representation of the Maya. Chávez (1979) utilized the *Popol Vuh* to represent the Maya and their literary contribution to the world. In the words of Carlos Guzmán Böckler (1979), "The originality of his work and his erudition has challenged the impositions of western linguistics. By presenting and using his own alphabet, he challenged intellectual colonialism."

While this was happening among the K'iche' Maya with Chávez, a younger generation throughout Guatemala gained the opportunity to be educated in urban schools with scholarships offered by missionaries. Some of those who graduated from schools run by these missionaries became involved in party politics, making Maya more visible as subjects of history. Since then, the indigenous people of Guatemala have carried out a campaign of autorepresentation, demanding their rights while becoming involved in national politics.

One of the first major efforts to push forward the process of self-representation was the formation of a political party, Frente Indígena Nacional (FIN; National Indigenous Front), by Maya intellectuals. Their strategy was to show pride in their heritage, and they presented themselves to the national community as "indios." This was the common term used by Maya leaders during the 1970s, since the term "Maya" was used by foreign scholars of the Maya to refer solely to the builders of ancient Maya civilization or to refer to Yukatek Maya.

Unfortunately, these Maya leaders fell into the trap of party politics, and the FIN ended up supporting the brutal and repressive government of Romeo Lucas García (1978–1982). With this coalition supporting a repressive government, the leaders of this political party were seen as opportunists, no different from ladino politicians. They wanted to obtain positions in the government, and so they allied themselves with the Partido Revolucionario (PR; Revolutionary Party), then headed by General Lucas García.

The proximity of Guatemala City to the territory of K'iche' and Kaqchikel leaders playing these political roles provided them with more opportunities and access to political power. At the same time, in the most remote areas of western Guatemala a different kind of cultural revival was underway, but on a more regional scale. In the Jakaltek region, two local and regional newspapers were founded, *El Jakalteko* and *Despertar Maya* (Mayan Awakening), which I edited in 1978. We had to cease publication of *Despertar Maya* because of death threats. The use of Mayan languages in these newspapers was not the immediate goal. At that time, it was more necessary to let people know that Maya culture was alive and that the people of the region were related to one another culturally. It was necessary to recover our Maya identity and be proud of it despite ladino discrimination. This Maya awakening after centuries of voicelessness and inaction was headed by Maya intellectuals, mostly schoolteachers. The idea was to develop the habit of reading among the Maya while making them aware of the local, regional, and national situation.

At the end of the 1970s, the existing indigenous organizations were forced to redefine their goals and strategies because of governmental repression against their leaders. Most of these organizations had ladinos as leaders, so it was easy for them to opt for a militant strategy and strong links to the guerrillas (Carmack 1988; Smith 1990; Perera 1993; Carlsen 1997). The divergent interests of the traditional and militant Maya became apparent, as some agreed with and supported the guerrilla movement while others continued with their nationalist and cultural agendas (Smith 1990). The so-called popular movement became nationally well known, and international solidarity organizations began to support it. Unfortunately, the agenda of the popular movement was mostly prepared by nonindigenous leaders who continued to manipulate the movement until the signing of the peace accords. The involvement of leftist non-Maya leaders in the decision making of these organizations was evident. For example, representation of the Maya by the umbrella organization COPMAGUA (Coordinación de Organizaciones del Pueblo Maya de Guatemala; Coordinator of Organizations of the Maya People of Guatemala) was weak, and stumbled because of the lack of solid Maya leadership. The desire for personal gain and political position by some of these leaders rendered the negotiating ability of COPMAGUA less than powerful as an umbrella organization.

At the same time, the leadership of the culturalist Maya movement was radicalized to the point that nothing could be accepted if it was not aimed at the creation of an autonomous Maya nationalism (Cojtí Cuxil 1996). The strategy for negotiation by these leaders was not appropriate, since they undiplomatically proposed bold radical changes in their relations with the non-Maya. At this political juncture, and after a bloody undeclared civil war between the army and the guerrillas that killed tens of thousands of Maya, it was not a convenient time for radicalized action, because the Maya majority was not fully represented by the political and cultural leaders of the popular and the pan-Maya movements.

I think it is important at this time to have a middle-ground leadership, which could be called "regenerationist." The regenerationist group should be flexible and careful about preaching an extreme nationalist ideology along Western lines. We must think about the multicultural and multiethnic reality of Guatemala. Maya must realize that not all ladinos belong to the elite and that they cannot be treated as outsiders either, since they share Maya blood. On the contrary, Maya may help them recognize their mixed heritage so that both may collaborate in the construction of a multicultural nation-state in Guatemala. The ladinos have long attached themselves to the ruling class and rejected their other side, the Maya component. They must search for their own identity and cherish the sources of their mixed blood equally in order to find that the Maya way is not backward or dangerous to the ladinos.

Similarly, the Maya must try to explain what it is to be Maya to these ladinos, to prevent mistrust of the Maya projects of revitalization. For this reason, the radical nationalism proposed by some Maya leaders as a solution to the Maya neocolonial situation cannot help in the implementation of the peace accords, but would only deepen the century-old division. The construction of a multicultural nation-state requires the contributions of all the ethnic groups in Guatemala to the consolidation of those nationalist-pluralist goals. We must think about the future in realistic terms. To use the metaphor of Eric Wolf (1982), we should not promote the creation of small independent nation-states that may clash continuously like billiard balls within Guatemalan territory. To create the Guatemalan imagined community (Anderson 1990) as a multicultural nation-state is to share and create the future from the contributions and particularities stemming from Maya and ladinos alike.

While talking to a high-ranking Guatemalan diplomat in the Alvaro Arzú government, I asked why President Arzú had not appointed any Mayas to positions of power in his cabinet, as he had promised to do before the elections. The diplomat answered that the Maya did not want the Secretaría Indígena that the president had proposed for them. The Maya argued that it was a form of separatism that they did not want, so the government stopped considering it and gave them nothing instead. The issue is not whether or not the Maya want the proposed *secretaría,* which should be called Secretaría de Asuntos Indígenas. The government has a responsibility to fulfill its promises to the Maya people, a majority of the population, and create institutions that benefit them. I believe that Maya leaders should have accepted the Secretaría Indígena and the political power that would have come with it, if run by Mayas. It is better to achieve something than nothing at all. I strongly believe that it is necessary to create institutions run by Mayas to deal with Maya issues. Maya are now considered Guatemalan citizens, but continue to lack the opportunities and rights enjoyed by citizens belonging to the dominant group. Maya should be equal partners in any joint projects for the future. It is time for Maya to be fully part of the nation, and not just part of the labor force (Peeler 1998). The efforts to achieve self-representation are advancing slowly, although some critics say that the paternalistic attitude of the scholars behind some Maya leaders shows that they cannot do things for themselves. This may be the case with a few Maya leaders, but the majority are really engaged in creating and producing knowledge. To do this, modern Maya are making use of the tools provided by print capitalism: they write books and make contributions to the Guatemalan media, projecting their ideas and enriching the Maya movement. Among such scholars are Estuardo Zapeta, an anthropologist whose polemical work is aimed at shaking the bushes of both camps, Maya and mestizo. Luis Enrique Sam Colop writes for the newspaper *Prensa Libre;* his articles are critical, and they reach the Maya population since he uses the K'iche' Mayan language in his editorials. Then we have the Maya writers who have published works that have been translated into other languages. Among the best known are Humberto Ak'abal (K'iche'), Gaspar Pedro González (Q'anjob'al) and Victor Montejo (Jakaltek).

In Chiapas, the Maya presence in the media is becoming more noticeable, and women are among those who are at the forefront of writing and producing theater pieces for public performance. As Warren (1998a:27) notes, "The production of cultural representation in a variety of media is used quite self-consciously by public intellectuals to support struggles for social change." The multiplicity of Maya voices and the lack of formal representations of Maya and their ideas for a unified Maya movement are due to the fact that the most visible leaders play opposite roles, siding with radicalized groups. For this reason, it is necessary for Maya to be represented by the voices of peasants, intellectuals, and students from rural and urban areas. We need to refine our rhetoric and create a middle position that is viable, nonviolent, and feasible for all Maya and non-Maya. Maya leaders must develop a new approach to their own linguistic communities, such as more direct consultation with the communities by using the traditional political forms of consensus making in order to reflect the concerns and needs of the community. This is one of the goals of the pan-Maya movement. Mutual respect within each Mayan linguistic community must be emphasized, as well as a commitment to their collective survival and resurgence (Wilson 1995; Montejo 1999a).

The early forms of pan-Maya associations can be traced to the special teacher institutes that train Maya women and men. Among these institutions have been the Instituto Indígena "Santiago" and the Instituto Indígena "Nuestra Señora del Socorro" (the latter for women). These institutes for secondary and vocational education were run as boarding schools by religious orders. The establishment of these Indian institutes was a result of the struggle against Communism in Guatemala by Bishop Mariano Rossell y Arellano after the downfall of the Arbenz government. This was a measure to stop Maya from falling into the traps of Communist manipulation. It is interesting to note that some of the most prominent Maya leaders of the present were trained in these institutes.

The functioning of these institutes, which brought together young men and women from most Mayan linguistic communities, opened up possibilities for becoming acquainted with other linguistic communities. Also, interethnic marriages took place, weakening the endogamous tradition that Maya communities have maintained for centuries. In other words, the migration of Maya to the cities for economic and educational purposes put them in contact with people from other Mayan linguistic communities, thus broadening their views of themselves, their people, and the country.

Attendance at universities also helped Maya academics construct an ethnic identity that encouraged pride in the Maya heritage. Better educated than previous generations, Maya after about 1950 began to rethink their position as mediators and interlocutors between the two worlds. They recognized and experienced the problems of the past, but now there was a possibility of influencing or at least envisioning a better future.

On the local and regional level, Maya revitalization is also occurring. One of the major symbols now used by Maya for self-representation is the Maya New Year ceremony, demonstrating that the revitalization of Maya religion and spirituality has become a powerful moving force for all Maya groups. The hope is to develop a Maya unity and consensus within the multiple ways of being Maya and to guarantee a better future for all Guatemalans. In this way Maya are reviving those values that emphasize respect for the land. The land is the source of their being and the place of their roots and identities. At the same time, they are developing a strong and respectful relationship with other ethnic groups beyond the borders of modern Guatemala.

Maya Political and Cultural Awakening

The major changes in Maya political views were generated during the brutal repression the people have endured since the 1970s. The massacre of one hundred Q'eqchi' Maya in Panzós in northern Guatemala in 1979 marked the beginning of a strong politicization of the Maya population. When news that the army had killed these Maya peasants spread throughout the country, so did condemnation of this criminal act. As a response from the communities, poems and songs were written honoring the victims of the massacre, denouncing this violation of human rights by the army. This was a wake-up call for the Maya, who began more fully to recognize the terrible restrictions and lack of opportunities to which they were subjected. Another event that had a national impact was the killing of radio announcer Timoteo Curruchiche. He had a Kaqchikel-language program listened to by Maya that addressed the problems of violence in the nation. The death of a voice with which people identified symbolized the death of their own voices, as Maya had become silent and fearful of death squads during the Lucas García regime. The cultural revitalization that was beginning to take place in most Maya communities during the 1970s stagnated, and its leaders were silenced. There was persecution of those who had denounced the aggression against peasants and indigenous people: university students, professors, missionaries, labor leaders, and politicians. The killings of Congressman Alberto Fuentes Mohr and the former mayor of Guatemala City, Manuel Colom Argueta, were a turning point in the political violence instigated by the government against those who opposed its repressive methods of control. Leftist Maya organizations such as the Comité de Unidad Campesina (CUC; Committee for Peasant Unity) were under attack, and most of its leaders went underground and became guerrillas to continue their struggle.

Ironically, an important development during this period of violence was an increase of the number of young Maya men and women pursuing careers in vocational schools in the cities. The Roman Catholic Church provided scholarships to Maya students to attend vocational institutes, seminaries, and universities. This was a major change in the educational structure for Maya communities, where schoolteachers had been ladinos from the cities who did not speak the local language or share the indigenous culture. Maya schoolteachers who graduated began to take jobs in their own linguistic communities, and there was an increase in the awareness of Maya values and pride in their cultural heritage.

With the awareness of their cultural heritage, Maya intellectuals began to organize their efforts for cultural revival and revitalization. The work of Maya writers was important; they concentrated on the use of the language as a means of ensuring that Maya culture and worldviews would be passed on effectively from one generation to the next. At the beginning of the 1980s, this organized effort led to the creation of the Academy of Mayan Languages of Guatemala (ALMG). The recognition of the ALMG in 1985 as an autonomous institution funded by the government was one of the major achievements of the Maya working for self-representation. The ALMG is a pan-Maya institution in which the twenty-one Mayan linguistic communities of Guatemala are represented (Warren 1998a). Another major achievement of the Maya movement was the organization of projects of cultural and religious revival by Maya religious leaders, such as the National Association of Maya Priests, the *ah q'ijab'* or experts on the Maya calendar. The so-called popular organizations also have a pan-Maya view, but operate mostly in the political arena. Maya umbrella organizations such as the COMG and COPMAGUA significantly influenced the negotiations of the peace accords. Although there has been a division of leadership within and among these organizations, their tenacity in mobilizing mass demonstrations has had its effect. The major achievement of these umbrella organizations is their recognition as institutions that voice the demands of indigenous people concerning the implementation of the peace accords.

In spite of its contribution to the Maya popular movement, COPMAGUA has lost its power of convocation and leadership by being seen as too attached to the left. On the issue of Maya identity, COPMAGUA organized multidisciplinary commissions to study and present proposals and projects for the implementation of the accords relating to Maya rights and identity. Unfortunately, the referendum or national consultation on May 8, 1999, failed when the voters said no to the proposed constitutional reforms. The rejection of the constitutional reforms made it clear that the majority of the population who had the ability to vote, mostly ladinos, did not want to give "more rights" to the Maya. According to them, all Guatemalans are equal under the Constitution, so changing it to accommodate indigenous rights meant dividing the nation. For this reason, those who opposed the changes argued that an ethnic war or an indigenous uprising against the ladino population might result. This was a manipulation to infuse fear in the population, and so those who could vote, voted against the reforms. The referendum was also proof of the discontent in the rural populations. There was an 80 percent abstention rate in the voting, which sent a message to the government and to the leftist opposition that the people were unhappy with the system and did not believe the politicians' promises.

Another important factor in the signing of the peace accords was the Asamblea de la Sociedad Civil (ASC; Assembly of Civil Society), which managed to push the agenda of indigenous issues in the discussions between the army and the URNG. Unfortunately, the ASC has disintegrated and cannot help monitor the implementation of the peace accords. But the formation of Guatemala's truth commission, the Comisión para el Esclarecimiento Histórico de Guatemala (CEH; Commission for Historical Clarification), brought some hope to the Guatemalan population. It was necessary to let the people know about the history of violence and its sources and to name the perpetrators of the crimes. Two Maya intellectuals were members of the truth commission, which documented the horrors of the violence experienced in rural Guatemala. But, as is usually the case with these investigatory commissions, those who organized and planned the investigation were mostly foreigners assigned by the United Nations; few Maya participated, except as informants. For this reason, the recommendations of the truth commission to follow up with a process of "reparation" to the affected communities has not been taken seriously by the present government of President Alfonso Portillo (2000–2004).

Similarly, the Catholic Church organized its own investigatory commission and publicized a document called *Guatemala: Nunca Más* (*Guatemala: Never Again;* REMHI 1998). This commission documented atrocities committed by the army and the guerrillas and named the perpetrators of these crimes. Both commissions carried out the tremendous task of calling for the Maya to write down their own stories so that the martyrs will not be forgotten. Unfortunately, the killing of Bishop Juan Gerardi a few days after he made public *Guatemala: Nunca Más* shattered the hopes of the Guatemalan people for a lasting peace. The document was a compilation of the testimonies of thousands of people who had been victims of the armed conflict. With the violent death of Bishop Gerardi, Guatemala is now concerned about the impunity with which those who have avoided justice are now committing new crimes.

The Maya: A New Force in Guatemalan Politics

At the present time, it is obvious that a new indigenous political front is developing. During the past elections (1999), most indigenous communities decided to support mayoral candidates who had been nominated by local civic committees. Some of these committees had links to the newly formed Frente Democrático Nueva Guatemala (FDNG).[4] An increasing number of Mayas are now interested in politics, although some favor the ideologies of the old right-wing political parties. In reality, these parties had not been interested in having Mayas in positions of power. This pattern was changed when the FDNG won some seats in Congress. The FDNG was seen as a democratic force with possibilities for promoting unity among Guatemalans for national reconciliation. Nevertheless, little has been achieved by the opposition parties, for the ruling party Frente Republicano Guatemalteco (FRG) has the majority of representatives in Congress. The signing of the peace accords, however, provided the Mayas with the possibility to speak up freely and without fear. Now they can tell their stories of how both sides, army and guerrillas, committed crimes against indigenous people. This is a positive result of the peace agreements, and now Mayas are voicing their concerns and breaking the silence imposed on them as a result of the armed conflict.

The 1999 election in Guatemala resulted in many changes in the political arena. Many old political parties died out (e.g., the Partido Institucional Democrático, PID) since they no longer provided alternatives for change and democracy in Guatemala. Maya communities in western Guatemala have benefited from this because the old local caciques who had strong links to the leaders of the national parties lost their power, and no longer could manipulate the

Maya peasants. The caciques that I am referring to here are strongmen who have served political parties for decades and are friends with the ladino mayors and secretaries of the towns. They were the only people knowledgeable about national politics because they were the parties' representatives in the towns. These old Maya political leaders were loyal to their parties and were feared by the communities. One of the strategies commonly used by the leaders of national political parties was to distribute communal lands among their followers. At present, some young leaders, mostly intellectuals, are taking their places, but they owe no loyalty to these new parties. These leaders can shift allegiance from one political party to another. They are interested in becoming mayors of their towns, and frequently become corrupt as they use the office for personal gain. Most other Mayan leaders in western Guatemala are reluctant to join political parties, preferring to organize civic committees and participate in elections. They are the ones who are likely to be involved in the revitalization of Maya culture, and they reject party politics.

The opposition parties have been widely divided ideologically and politically. The FDNG leadership, for example, reached out only to those members who were already identified with the left. Because of its limited political strategies and vision, the FDNG lost all that it had gained as a political party and also became extinct after the November 1999 elections. I would say that the URNG, which became a political party after the signing of the peace accords, has been stillborn as a political party. A major problem has to do with its name, which symbolizes combat and clandestine activities, carrying with it the stigmatizing associations of war, violence, and failure. Similarly, General Efraín Ríos Montt's political party, Frente Republicano Guatemalteco, which reminded people of military repression and massacres, against all odds won the presidential elections of 1999, with Alfonso Portillo as its presidential candidate. Some Mayas won seats in Congress by supporting the FRG; the most intriguing event after the election was the appointment of Maya critics to the governmental cabinet, as a form silencing Maya leaders. Despite this, I believe that Maya intellectuals should get more involved in politics and seek positions in government. Maya should be able to represent themselves and be in charge of the decision making that will affect their own future.

Pan-Mayanism: Maya Self-Representation

As I have mentioned, there are several Maya projects concerned with cultural revival. These achievements are astonishing because of the restricted spaces

Second Congress on the *Popol Vuh,* Quetzaltenango, May 1999; *left to right:* Miguel
Ángel Velasco Bitzol, Rigoberto Quemé Chay, Robert M. Carmack, Victor Montejo,
and Kay B. Warren (author's photo)

and limited resources out of which they have been developing. The new Maya
movement is emerging from the ashes of the thirty-six-year armed conflict
that finally came to an end in December 1996. In this context, the Maya have
shown a powerful will to survive in the midst of extreme political violence.
Once again, the resurgence of Maya culture is underway, responding to the extreme pressures imposed upon indigenous cultures during the past decades —
for instance, the massacres that disrupted Maya worldviews and traditions. The
present revitalization of Maya culture is also a reflection of the continental mobilization of indigenous people to achieve self-determination. On the cultural,
linguistic, political, and religious levels, Maya are engaged in the process of unifying the diverse Maya ethnic groups or Native Nations into a pan-Maya movement of cultural revitalization and resurgence (Warren 1998a; Montejo 1999a).

The current process of building a coordinated effort for subsistence and
cultural reaffirmation among these Mayan linguistic communities (pan-
Mayanism) results from the violent history of the past decade through which
they have lived. Maya culture was affected dramatically during the military
confrontation between the army and the guerrillas, so now Maya are in the
process of organizing themselves into a cultural movement concerned with
self-representation. This cultural resurgence emphasizes the necessity of Maya

First Congress on Maya Education, Quetzaltenango, August 1994; anthropologists
Kay B. Warren and Margarita López Raquec (author's photo)

being allowed to express themselves freely and to contribute from their own
knowledge system, ideology, and communal politics to the construction of a
multicultural Guatemalan nation-state.

Pan-Mayanism is a cultural movement focused on self-understanding and
the validation of Maya heritage (Montejo 1997). Maya prefer to call their own
efforts a process of self-determination that will help to create a pluralistic Guatemalan nation-state. Pan-Mayanism is the basic first step for achieving further
goals. This is because, first, Maya must take pride in their Maya culture in order
to promote it as a source of powerful identities. And second, the stereotypes
and images embedded in the minds of the different non-Maya groups in the
nation-state must be radically changed to positive ones, with an appreciation
of Maya history and culture, past and present. The construction of a Guatemalan nationalism must come from a compromise between Maya and non-Maya.
If Guatemala wants to continue proclaiming its uniqueness as a nation by using
Maya elements and symbols, it must recognize the active role of Maya culture
as an integral part of the process of nation-state building (Smith 1991).

It is evident that Maya culture is very complex. It is the expression of various levels of understanding or worldviews being reworked by each Mayan linguistic community. It is also the expression of different sectors of the Maya
population, such as intellectuals, advocates, peasants, and traditional religious

leaders. All voices must be heard so that action is not radicalized. Otherwise, only one highly politicized sector will prevail, limiting the ability of other sectors of the Maya people to express themselves. Maya must understand and be aware of the political environment, nationally and internationally. The world is changing dramatically, and each sector must strengthen its national feelings through the recognition of other ways of thinking and being Maya. The distinctiveness and cultural expression of each Mayan linguistic community is being recognized and valued within the developing pan-Mayan movement. Pan-Mayanism recognizes the way different Mayan linguistic groups have contributed to the continuous transformation and maintenance of Maya culture as a whole.

The diversity of Maya culture should be seen as an advantage and not as an obstacle. This is a healthy sign, which affirms the continuity of Maya culture despite centuries of violence and forced assimilation. Similarly, we must insist that Maya identity be historically based and that contemporary Maya continue to sustain and recreate it. But as Joane Nagel has argued for Native Americans in the United States:

> The knowledge that Native American ethnicity is historically based, however, must not obscure the fact that Indian ethnic boundaries and identities are continually socially constructed and negotiated. It is important to note that for both traditional and emergent Indian communities, the work of social and cultural survival represents an ongoing challenge. There is nothing "automatic" or "natural" about Native American tribal or supra-tribal ethnicity. No matter how deeply rooted in tradition, Indian ethnicity, like all cultures and identities, must be sustained and strengthened. (Nagel 1996:9)

The Maya definitely need to sustain and strengthen their Mayaness. Maya must write and rewrite their own histories in order to eliminate the negative images imposed on them. This is possible since Maya, now more prepared and sophisticated, make use of modern technology and media information to promote their own views of themselves.

Conclusion

The recognition and value of the cultural distinctiveness of each Mayan linguistic community makes pan-Maya identity very strong and complex. Pan-

Mayanism argues for a common Maya global identity, that is, a sharing of the base Maya culture. Pan-Mayanism also values and recognizes that diversity greatly increases the probability that Maya culture will continue in the future. Pan-Mayanism is not about a political imposition that dictates the role that each Mayan linguistic community must play, but rather about the shared recognition that each community values its own share of Maya civilization.

The position of the movement for pan-Maya identity can be summarized as follows:

1. Today's Maya should be recognized as such because there are elements that strongly link them to the millennia-long history and tradition of their Maya ancestors.
2. Pan-Mayanism is an effort to make the diversity of Maya cultures strongly visible, reaffirming their presence as Maya in the present century.
3. Pan-Mayanism is an interethnic movement valuing and recognizing the importance of diversity in the unity of Maya culture, including those communities in Mexico, Belize, and Honduras.
4. Any and all ruthless violence affecting a particular Mayan linguistic group must be considered as an attack against Maya culture as a whole; this will bring broader international awareness of Maya culture.
5. Stereotypes found in different Mayan linguistic communities are the result of their forced isolation from other groups. All Maya should understand and recognize that there are different ways of being Maya.
6. Defense of the cultural heritage of the Maya must be seen as a global concern of all Mayan linguistic communities. In some areas, like Chiapas, Mexico, the recognition of the uniqueness and diversity of Maya culture and the respect of those differences and autonomies are being created.

Thus Maya must seek this pan-Maya identity in order to legitimize their cultural projects of revitalization within and outside the nation-state. The pan-Maya cultural and political movement is being extended to other Mayan communities in Mexico, Belize, and Honduras as they develop projects of cultural revival like that of the Guatemalan Maya. The recognition of belonging to a common root or base culture as Maya and developing a pan-Maya solidarity must be encouraged (Montejo 1999a). This cooperation will provide the basis for a more permanent peace and security instead of a continuation of the unequal relationship imposed by elite ladino nationalism. Maya do not want to isolate themselves into little nation-states. We don't need to create a new Yugoslavia or replicate the ethnic warfare and tribal conflicts raging on the African continent. All Guatemalans, Maya and non-Maya, must work toward the construction of a pluralistic Guatemalan nation-state.

In the construction of a global pan-Maya ethnic identity, the role of Maya organizations and the media is essential since they help promote the revitalization of Maya culture. Among the organizations dedicated to the diffusion of Maya ideas and information are at least two publishers, Cholsamaj and the Yax Te' Foundation, as well as the multilingual weekly newspaper *El Regional*. Similarly, the work of Maya leaders at the national and international levels is also important. One of these Maya figures is Rigoberta Menchú, winner of the Nobel Prize for Peace, whose efforts have helped bring indigenous issues to the forefront of discussion in Guatemala and elsewhere. Similarly, the role of the spiritual leaders has become a symbol for the revival and unification of Maya culture nationally. It is my hope that the current demands of indigenous people for their self-determination, supported by the United Nations, will help Maya to coordinate efforts to know and value their own uniqueness, a great asset for the multicultural nation-state building in Guatemala. There is still much to be done for the resurgence of Maya culture in the whole Maya area. At this point, Maya are becoming aware of their cultural heritage and focusing on the revival of institutions and ceremonies.

Unfortunately, the Maya movement is divided and has a weak leadership. There are at least some 200 Maya organizations in Guatemala, each with its own agenda. Some are offshoots of political parties, members of NGOs, and religious Maya and non-Maya organizations. The Maya organizations with strong links with the left, like the URNG, still use confrontational rhetoric in their demands and promote the invasion of lands and ecological reserves. It is unfortunate that members of Congress have not come out with legislative initiatives that attend to the demands of the Maya population. Even worse, the current government of the FRG is not interested at all in the implementation of the peace accords.

Nevertheless, the Maya continue their struggles to make their presence visible. Among the projects being contemplated by the Maya is the creation of a Maya university. It is imperative that the leadership of the Maya movement achieves higher education in order to develop a critical vision of the educational system. They must have the freedom and power of decision making in the elaboration of educational curricula that are more global and inclusive. Similarly, the organization of a Maya political party (but one not exclusive of ladinos) seems appropriate at this time, when Maya have come to realize that they have been used by political parties, by institutions, and even by the contenders in the armed conflict. Maya must bring their creativity to the forefront and make their presence stronger and more visible. Also, a regenerationist Maya leadership should organize a Maya commission to monitor the implementation of the peace accords. The Maya must be in charge of developing and implementing projects for reparation to the communities affected by the recent armed conflict.

In order to achieve any level of political and cultural autonomy and self-determination, the Guatemalan Maya movement must put an end to the centuries of silence. Maya must speak and write about everything because we have been affected on every political or institutional front. Yes, the Maya need lawyers, anthropologists, Maya priests, educators, politicians, poets, and writers. We are a civilization that must flourish in all of its creative expressions. All Guatemalans must recognize that Maya culture is a vital part in the current efforts to lead the country to sustainable development and positive historic change. This is the challenge that Maya leaders and organizations confront now at the beginning of this new millennium.

CHAPTER 5

Truth, Human Rights, and Representation
The Case of Rigoberta Menchú

The Truth and Testimonies

Despite anthropology's critical view of itself as a discipline, dealing mainly with the problems of representation and misrepresentation of indigenous cultures, once again here we are engaged in the same problem. In terms of the truth, anthropologists have tended to impose their own views on indigenous people and not to respect the indigenous people's truth on its own terms. It is the practice of anthropologists to search for the truth, and some expect that it will come in only one version. But with human cultures and behavior, the situation is different, and there may be as many interpretations of events and actions as there are different worldviews. In the case of Rigoberta Menchú, many elements are at play in her testimony: death, memory, army violence, fear, leftist ideological conditioning, exile, and so on.

Perhaps the theorists of testimonial literature have pushed us too far in believing that testimonies are infallible stories or eyewitness accounts. For this reason, some of Menchú's supporters believed that she had told the absolute truth, and they cannot accept that she has added elements to her stories to make them more dramatic and appealing to international solidarity organizations. On the other hand, I recognize the difficulties of writing and presenting the facts of such a violent and genocidal war to the general public. For those of us who have written testimonies, it has been necessary to be in a secure place in exile in order to write these eyewitness accounts. Here, the protagonist has to rely on his or her memory in order to recount the events. In this process of forcing the self to relive those moments of desperation, pain, and death, the mind tries to recall the strongest images of death and destruction experienced collectively. This may explain why Rigoberta Menchú added images of cruelty—seeing her brother burned alive—to her own account, which by itself was already so dramatic. For those who lived through those moments of despair and massacres, this is an effort of the part of the unconscious mind to ensure that one's voice is effectively heard, that the voice elicits a strong commitment and solidarity from those who may respond immediately to these human rights abuses. In the case of Rigoberta Menchú, besides these internal and psychological pressures, she had to answer to her editor, Elisabeth Burgos-Debray, and to the guerrilla leaders who approved the final text (see Taracena 1999).

Some of her followers argue that Menchú's authority as a Nobel Prize winner is being undermined as a result of her work being scrutinized or challenged. The problem of isolation that Menchú is currently facing is not because of her book, but because of her lack of presence in Maya communities. Even some of those who worked closely with the popular left and guerrilla organizations now argue that she does not represent them. Everybody agrees that she is an international figure with a limited presence in Maya communities. In other words, her name and image were not well known by the indigenous people in Guatemala.

Despite the criticisms against Menchú in Guatemala, she is still a strong figure who has confronted the Guatemalan government because of its lack of seriousness in developing projects of reparation and implementing the peace accords. In a recent interview, Menchú said, "I cannot pardon those who killed my parents. To pardon is to know the names of the criminals, to know that they recognize their crimes" (Menchú 1999). Her strong voice on this issue of the historical clarification of genocide is important for the future of reparations in the communities massacred during the armed conflict. Meanwhile, the political left is trying to distance itself from her. This distancing by the left will, in the long run, be more beneficial for Menchú since she will be closer to the general Maya population of Guatemala and not only to the most radicalized peasants.

Historically, the work of Menchú and others who write testimonies is very important. Their works resemble those of the Maya who denounced the atrocities of the Spanish invasion during the early sixteenth century. Christopher Lutz and Karen Dakin's book *Nuestro pesar, nuestra aflicción* (1996:5) contains the testimonies of Maya telling the king of Spain about their suffering under colonial rule:

> Now, you should know that the Auditors came here to the city of Santiago de Guatemala to bring the Audience. They brought us too much suffering. They brought a great affliction to us, those *alcaldes* and councilmen. This is how they forced us to live in slavery. They did not have pity on us. It is in this way that we lived, as slaves. . . . For all this, it is so overwhelming, the affliction that they have caused us. (my translation)

At the same time, Bartolomé de Las Casas wrote to the king of Spain denouncing the crimes and tortures that the Spaniards committed against the Indians. In his *Brief Account of the Destruction of the Indies,* Las Casas mentioned that the Indians were subjected to inhumane treatment by the Spanish lords (Las Casas 1989). Because of these denunciations, Las Casas's account was attacked as a lie and considered a "black legend." Those who opposed Las Casas called his account an unfounded accusation against the Spaniards and a major insult to Spain.

The book of Rigoberta Menchú, then, has played an important role in making public the plight of the indigenous people of Guatemala. That is why David Stoll's book has created a fuzzy environment around Menchú's testimony. No doubt the right-wing sectors of Guatemala, especially the army, which was involved in these crimes, may soon consider her story a "black legend" too. Fortunately, the REMHI and truth commission's reports are conclusive proof of such atrocities. Indeed, these reports refer to the massive massacres by the army and the guerrillas as "genocide."

The Maya Situation

The 1970s and 1980s resembled the years of the 1950s during the Arbenz government. Anthropologists John Gillin (1960) and Richard Adams (1960) said that during the Arbenz government many of the younger and better-educated Indians and lower-class ladinos were drawn first into political activity and then into more "radical" movements. This is what happened to the indigenous population of western Guatemala during the 1980s with the Committee for Peasant Unity (CUC). This is the historical context in which Rigoberta Menchú played an important organizing role, as stated in her account.

The late 1970s and the 1980s were a very difficult time for the Maya of rural Guatemala. Freedom of speech and the civil rights of Guatemalans were strictly controlled by the successive military governments. The legacy of these years of *la violencia* was silence, fear, and intimidation (Warren 1998b). During the violence, it was dangerous to write about these massacres, and I am among the few who wrote testimonies in exile. We had to rely on oral tradition to pass on the information, and we had to find mnemonic devices to fix and remember those dates and events that were the most violent in modern Guatemalan history (Montejo 1999a). But no attention was paid to other testimonies, because the popular-guerrilla movement decided to promote only one testimony, thus making Menchú the only indigenous voice for the Maya. In this way they consecrated Menchú's testimony as the sole truth to be preached for eliciting international support. Of course, this was not Rigoberta Menchú's fault; she did not say that her account contained the gospel or absolute truth. It was the popular movement, some left-leaning university professors, and international solidarity organizations that themselves made it a sacred text. So when anthropologist David Stoll came out with a devastating deconstruction of the text, they were scandalized. For international solidarity organizations and academics, Stoll committed a sacrilege by questioning Menchú's stories. They have forgotten that all writings are "suspicious" and that they represent the political or ideological conditioning or tendencies of the individual who produces them. Even the Bible has its critics, and this tells us that we must learn to take criticisms constructively.

Let me comment briefly on Menchú's autobiography. To me, the first part of the book, which describes the cultural traditions and ceremonies performed in the villages during birth and infancy, is the most important part of the text. Here it is Rigoberta who speaks with her own voice and knowledge. This is the true Maya aspect of her culture depicted in the book. But when she enters into telling her stories about the plantations, the Maya themselves who have gone there start to feel uneasy with her stories. This is where she began to respond to a different agenda, the revolutionary agenda, which sought to bring and integrate indigenous people into the two major guerrilla fronts in rural Guatemala, the Ejército Guerrillero de los Pobres (EGP; Guerrilla Army of the Poor) and the Organización Revolucionaria del Pueblo en Armas (ORPA; Revolutionary Organization of the People in Arms).

In addition, Menchú provided an oral account to Burgos-Debray, which became a fixed text. The creation of this text brings us to the problems of representation, history, ethnographic authority, military repression, guerrilla warfare, and the truth. Obviously, Menchú was not completely in charge of the representation of the Maya or the description of the events. Her account is controlled by an anthropologist who is an outsider (Burgos-Debray has stated that she had never been in Guatemala). Then we have the problem of history. Who is writing this history? Who decides what is to be said and how? Here we have the leftist view of the history of Guatemala, the revolutionary point of view. With the publication of the book, Menchú's account and painful experience became a political and revolutionary tool. The problem is that Menchú was not in charge of writing her own account, although she may have agreed with the final product.

The book has served its purpose, and now we are in the process of revising

history. Those who attack David Stoll as the antichrist of anthropological research are fossilized in time. With the publication of his book, *Rigoberta Menchú and the Story of All Poor Guatemalans,* a firestorm of controversies has been
burning in the United States among activists and left-leaning academics. Stoll
is being demonized for revealing what he heard among the K'iche' people who
are depicted in Rigoberta Menchú's book. Now the debate has turned into Stoll
versus Menchú; American anthropologists versus ladino anthropologists; left-
wing versus right-wing intellectuals, and so on. Why is it that Stoll's findings
are so cherished by right-wing intellectuals and so damaging to the left and
revolutionary supporters? I ask myself, "Where are the Maya people in all of
this?" One side takes Stoll's book as proof that Rigoberta—and by extension,
any indigenous person—is a liar. The other side believes that *I, Rigoberta Menchú* is a sacred document that does not contain mistakes or distortions. And
even if they recognize that Stoll has valid information that supports his claims
for such distortions, the left does not want to admit that there are mistakes or
problems.

This is a very entertaining debate, but I would like to remind my colleagues
that we are missing something important. Don't we realize that the report of
the Commission for Historical Clarification (CEH) has made public the fact that
the army committed 93 percent of the massacres and the Guatemalan National
Revolutionary Unity (URNG) 3 percent; that both armed groups did damage
to indigenous communities; and that Maya now need to reconstruct their lives
by trying to remove themselves from those who brought the guns and did the
killing? The Maya now want to remember the last words of Monsignor Juan
Gerardi, who called for peace and justice in the report *Guatemala: Nunca Más.*
In this cry for justice we can also hear the voices of the thousands killed in this
war. The problem that we are witnessing in this debate is internationalist and
leftist revolutionary nostalgia; they do not want to let their baby, the revolution, go. They hoped to free the oppressed and have a free Guatemala, but in
the process they, too, became part of the problem that they were struggling
to solve.

I, Rigoberta Menchú, *the Book*

I will now focus on the construction of the book *I, Rigoberta Menchú,* edited by
Elisabeth Burgos-Debray. The problems in this book appear right at the start. I
am talking about the original Spanish version (1985), because the English edition has been slightly changed. The original title of the book was *Me llamo*

Rigoberta Menchú y así me nació la conciencia (*My name is Rigoberta Menchú and this is how my consciousness was born*). This title is very expressive of revolutionary slogans because she talks about revolutionary consciousness, *conciencia de lucha,* as if the Maya were not conscious of their situation but passive and opposed to change, as Marxist thought would assert. Appropriately, the title was changed in the English translation to *I, Rigoberta Menchú: An Indian Woman in Guatemala.* Also, in the original version the guerrilla movement, and the CUC as one of its civilian fronts, included a pamphlet as an appendix to the book. This does not appear in the English version. Now we know, according to Arturo Taracena's interview, that the book was processed by Burgos-Debray and revised by guerrilla leaders before its publication to make sure that it said what they wanted people to hear. The issue of representation, then, becomes problematic. According to Kay Warren, "questioning the politics of who speaks for whom will always be important for insiders and outsiders alike. It raises the issue of representation in both senses: who claims the authority to craft representations of ongoing social and political realities and who gains the position to represent others in public affairs?" (1998a:20).

So the problem of representation is evident in Menchú's book. I agree with Stoll that not all Maya sided with the guerrilla movement as it is portrayed here. The participation of indigenous people varied from place to place or region to region. Also, those who had some political education were involved in events promoted by the CUC to raise consciousness. The majority did not care about the revolution, and they were afraid of both armed groups. I have written about the history of these conflicting relationships between the army and the guerrillas as the war took its toll on indigenous people (Montejo 1999a). Rigoberta Menchú and her family, like thousands more, are definitely victims of the army. Perhaps we could say that the guerrillas, too, kept Menchú tied to their agendas as a result of the death of most of her family members.

So what is the problem here? One of the problems is making a static icon of Rigoberta Menchú. The political and academic left has singled out Rigoberta Menchú as the only voice for the Maya movement, and that is why they are now afraid that the extreme right might destroy the movement by discrediting her. But the Maya movement is not only represented by the popular movement, which is guerrilla-oriented. This difference is what the left and the right often confuse. First, the Maya movement referred to in this debate is not necessarily the popular left movement championed by Rigoberta Menchú. We all know that the guerrilla leaders did not want to hear about Maya culture and its diversity as a positive contribution to the guerrilla struggle. Too many languages, too many forms or expressions of Maya culture were seen as obstacles to the guerrilla movement. That is why the Maya culturalist movement worked patiently to promote Maya culture, while the left promoted revolution and armed struggle with no interest in Maya culture.

Second, it has always been a strategy of the left to have a unified, controlled voice or spokesperson. This was the role of Rigoberta Menchú in the popular movement, which is now called the Maya movement. This guerrilla strategy has been a danger to the real Maya movement. If you have one voice and if that voice is not free to say things unless approved by partisan interests, then it becomes ineffective. This is what happened to Rigoberta Menchú. The popular movement and the guerrilla movement wanted international solidarity support and created one voice, which became the only voice for all the Maya. The extreme right understands this strategy, so it is now focusing its efforts on undermining that one voice and discrediting the Maya movement. It is, then, very important to recognize the complexity of the Maya movement. "In the post–Cold War era, with the transition to civilian governments and the signing of the Peace Accords, it is particularly important to hear other voices and grammars of dissent" (Warren 1998a:117).

Much like the Zapatista uprising in Chiapas, the Menchú case is a cyberspace intellectual war in which some speak in desperation to "protect" Menchú while condemning Stoll. It seems that those who promoted the guerrilla war internationally now have little to do, and this is the opportunity to keep fighting and firing from their computers. They are not really interested in the problems that Maya are facing now in Guatemala. For the Maya, the ex-guerrillas and the government are seen as political tricksters who have been deceiving the people.

The Maya want to be in charge of their projects and now are struggling to make the Guatemalan government comply with the peace accords and the reparation recommendations of the CEH. The Menchú-Stoll controversy is only entertainment for academics and politicians who want to accuse each other or themselves of what they have failed to do, namely, to work with indigenous people.

The Menchú-Stoll Controversy

The responses to Stoll's book have been diverse, ranging from right-wing approbation to leftist accusations that Stoll is working for the CIA. In between are the Maya people whom both camps seem to dismiss without care or consideration. They tend to forget that there is a Maya movement directed by the Maya and that it is represented by multiple voices. As I mentioned, the left has glorified an individual to the point of apotheosis. On the other side of the camp are those who consider Stoll's book an invitation to dismiss Menchú's arduous work for human rights and to accuse her of being a "shameless liar" and a "Marxist terrorist" (Horowitz 1999). Eileen Mulhare has said that the people who have externalized their opinions with anger have not read Stoll's book carefully, or they have only a one-sided view of the Guatemalan situation (Mulhare 1999). As both an anthropologist and a Maya who suffered the violence that scholars here are disputing as an academic pastime, I believe that Maya self-criticism is important at this point. Well-meaning, left-oriented anthropologists have been defending Menchú's book, but in the meantime she has tried to distance herself from it.

Here we have foreign anthropologists speaking for Menchú and for the Maya. To engage in this kind of debate is to distance ourselves from the reality that indigenous people are living. We know that they suffered the most and that because of their ethnicity they were targeted for destruction. And we are aware that no one is being prosecuted for these criminal actions. In fact, there is no reparation project in place to heal the wounds of the survivors of this armed conflict.

Now is the right time to focus on these pressing issues for the Maya. We should insist on the implementation of the peace accords. We must teach human rights in our universities. We should help the Maya, and not just the politicized sectors, in this process of reparation that is necessary for healing the wounds of thirty-six years of war and the destruction of Maya cultures. We should spend our energy on initiatives that will support the Maya movement. We have to see this Menchú-Stoll debate as a problem not of the integrity of Menchú, but of the revolutionary movement and its relationship with indigenous people. It is unfortunate that Menchú started too late to remove herself from the guerrilla conditioning, because in the countryside indigenous people still identify Menchú with the guerrillas, and that is why they doubt her leadership.

The concern of many is that Stoll's book will have a negative impact on the Maya movement. This may not happen, because the current Maya movement does not rest on one individual. Just think of the four hundred or so Maya organizations struggling today to express their disagreements with the two major players of the armed conflict, the army and the URNG.

Meanwhile, the Menchú-Stoll controversy has been followed by scholars and intellectuals in the Americas and Europe. One of these is the Uruguayan writer Eduardo Galeano. In his article "Let's shoot Rigoberta," which appeared in *La Jornada* (January 1, 1999), he responded to David Stoll's book: "Lying that she witnessed her brother's being burned to death is insignificant," adding that "it is one of the hairs in the soup." The major problem, according to Galeano, is that "these people discredit the indigenous movement of resistance" by calling Menchú a liar (Galeano 2001). Galeano is right that people may dismiss the effort of the Maya to continue their struggle against racist discrimination and violence, but this does not discredit the movement. Rigoberta Menchú represented only one sector of the indigenous movement, the so-called popular movement. The Maya movement is very complex, and now it has given rise to the pan-Maya movement, which is focusing on culture and identity as major sources for its revival. Now we can argue that there are multiple voices supporting the Maya movement, and Rigoberta's is just one of them. Galeano also questions Stoll's ethics by pointing out his links to the army. Galeano wonders what documents and archives Stoll investigated. The army archives? But by reading Stoll's book we can find out that indeed the colonization of the national lands in northern Guatemala was common during the 1960s and 1970s, and Stoll makes reference to the records in the archives of the Instituto Nacional de Transformación Agraria (INTA; National Institute for Agrarian Transformation).

Among the North American anthropologists who responded to Galeano's article is Eileen Mulhare, who says that Galeano did not read Stoll's book before criticizing its findings. Mulhare tried to represent the middle ground, and includes the criticism of Dante Liano (1999), who argues that Stoll "came to Guatemala to study us as insects." That's right, this is the traditional critique of anthropology as a colonialist discipline. Mulhare defends anthropologists by stating that thanks to foreign anthropologists the world knows more about the current life of the Maya. This is true, but Mulhare forgot to add that archaeology has fossilized the modern Maya while giving life to the ancient past as reconstructed by the archaeologists to attract tourists. The anthropologist's role is to write about Maya culture, and then what? Little has changed in the oppression of indigenous people, even if foreign and ladino anthropologists have been studying them for a century. But Mulhare gets into difficulty with the Guatemalan ladino academy when she states, "Those who have the tradition of studying them [the Maya] as 'insects' are the Guatemalan ladino scholars" (Mulhare 1999).

Obviously, this accusation against ladino anthropologists is false. It is fair to say that the ladino academics have few opportunities for funding to carry out research. On the other hand, foreign anthropologists have studied Maya culture mainly to write dissertations and to get well-paid jobs at prestigious universities. But let us not forget that, as in the case of the ladinos, some foreign anthropologists, including Mulhare, have worked for human-rights issues also and have produced books denouncing the genocide suffered by indigenous people (Manz 1988; Falla 1994). Mulhare mentions the volume edited by Robert Carmack, *Harvest of Violence.* In this book, David Stoll also wrote an article denouncing the role of Protestantism and the CIA in helping the army repress the indigenous population.

Mulhare makes reference to the current dialogue between foreign anthropologists and indigenous people. But there are very few indigenous scholars who are also writing about their own cultures, and this situation has to improve. The truth is that there are North American people who are helping indigenous people in their struggle for their rights and self-determination. I agree with Mulhare on certain points, but her statement that the life history of Menchú is mythical does not convey a full appreciation of the situation. Menchú did suffer greatly, and the death of all of her family is not a myth.

Mulhare's critique of ladino anthropology brought another dimension to the debate. A Guatemalan anthropologist, Carlos René García Escobar, at the Centro de Estudios Folklóricos of the University of San Carlos, circulated an angry attack on foreign anthropologists in his 1999 article "Antropólogos gringos vs. antropólogos chapines." This article shifted the debate from Stoll versus Menchú to American versus Guatemalan anthropologists.

García Escobar argues that Mulhare attacked and made incorrect references to ladino academics in Guatemala. He said that she is wrong because she does not know them and their intellectual background. He argued that Mulhare is wrong on several issues. First, "It is not true that only the gringo anthropologists consult the Maya and live with them." Then he said that ladinos have lived with the Indians; that they do not have the difficulties that foreigners have in reaching and living with them; that

> foreign anthropologists have penetrated our territories to obtain information and inform their institutions while obtaining a Ph.D. at their universities. They serve as spies or secret agents providing information, free or paid by the institutions where they work. As tourists, they also plunder the national heritage, be it by buying or stealing archaeological objects and smuggling them out of our country. (García Escobar 1999)

Is this accusation against foreign anthropologists fair? To me, both groups, ladino anthropologists and foreigners, have a fundamental problem here. In his statement, García Escobar indicates that the ladinos see Maya culture and people as objects or separate entities that have to be studied by anthropologists, whether they be national or foreign. It seems that he is trying to argue that ladino anthropologists have more control and "ownership" of indigenous cultures than foreigners do. Thus, there is no difference between the ladino conceptualization of indigenous people and that of foreigners, who see them as "informants" and creatures to be studied. Both groups, I believe, obtain their degrees by studying indigenous people. In this same paragraph he stated that U.S. anthropologists are disguised agents who supply information to their institutions. We may think of CIA agents in this case. Certainly, some are involved in intelligence gathering, while others are just anthropologists studying Maya culture. Once again, we see that some Guatemalans, such as army intelligence officers, are on the CIA payroll to gather information.

García Escobar is right when he says that during the revolutionary government of Jacobo Arbenz Guzmán there were efforts to improve the life of indigenous people; that the CIA helped overthrow the Arbenz government and placed in power ladino authorities; that these leaders became worse tyrants over the indigenous people and maintained the structure that precipitated the civil war that began in 1960. I recognize the frustration of García Escobar, but to compare the University of San Carlos with foreign universities does not fix the problem. It is better to focus on the systematic development of curriculum in the national universities as a starting point, in collaboration with foreign universities.

The Extreme Right and Left Positions

Of course Stoll's book fueled fierce attacks against Rigoberta Menchú. The director of the right-wing Center for the Study of Popular Culture based in Los Angeles placed advertisements in campus newspapers calling Rigoberta Menchú a "Marxist terrorist." The extreme interpretations of Stoll's book are dangerous for indigenous and minority people on campuses. Any kind of vindicating struggle will be dismissed as "terrorism," and these right-wing critics will accuse professors and students who sympathize with third-world struggles of being terrorists. David Horowitz, president of the center, asks the question: "Why are they teaching something that is patently false and intellectually dishonest?" Responses like this are problematic for Menchú's integrity. Most of these right-wing people do not bother to learn about the historical subjugation of indigenous people in the Americas. For this reason, Stoll's book furnishes ammunition to those who hate dealing with the truth and the sources of misery that affect the life of those about whom they write. David Stoll argues for a loyalty to the truth and not to a political viewpoint. But unfortunately, there will be multiple readings and meanings derived from his book.

In Guatemala, elite ladino people who do not want the Maya holocaust to be made public also argue in favor of David Stoll. Alfred Kaltsmith, who was a director of the Fundación de Ayuda para el Pueblo Indígena (FUNDAPI; Foundation for the Aid of Indigenous Peoples) and coordinated aid to Maya communities as part of the hideous "Bullets and Beans" program of Ríos Montt, said in an article in *Siglo Veintiuno* (July 11, 1998): "Stoll's book, the product of ten years of careful and extensive research, acquires credibility while Menchú's book loses credibility." For people who worked with Ríos Montt, Stoll's book has come as a delicious aftermath to the conflict. But then, it is truly unfortunate that there are many inconsistencies in Menchú's testimony and that Stoll has decided to chase them down. The winner in all of this turmoil is the Guatemalan army and those who were responsible for committing the massacres reported by the CEH. A *Los Angeles Times* article, "The Truth Is Enough (December 25, 1998)," represents more impartial reporting, stating:

> Fiction is fiction, there is no way around it, and we now discover that Rigoberta Menchú, the winner of the 1992 Nobel Peace prize, concocted many of the events in the autobiography that brought her fame and adulation. But that does not lessen our need to learn what happened in the bloody war in the highlands of Guatemala during the Central American wars of the 1980s.

I agree. Even if Stoll's new study takes away the merits of Menchú's book as a truthful eyewitness account, it should not lead us, according to this columnist, "to reject the book as a pack of lies." And, as all of the scholars of the Maya have argued, the war did occur and the army did commit those horrendous massacres. Menchú had the courage, as did few other Maya, to tell her story and fight against these injustices.

On the other hand, the extreme left has its own arguments against Stoll and in favor of Menchú. César Montes, an ex-guerrilla, tried to justify Menchú's mistakes by using revolutionary arguments. In an article published in *Siglo XXI* he stated:

Very often we receive information about the death of our brothers clandestinely and in an inexact form. And we transmit the information like
this. Not because it is inexact does it become a lie. Perhaps her brother
did not die in the way she described in the book. But the fact is that he
was assassinated by the repressive members of the army. (Montes, n.d.)

Montes is arguing about something that Stoll already understands. Nobody
doubts that Menchú's brother died and that the army is repressive. Stoll explains this, although not forcefully. Then, Montes links her to the guerrillas
when he says that "we receive information . . . clandestinely." Menchú's problem is that she had to say this to suit the needs of the revolutionary movement.
Montes then says that the efforts of the compiler, Burgos-Debray, may have
been to emphasize the suffering of those thousands of Indians who live in extreme misery. Here, he tries to suggest that Burgos-Debray added more than
what she was told by Menchú. He also recognizes that Menchú's book was written on the basis of verbal accounts, which were taped and then transcribed, so
it cannot be rigorously exact.

Certainly one may agree with this explanation, that Menchú may have not
said everything that is in the book and that some things may have been added
during the editing of the manuscript. This is what I believe personally, but then
she repeated her stories in other media. She tells the same story of the murder of
her brother on TV and in the film *When the Mountains Tremble*. So the story of
the death of her brother being burned alive is not Burgos-Debray's fabrication.
Stoll is then telling us that in the book there are accounts that did not happen exactly as they are written. Even Rigoberta Menchú admitted in the *New
York Times* (December 2, 1999) that she used the experiences and testimonies
of others to weave her story.

To me, this is what Stoll is trying to explain to the readers of Menchú's book.
He is not denying that the army killed or burned its victims. The army was
criminal and genocidal, and those responsible should be prosecuted. The problem that he is trying to clarify is that in Rigoberta's account there are pieces
that do not fit. This, then, confirms what most scholars of the Maya have argued: that the left created only one voice and obfuscated or dismissed other
voices that did not fit their plans or that they could not manipulate and control. The accounts of those Maya who wrote and talked about the violence from
their own initiative and convictions were not taken into account. Definitively,
this restriction of other voices affected the Maya movement because there were

multiple voices denouncing the atrocities, but they were not given attention or importance.

More on the Academic Camp

Because an anthropologist wrote *I, Rigoberta Menchú* and an anthropologist challenged some facts in it, the book has become a source of entertainment and debate for anthropologists. Some express their views with sobriety and some with anger against David Stoll. I think we should understand the viewpoint of Stoll and his research, even though it may affect the image of Rigoberta Menchú. On the other hand, we are talking about Rigoberta's book and not about her dignity as a person or as a major Maya leader. We know, as suggested by Diane Nelson, that her book is "an explicitly political book, seizing hold of memory in a moment of extreme danger" (Nelson 1999a). I would add that the book was also a political propaganda piece forced out of her by the political strategists of the EGP and Burgos-Debray. Perhaps we have to recognize that she, too, suffered manipulation by the same guerrilla movement that she was supporting.

But Nelson rightfully asks the question of Stoll's undermining of Menchú's credibility. "Will it [Stoll's book] support the struggles of indigenous and poor peoples?" Obviously not; this is just another academic work. The right wing and the Guatemalan oligarchy are very happy with Stoll's book, and the spaces that were open for the implementation of the peace process are now being closed. Even in the United States, Victoria Sanford (1999) has indicated that some individuals are already using it to discredit the importance of multicultural education. Jeffrey Hart, a columnist for the Dixon, California, town newspaper, the *Independent Voice,* published an article about Rigoberta Menchú's book with the title "A Classic of Lies." This is very unfortunate, because in Guatemala the oligarchy is now accusing Menchú of being an Indian liar, reinforcing the stereotypes imposed on indigenous people.

An article appearing in the *Nation* by Greg Grandin and Francisco Goldman said that Menchú's book was a "piece of wartime propaganda designed not to mislead but rather to capture our attention" (1999:25). I think this critique is right on target. The guerrilla movement was more successful with the written word than with its weapons since it lacked an understanding of Maya people and their cultures.

As an anthropologist, David Stoll is free to write about issues that he thinks are challenging. Similarly, I want to make clear that the role of the guerrillas in fighting the monstrous Guatemalan army is a positive historical event. Many non-Maya as well as Maya gave their lives for this revolutionary ideal, and they must be remembered with pride and honor.

I am not defending Stoll's book either, because he, too, has many misrepresentations of Menchú and the Maya people. He does not really understand what it means to be persecuted by the army and to be in danger of being killed. Stoll also says that Menchú learned Spanish earlier with the nuns, despite her "repeated claim that she never went to school and learned to speak Spanish only recently, *as if this was a point of pride*" (Stoll 1999:159; emphasis added). Of course this is not a point of pride. She was trying to let people know that she is using the language of the oppressors and that she speaks it with some difficulty. She needed to justify herself to the international community, which was listening to her voice as that of an international spokesperson.

To avoid returning to these heated debates about an individual, it is important that solidarity organizations, scholars, and activists also recognize the contributions of other Maya. We tend to focus only on one voice, and that is why people fear that the Maya revitalization movement will be destroyed. It is as if Maya culture were resting on a single pillar. The truth is that thousands of Maya are working to promote their culture, and they are not given credit for their contribution. Academia creates icons and talks about one voice, one representation, and one Maya movement. But the Maya movement has multiple voices, multiple actors, and multiple expressions, so it is difficult to keep up with it.

For this reason, I think it is necessary to have Maya views and self-criticism of the events. It is our fault that others have directed us to violence and have represented us in this struggle. Even in the national dialogue for the peace accords, others represented the Maya. I am sure that those who were named as responsible for the massacres—and not those who were affected by the violence—will be again in charge of projects for reparation. It is time to be more impartial and support the Maya in their efforts to represent themselves. Former president Arzú remained silent about the truth commission's report.[1] The government is now saying that it has already done what was needed, so there is no need for reparation. For this reason, those scholars who are engaged in the Stoll-Menchú controversy need to focus their attention on current issues concerning the Maya people. The revitalization of Maya culture requires their support, and anthropologists can contribute their knowledge to projects that will benefit the affected communities. Anthropologists have been studying Maya cultures for so long; now let's confirm the usefulness of anthropology.

Generally speaking, *I, Rigoberta Menchú* has fulfilled its mission. It can still be useful in the classroom, especially the part that talks about Menchú's K'iche' culture, because this is the culture that she lives and cherishes. For the second part, which is about the guerrilla movement, there are other works that we can use to complement her text, which may be more impartial concerning the roles of the army and the guerrillas. Fortunately, more Maya are writing for them-selves, being in control of their own ideas and of what they write. We should be owners of our own voices and thoughts and move away from this intellectual and ideological colonialism that we are still living. Most importantly, I agree with Paul Sullivan, who wrote in the UC *Mexus News* (Winter 1999:5): "One cannot help but wonder who is being silenced when only certain indigenous voices are enabled by outsiders to speak." This is the case of Rigoberta Menchú, considered by the left to be the only voice of the Maya people. In other words, the controversy involving this book falls into what Marcus and Fisher call the "crisis of representation" (1986). On the other hand, Stoll is not an evil person who wants to destroy Menchú for winning the Nobel Peace Prize. He is follow-ing the rules of scientific inquiry, which require him to test his hypotheses. In the end, his work confirms the failure of anthropology: these anthropological works only fulfill academic curiosity and are irrelevant for indigenous people.

One thing is certain, though: in Guatemala most indigenous people are questioning Menchú's role. By being part of the popular left movement, which gave her a position, the guerrillas have also damaged her image as she now tries to become her own voice. The indigenous people have doubts about her, mainly concerning her links with the guerrillas. Stoll is not the only person who says that the people in her village do not totally support her accounts. This is what Maya women in the K'iche' region say: "She likes the foreigners more than she respects her own people." I think Rigoberta Menchú recognizes this criticism and is now living and sharing with the Maya inside her own country.

Conclusion

Returning to Menchú's autobiography, I truly believe that the first section of the book requires more attention by scholars who use it in their classrooms. The human relationships with the land and issues of respect and child rearing are very important for understanding indigenous cultures. Hopefully, scholars will recognize that we cannot teach Menchú's life story as the sole "truth." The Maya have multiple voices, and we must listen to other voices. It has been the tactic of the revolutionary movements to create one voice so that international support hears the same message. They had the ability to neutralize other voices that were not in conformity with the political and military goals of their high command.

A final criticism of Stoll is the use of the photograph of Menchú on the front cover of his book. For those who have books published, we know that editors and publishers have much to say about the front cover because they wish to market the product. But this is a demolishing critique against a Nobel laureate, and so it could be considered unethical to use her picture on the cover of the book. First, the context in which she appears in the photograph is a protest of the murder of Bishop Juan Gerardi. Second, the use of indigenous people to market a product is wrong because it makes them be seen as objects to be consumed. Third, by presenting Rigoberta Menchú on the front cover of a book that undermines her credibility is like saying, "Here is the liar I am talking about." This may be one of the readings of Menchú's photograph used in Stoll's book. Stoll may have been unaware of the decision to use Menchú's photograph on the front cover, but if he knew about it, he should have asked that the photograph not be used. It would have been better if Stoll had used one of his own photographs and changed the title of the book. But here we have the common practice of using indigenous people's images to market ethnographies. This is quite a contradiction because at least in the first (Spanish) edition, the front cover has a drawing of Rigoberta's face and not a photograph. The same with the English edition of the book, which uses a new drawing of her face.

Finally, I would like to address the most current questions of scholars regarding Menchú's book. If *I, Rigoberta Menchú* has problems, how can we now use the book as a college text? This is a legitimate question by those who have used the book as a tool to show their students the magnitude of the armed conflict suffered by the Maya and other poor Guatemalans. But if we know that the book has problems, how can we use it as a text? This is what David Stoll was asked during a conference in Berkeley at which I was a participant. Stoll said that he had heard someone propose that the best way to teach it is to treat Menchú's biography as an epic novel. It is the truth, but mythologized: call it a myth-history. We may treat the book as a collection of stories falling into the category of what Miguel Angel Asturias called magical realism. I think this is a postmodern trick that will push back in time and make unreal the pain and suffering of the Maya. Thus, it will be easy to forget that the reparations recommended by the truth commission have not yet been carried out. According to the epic approach, we can now read the Menchú book like *El Poema de Mio Cid, Roldán,* or even the adventures of Don Quixote. To imagine the recent Guatemalan holocaust as an epic is to remove ourselves from the reality of this genocide that has left two hundred thousand dead, a problem that is still latent and that remains unresolved.

I think the two books and many more on these issues should be consulted in order to see that history is reconstructed with multiple voices and not by a single voice or truth. This may be one of the messages to be learned if we want to be impartial. Perhaps the left and the right must stop conditioning people to think in black and white, or in binomial appositions such as good-bad or left-right. The Maya people and their culture are in the middle of this intellectual debate, which has become highly abstract and removed from current Maya reality.

CHAPTER 6

The Ethnohistory of Maya Leadership

There is no doubt that the Maya, under the direction of political leaders, spiritual guides, military strategists, and extraordinary intellectuals, constructed one of the most brilliant civilizations in human history (Morley 1983). We, like millions of other tourists, can admire their achievements in the remnants of their classic cities. But it is difficult to speak with any certainty about pre-Hispanic Maya leadership because we still lack so much knowledge about past Maya civilization. Archaeologists, epigraphers, and historians, through the study of Maya art, architecture, and iconography, have told us something of the Maya rulers whose portraits appear carved on stelae and archaeological monuments. Little is known, however, about those other leaders who contributed much to the flourishing and survival of Maya people and culture but whose rank did not merit portraiture or glyph.

Anthropologists and epigraphers provide us with different theories about Maya society and government. Some have argued that the Maya formed a theocratic society, peaceful and meditative, led by a priestly class. One of the early "mystiques," traceable to Alfred P. Maudslay, Alfred Tozzer, and particularly to J. E. S. Thompson, was that the Maya—and especially the classic Maya—were not plagued with the warfare and militarism characteristic of other complex societies, but that they somehow, with their special genius, had developed modes of interaction that stressed amicable cooperation and avoided competition and aggression (Webster 2002:417). Others argue that the Maya leadership was militaristic and bent on conquest (Schele and Miller 1986; Webster 2002; Schele and Freidel 1990; Demarest 1992). And there are some who argue that "Indians" could not have been the creators of the Maya civilization, but that these ruins were the remains of a culture left by extraterrestrial astronauts (Argüelles 1987). Theories that deny the intellectual capacity of indigenous people ask how is it possible that Indians, whose descendants still live in these territories, constructed an architecture as monumental as that seen at Palenque, Tikal, Copán, or Uxmal? There is no doubt that those who forged the ancient culture now known as the Maya were human beings whose sophisticated leaders mobilized their people to construct not only buildings and cities, but also the sciences, arts, and spirituality that are still admired today. Maya leaders and intellectuals developed mathematics, architecture, medicine, astronomy, philosophy, and political science in their highly expressive forms during the Maya classic period (AD 250–900).

The elite leaders best known to us were rulers, and their portraits were sculpted on stelae or painted in hieroglyphic texts to recount their rule and document their history. These are seen in front of the temples at the larger Maya centers of Palenque, Uxmal, Tikal, Copán, Quiriguá, or Piedras Negras. Except for what the stelae and glyphs tell us, we know very little about these commanders, military chiefs, or politicians who directed the destiny of their people in ancient times. And often the interpretations of hieroglyphic texts are speculation on the part of the epigraphers and archeologists. Because of their expertise, however, their readings of vessels and archaeological pieces become the "true" history of the Maya. Although we are grateful for what they can tell us, we must be aware that they are also responsible for romanticizing the past, creating mythical Maya from the classic period who are not easily comparable to the malnourished "Indians" of today (Otzoy 1999).

Hieroglyphic texts and the relief work on the stelae and murals of the Maya temples and palaces depict rulers, both men and women, of extraordinary power. These rulers commissioned the stelae that glorify themselves, leaving us with a skewed vision of Maya society and its governors. The same texts show us that, as is often the case in expanding empires, wars of conquest and annexation were fought in the *Mayab'* territory, the region of Mayan speakers. It is not surprising, then, that many experts have exaggerated their interpretations of this warfare and given their imaginations free reign when describing the war events of the past. *A Forest of Kings* (Schele and Freidel 1990) contains sections I would call "archaeological novellas." The writers, at the behest of their publisher, wrote short fictionalized stories that elaborate without evidence the adventures of classic-period rulers. Chapter 4 contains a particularly funny account of the "war of conquest between Tikal and Uaxactún." According to the authors, Tikal's attack on Uaxactún was a surprise. The ruler of Uaxactún was in a dark sanctuary when suddenly, to his horror, he heard the victory cries of the Tikal warriors as they entered the center of the city of Uaxactún:

He emerged into the blinding light, and as his vision cleared, he saw smoke billowing from the fires of destruction, which consumed the spa-

cious homes and public halls of this city's center. Screaming taunts of
desperation, the lords of Uaxactún gathered on the sides of their living
mountains, throwing their stabbing spears, rocks and finally their bodies
at the advancing and implacable Tikal forces. In spite of all their efforts,
Smoking-Frog and his company swirled around the base of the king's
pyramid, killing and capturing the valiant warriors of the Uaxactún royal
clan. The king and his men fought to the last. At the moment of his capture, the king of Uaxactún reached furiously for Smoking-Frog's throat.
Laughing, the Tikal lord jerked him to his knees by his long, bound hair.
(Schele and Freidel 1990:152)

Some researchers enjoy writing these archaeological stories, perhaps because
they wish that they, like Indiana Jones, could have experienced these historical
events that they paint with such lively descriptions. But in spite of the exag-
gerations, we are sure that there were great leaders of the Maya people who
brought their civilization to its peak, and these were not necessarily the ones
whose names are carved in stone. No civilization as finely wrought as the classic Maya could have arisen solely on the strength of warfare and conquest.
Those who built and carved and painted, those who planned and planted and
traded, all unknown to us today, were also leaders during those times. Some
scholars of the Maya, like Eric Thompson, believe that the so-called collapse
of classic Maya culture was due to an uprising of the working class against the
dominant elite, which abused its power, an event not uncommon in other empires and political hegemonies (Thompson 1954). There is no doubt that there
were wars and internal conflicts, but the collapse of the great classic Maya culture, if indeed it was a collapse, was a product of many factors (most recently,
drought has been proposed) and not just the result of internal wars (Culbert
1973; Webster 2002; Lucero 2002).

Maya Leaders at the Time of Contact and Conquest

Shortly before the conquest, Maya leaders and their rulers, especially with the
help of spiritual guides or *ajq'ij,* predicted the arrival of the Spanish and prepared their people to receive the invaders and to bear the great suffering that
this invasion would bring with it. In the books of the *Chilam Balam,* the Maya
priests, leaders, and spiritual guides bemoaned the arrival of the conquistadors
and the events to come.

Ay, my poor
Little brothers
Who on the date 7 *Ahau katún*
Will suffer an excess of pain
And an excess of misery
Due to the tribute gathered
With violence
And above all delivered quickly
A different tribute tomorrow
And the day after you will give
This is what is coming, my children
Prepare yourselves to bear the weight of misery
That is coming to your people,
Because this coming katún
Is a katún of misery,
A katún of fighting against evil,
Fighting on the day 11 Ahau.

(Barrera Vásquez 1963:68–69)

Unfortunately, the first missionaries who came with the conquistadors were not concerned with preserving indigenous knowledge, and instead they ferociously persecuted the intellectual and spiritual leaders who served as guides for the people. They accused the indigenous people of practicing witchcraft and following the teachings of the devil. In the Yucatán, Bishop Diego de Landa was the executioner who destroyed the long-maintained bridge of wisdom with the past by burning the Maya books of hieroglyphic writing from the classic and postclassic periods. He effectively demolished Maya arts and sciences in the Yucatán region. Later, Landa himself rewrote the history of the Yucatán people in his *Relación de las cosas de Yucatán* (1560/1900), telling us about some of the destruction he committed. In this work, he refers to the roles that the intellectuals, rulers, and spiritual guides played in preconquest times, relating how the rulers "used to search in the villages for cripples and blind people and give them whatever they needed." About the education provided by these leaders, men who often served in all three capacities, Landa tells us:

And these provided priests for the people when they needed them, examining them in their sciences and ceremonies and entrusting them with the

articles of their office and the good example for the people, and they provided their books in addition to attending to the service of the temples
and teaching their sciences and writing books about them. (Landa 1983
[1900]:21)

Maya autonomy suddenly disappeared in 1524 in the total subjugation de-
manded by the Spanish. The Maya lost their lands, their liberty, and their own
forms of government. Accounts of the conquest written by conquistadors and
Spanish historians record that point of view. But the indigenous people who
soon learned the Roman alphabet also wrote their stories, documenting the
destruction of their communities, not only through the wars of conquest and
through slavery, but also through the epidemics that devastated all the indigenous peoples of that time. Among these books we have the *Popol Vuh, Annals
of the Cakchiqueles, Title Deeds of the Lords of Totonicapán,* and the books of
the *Chilam Balam.*

Concerning Maya leadership in ancient times, the *Popol Vuh* is an essential
document that tells of the battles of the Maya heroes against the forces of evil.
The *ahtzib',* or Maya scribe, who preserved these stories and committed them
to writing was a true intellectual leader who fought to ensure the continuity
of the religious, political, and historic traditions for posterity. By writing in
Mayan using Roman letters, this intellectual leader challenged the rash policy
of destruction carried out by the Spanish religious and political authorities to
eradicate what they called the devil's teaching among indigenous people (Tedlock 1985). In his prologue to the *Popol Vuh,* Father Francisco Ximénez wrote
that "one should not give this more credit than that of Satan, the Father of Lies,
who no doubt is its author in order to trick and to mislead these miserable
people" (Estrada Monroy 1973:11).

The *Popol Vuh* describes the mythic adventures of the hero twins, Hunajpu
and Ixb'alamke, and of the ballgame against the lords of Xibalba, the underworld. The twins were very intelligent characters, and they knew how to avoid
all of the dangers they were subjected to and how to beat the lords of Xibalba,
who were busy causing sickness and death on earth. The mother of the twins,
Ixk'ik', even came out of the underworld to give birth to them on the earth.
In indigenous stories, women leaders often play important roles in defeating
the forces of evil. The twins present images of heroes and leaders who worked
cooperatively and who could intuitively perceive danger and avoid it. These
leaders also collaborated with other beings, messenger animals, in order to

overthrow the lords of Xibalba. The leaders defeat the enemy and show the right road to follow; the day dawns, and the sun and moon appear in the sky that was once dark.

The last, historic part of the *Popol Vuh* contains the genealogy of the K'iche' royal family up to the succession of the rulers 'Oxib-Queh and Beleheb Tzi', the twelfth generation of that dynasty. These kings were in power when Dunadiú, the K'iche' name for Pedro de Alvarado, arrived, and they were hanged by the Spanish (Recinos 1978:150).

From a slightly later date, other books from the indigenous point of view bear witness to the wars of conquest, including one relevant to the struggle of Maya leaders to protect the freedom and sovereignty of their people and territories against the invaders. The *Title Deeds to the House of Ixquin Nehaib, Lady of the Otzoya' Territory* (León-Portilla 1974; Recinos, Goetz, and Morley 1983) relates the hand-to-hand combat between Tecún Umán and Pedro de Alvarado, and the "white lady" who protected the conquistador. According to the myths (and the way oral history is woven), it was captain Ixquiin Ahpalotz Utzaki-balha, also called Nehaib, who was transformed into a lightning bolt and first attacked the Spanish, but he was blinded and wasn't able to defeat the enemy because a dove or a very white lady protected them. This captain tried several times to attack in the form of a lightning bolt, but could not defeat the enemy. Then, Tecún Umán arrived at the battlefield dressed in his war regalia to confront Tonatiuh, the Kaqchikel name for Alvarado.

And then Captain Tecún took flight and came as an eagle full of feathers that came forth of themselves, that weren't artificial. He had wings that also grew out of his body, and he wore three crowns, one of gold, one of pearls, and one of diamonds and emeralds. The captain came to try to kill Tonatiuh, who came on horseback, and he hit the horse instead of *el Adelantado,* and he beheaded the horse with a lance. It wasn't an iron lance but rather one of mirrors, and the captain did this through enchantment. And when he saw that it wasn't el Adelantado but only the horse that had been killed, he once again took flight upward and from there he came to kill el Adelantado. Then, el Adelantado waited for him with his lance and ran it through the middle of Captain Tecúm. After that, two dogs came—they had not a single hair, they were completely bald—and they grabbed the Indian to tear him to pieces. But since el Adelantado saw that this Indian was very gallant and that he had the three crowns of gold, diamonds and emeralds, and pearls, he defended him from the dogs and slowly looked him over. He was covered with quetzals and beautiful feathers, and this is why the town was named Quetzaltenango, because this is where the death of Captain Tecún took place (in Leon-Portilla 1974:99–100).

As one can see, this document is a lively story of the actions of the Maya army leaders who clashed with Alvarado's hosts and his Mexican allies. This indigenous history is very important and has become a myth through the process of oral tradition.

The Kaqchikel Maya also have their own stories of the conquest, retold in the *Annals of the Cakchiquels* and documenting the invasion and the slavery of the people when the conquistadors imposed their tributes. The *Annals* contain the laments of the rulers as they see the suffering of their people.

> During this year, terrible tributes have been exacted. Tunatiuh was paid tribute in gold; he was given four hundred men and four hundred women to go and wash gold. All of the people were extracting gold. Four hundred men and four hundred women were paid in tribute to work in Pangán by order of Tunatiuh in the construction of the Lord's city. All of this we saw, oh my children. (Recinos 1980:33–34)

Pedro de Alvarado was called to the Spanish court to defend himself against thirty-four charges of cruelty and abuse, including the burning of the K'iche' rulers in the city of Utatlán or Gumarcaaj, an action that Alvarado himself told about in his reports by letter to the king and to Hernán Cortés. With regard to his encounter with Tecún Umán, Alvarado only gave us a brief statement about the combat at Quetzaltenango, saying, "one of the four chiefs of the city of Utatlán was killed, who was the captain general of all of these lands" (Alvarado 1924:58).

Maya literature produced during the colonial period is minimal, and there are very few stories from the Maya themselves. We know that the forced labor on the encomiendas was very hard and that indigenous people had neither time nor opportunity to write their histories in their own languages. No Spaniard would condescend to learn Mayan, and the Spanish language was imposed on the Maya, further distancing them from their roots and history. One record available from this era is the letters or *memorias* that indigenous leaders sent to the king of Spain denouncing the atrocities that they suffered. *Nuestro pesar, nuestra aflicción* (Lutz and Dakin 1996) contains a collections of these letters, written in Nahuatl by Maya mayors and *regidores* (councilors) in 1572 to King Philip II of Spain, complaining of the hardships and mistreatment they received from the hands of Spanish landlords and authorities.

Now you should know that those judges arrived here at the city of Santiago de Guatemala to bring the court. They have caused us a great deal of suffering. The mayors and aldermen brought a great affliction to us, the mayors and aldermen. They make us live in slavery. They have no pity on us. We can only live in this way, in slavery. Because of all this, the affliction that they cause us is very great. (Lutz and Dakin 1996:5)

The *Chilam Balam de Chumayel,* a Yukatek Mayan text, shows the preparation and wisdom Maya leaders needed before they undertook positions of authority. Their knowledge encompassed Maya history and culture, and the *Chilam Balam* contains a section of tests to determine the intellectual capacity and maturity of young leaders (Mediz Bolio 1941). The questions are in a figurative language called the "language of Suyua." The interrogation of potential leaders determined if they merited leadership responsibility and remembered their origins, lineage, and traditions.

The *Kaat Naat,* the Questioner, comes in the katún that has just finished. And he arrives at the time when the princes of the communities must be asked about their understanding; whether they know how their lineage and their lords descended from ancient times; the order that their princes and kings came in; and whether they are of a prince's or king's caste. And they must prove it. Here is the first puzzle they must solve. They will be asked for their food. "Bring the sun," the True Man will say clearly. And the Princes will be told the same: "Bring the sun, my children. And spread it out on my plate. The lance of the sky is stuck in it, in the center of its heart. The Great Tiger must be seated upon the sun, drinking its blood." The figurative language must be understood. Here is the sun that they will ask for: the sacred fried egg. Here is the lance and the sky cross, stuck into its heart: what we call the "blessing." Here is the green tiger, crouched on top, drinking its blood: the fierce green chili. This is in figurative language. (Mediz Bolio 1941:38)

From this time there are also the indigenous *Títulos,* only some of which are well known. These documents were written by Maya people to establish their property rights and their centuries-long occupation of the territories that were being expropriated from them by Spanish decree or colonial authority.

Toward the end of the colonial period, great Maya leaders emerged to lead uprisings against the *criollos,* the American-born Spaniards, who continued to exact tribute from indigenous people even after the king of Spain had abolished the practice. The two best-known leaders of this period were Atanasio Tzul and Lucas Aguilar, who were *principales* or elders of the town of San Miguel Totonicapán. In his work *An Indigenous Rebellion in the Totonicapán District,* J. Daniel Contreras (1951) tells us that Atanasio Tzul would have been about sixty years old at the time of the rebellion. As early as 1816, Tzul, in his position as mayor of the town, tenaciously opposed the collection of royal tributes and allowed only those taxes that would serve the community or benefit the church. In 1820, many Maya communities were in a state of unease. Rumors circulated widely that the king had abolished tributes but that the criollo authorities were suppressing the reading of the royal decree. When unrest spread in Totonicapán, Tzul insisted that the indigenous people know the truth of the decree. The Spanish authorities set a date for the reading of the constitution and the new laws, believing that these papers would pacify the rebels. But far from keeping people quiet, this information gave the event a different trajectory and meaning. Once having the papers in hand that would free them from tribute and more forced labor, the people thought it was time to reform the local indigenous officials who collaborated with Spanish misrule. Lucas Aguilar brought to justice those indigenous officials who had falsely collected tributes in the name of the Spanish authorities. He forced them to return these tributes under threat of punishment, including whippings and imprisonment. Many of the justices and all of those who had collaborated with the ladinos complained of having been beaten by Aguilar himself.

The reprisals against the indigenous officials and the expulsion of local Spanish authorities and their collaborators aroused fear in the criollos of the region. The bid for self-determination in political and government matters raised by the Totonicapán leaders forced the commissioner of public order in Quetzaltenango, Lieutenant Colonel Prudencio Cózar, to bring troops to invade the town. On August 3, 1820, Cózar's troops entered the town and treated every indigenous person who crossed their path with great cruelty (Contreras 1951). The rebels of Totonicapán, armed only with sticks, rocks, and machetes, were easily defeated, and the elders of the movement, Atanasio Tzul and Lucas Aguilar, were captured and taken as prisoners to the jail in Quetzaltenango. They were not released, and petitions for their freedom went unanswered. The accounts of that time are silent about their fate.

Although Aguilar seems to have been the more active player, it is not apparent that Aguilar took advantage of Tzul's prestige in these events. The actions briefly summarized here make it clear that both fought for collective goals, not personal ones, and that the abolition of the tributes was a matter that weighed heavily on all the indigenous people of Guatemala at that time. The opposition to the royal orders and the radical changes that Tzul and Aguilar began to put into effect, such as jailing indigenous officials opposed to the movement and expelling Spanish authorities from their positions, gives us an idea of the dimensions that the movement was beginning to acquire. The revolutionary uprisings, at first purely local, expanded to more extensive regions. Sacapulas in the same year, 1820, followed the example of Totonicapán, as this discontent was common to the entire kingdom. Manuel Tot, a leader in Verapaz, is not as well known, but was also involved in the same independence movement.

Although the sparse written record allows us only glimpses of these colonial-era Maya leaders, they were not the only people working to counsel the Maya people. Just as in the classic period, many unnamed Maya leaders continued to guide the people, their anonymous lives receiving no comment in the histories written by the Spanish. Maya leaders helped people cope with the Spanish-imposed systems of forced labor and forced tribute. They eased the adjustment to the intrusion of priests and colonial authorities, or they led the people to flee from forced relocations. They helped maintain both people and culture in a period of wrenching dislocation, devastating illness, and vital accommodation for survival.

Postindependence Maya Leaders

After independence from Spain, indigenous leaders of many communities participated in the rebellions and uprisings in support of the conservative *caudillo* Rafael Carrera. For indigenous communities, liberal governments were a greater threat than conservative ones — which allowed indigenous people to practice their culture and daily life without forced labor — so indigenous people participated in efforts to overthrow the liberal governments in Guatemala. Maya communities in western Guatemala joined the forces of Rafael Carrera *en masse* in 1840. Carrera was a man who claimed (or at least didn't disavow) Indian blood in his heritage. The dominant class and the liberal government were alarmed when the "Indian" Carrera entered the capital with his unruly hosts and managed to overthrow the liberal government of the time. Although the criollos and ladinos complained about the resurgence of the indigenous forces, Carrera gave indigenous people the opportunity to return to their traditions and did not persecute them as fiercely as the liberal governments had. Ralph Lee Woodward tells us that "the conservatives, on the other hand, presented themselves as the followers of the tradition of Bartolomé de Las Casas, the sixteenth-century Dominican monk who defended the indigenous people against the excessive abuses of the Spanish conquest in Guatemala" (Woodward 1993:125).

Thus, during the government of Rafael Carrera the indigenous leaders revived their local community governments of principales and the egalitarian cargo system (a political and religious office based on the power and knowledge of the elders). The elders of the communities went back to practicing their ceremonies, and the *alcaldes rezadores* (prayer-makers) continued their ancient tradition of serving the people through their politico-religious functions. The alcaldes rezadores placed emphasis on the celebration of the Maya New Year (*Hijom Habil*) or Year Bearer, the ceremony of spiritual and government renewal practiced according to the ancient Maya calendar.

With the end of Carrera's reign and the return of liberal governments, particularly under the dictator Justo Rufino Barrios, indigenous people were once again subjected to the expropriation of their land and the exaction of unpaid labor. The liberal government created laws to justify these abuses, including antivagrancy laws and the *mandamiento.* The liberal elite did not forget Maya participation in Carrera's rise to power, and they tried to ensure their control over indigenous communities, fearing that the Maya, the majority of the population, could again unite with their ladino allies and overthrow the dictators. In the Maya communities of western Guatemala, many indigenous leaders were shot, just as happened eighty years later after the overthrow of Jacobo Arbenz in 1954 (Grandin 2000).

Until the 1940s, dictatorial liberal governments imposed ladino authorities on Maya communities, curtailing the ability of indigenous people to govern themselves and installing a bulwark of non-Maya local control. For the most part, these ladinos administered the interface between the Maya community and regional and national powers, dominated commerce and trade, and brought racist and discriminatory behavior into their dealings with Maya residents. The Maya leadership during this time maintained the religious part of the cargo system and accommodated and modified other local activities to adapt to these patterns of ladino control.

Maya Leadership from Midcentury to the Present

Ladino power in Maya communities began to be checked during the "Ten Years of Spring" under the presidents Arévalo and Arbenz, when the *intendentes* of the Ubico regime were eliminated, forced labor was abolished, and political parties were allowed in all areas of the country. Maya mayors were again elected to lead Maya communities in many of the highland towns, and local efforts to expand schooling and improve local conditions were again led by Mayas. But these new leaders were not the traditional elders of previous years. During this period and into the following decades, many young Maya, both men and women, received training from church groups, political parties, or international NGOS, and they brought new ideas, resources, and organizing skills to work on long-standing problems in Maya communities. Their activities sometimes provoked strains with older Maya leaders and often produced tense encounters with local ladinos, particularly when cooperatives or economic ventures competed with ladino sources of revenue (Brintnall 1979; Handy 1994). By the 1970s many indigenous people had began to attend universities, and the conceptualization of the indigenous person as irrational had started to change. Indeed,

> the arrival [at universities] of indigenous people who had no intention of hiding their ethnic identity and who energetically defended themselves against racism, shook the university environment during these years and opened a polemic debate among the urban and ladino intelligentsia regarding the situation of the indigenous people in the country. (Arias 1990:236)

In 1954 the Ten Years of Spring came to an end with the U.S.-sponsored coup that replaced the democratically elected national government with military rule and a brutal repression of the gains made during the previous ten years. The struggle of the past fifty years has been to return Guatemala to a civilian and democratic government, a struggle that has involved both ladinos and Maya. The first major insurgency against the military government came in the 1960s and was led by disaffected junior army officers. They based themselves in eastern Guatemala, a poor ladino area, but their plans for an uprising were quickly and violently quashed by a Guatemalan army equipped and trained by the United States. Almost immediately thereafter, the remnants of this rebellion began again to raise the call to revolt (Handy 1984).

During the 1970s the army began a campaign of repression against those it called subversives, targeting former Arbenz supporters and any whose actions challenged the political or economic status quo. At first these attacks—death threats, kidnappings, denunciations, extrajudicial executions—were directed at students, labor leaders, teachers, health-care workers, agronomists, journalists, and opposition politicians in the urban areas of Guatemala. But by the mid-1970s, these attacks moved into Maya communities, and many of the new young Maya leaders disappeared from their communities, their bodies later found bearing marks of torture. It does not stretch the truth to say that in some areas of the highlands an entire generation of young Maya leaders lost their lives in the decade of the 1970s (Davis and Hodson 1982).

One response to this barbarism was the increased activities of insurgent guerrilla forces, and their presence provoked the development of an intensified counterinsurgency war. The guerrilla revolutionaries this time saw the need to involve the majority of the Maya population, but many continued to consider the indigenous people incapable of thinking for themselves, at least in a revolutionary way, and believed it was necessary to "raise their consciousness" (Burgos-Debray 1983). Maya men and women began to take positions within the revolutionary movement. International aid via supporting organizations helped the revolutionaries attain the visibility they sought. Unfortunately, with a few exceptions, Mayas were not in upper leadership positions within the guerrilla organizations, but were almost always in subaltern positions to the commanders of the Unidad Revolutionario National Guatemalteca (URNG), the united guerrilla command. Most Maya served only in supporting positions or as guerrillas who offered their lives for a cause they barely understood. There were, of course, some who understood and promoted the revolutionary struggle on a national and international level. One of these was the most prominent Maya leader of the war, Rigoberta Menchú, who was awarded the Nobel Peace Prize in 1992, the year celebrating the quincentennial of the European "discovery of the New World" (1492–1992). Her Maya heritage made her a symbolic selection for the Nobel Prize in that year, but many also saw it as a gambit to influence the peace negotiations that were underway in Guatemala that year (Arias 2001). Given Guatemala's underlying racism and discrimination against indigenous people, it was to be expected that certain ladino sectors would oppose Menchú's nomination for the Nobel Peace Prize. She was able, however, to inform the world about the painful situation of Maya people living in Guatemala.

As the war wound down and civilian governments provided a façade for military rule, other Maya women achieved some national prominence, including the former congressional representatives Rosalina Tuyuc, founder of the Guatemalan National Widows Coordination (known by the acronym CONAVIGUA), and Manuela Alvarado. Many other Maya carried out work within the government bureaucracy, where their efforts were limited by their need to favor the dominant parties and politicians of the moment, but very few of these have been able to respond to the needs of the Maya people themselves. Others have managed to project a national presence by participating in electoral contests via civic committees, including Rigoberto Quemé Chay, the mayor of the city of Quetzaltenango, the second-largest city in Guatemala. Quemé Chay ran as a presidential candidate for a small political party that evolved from his local civic committee, Xelju, though he later dropped out of the race.

In Guatemala today a wide assortment of Maya leaders espouse a variety of political stances, right, left, and middle, and as in the past, there are also many community leaders whose names are not prominent and who do not take any particular political side. Some indigenous leaders dislike all talk of left and right, but most political dialogue has, of necessity, fallen into those categories since the war. There are leaders from farming communities who are not academics but who have demonstrated extraordinary valor in their struggle against oppression, as happened when the Tzutujil Maya community of Santiago Atitlán united to drive the army out of their community in December 1990. And there are Maya human-rights workers and lawyers whose lives are again threatened because of their work seeking justice for the victims of past wrongs. One current problem for all Maya leaders is the ongoing search for ways of developing supportive organizations that encompass the multiple Maya leadership voices of today, organizations that can articulate Maya positions within national debates and struggles, that can work for Maya civil and human rights, and that can enforce the implementation of the peace accords.

CHAPTER 7

Theoretical Basis and Strategies
for Maya Leadership

Although the Maya culture is important in Guatemala, there has been little sociological, political, or ethnographic literature on Maya leadership. What studies exist are primarily analytical ones of the Maya movement by foreign scholars (Smith 1991; Perera 1993; Fisher and Brown 1996; Warren 1998a; Nelson 1999b). It is not a subject yet developed by Maya writers. Introspection and self-analysis are necessary if the Maya revitalization movement is to understand its current contributions and its limitations. Maya leadership in Guatemala, in spite of its present form and strength of expression, is a subject that has not been addressed in depth. This chapter aims to present a more systematic and diachronic study of Maya leadership, its roots in ancient times, and its many forms and connections to the current Maya movement. Although my perspective is interior, or that of a Maya native, this first attempt to explain the complexity of Maya leadership cannot be complete since there are more than two hundred organizations promoting and revitalizing Maya culture. Maya leadership is bound up with the politics of the Maya people and their self-representation as a culture with millennia-deep roots. Any analysis must put Maya leadership and its politics of self-determination into a historical context.

One purpose of this chapter is to explain the present revitalization of the Maya culture in terms of its place in history, as occurring in the "prophetic" cycle of time, *oxlanh b'aktun*. A second purpose is to discuss some perceptions that ladinos hold of Maya leadership and how, in some cases, that leadership was promoted, used, manipulated, and taken advantage of by some ladinos in order to promote their own political actions in the revolutionary movement (the guerrillas) and in the popular movement (leftist civilian organizations). A third purpose is to ask some challenging questions about the present Maya leadership crisis, to stimulate discussion among Maya groups, and to draft some directions for its future development.

One weakness of the Maya movement is that its achievements (and, of course, its failures) have not been systematically documented. The atomization of the Maya movement and the great diversity of leaders with multiple agendas, especially those that obey foreign ideologies such as those put forth by Marxist-Leninists, have created a situation that makes documentation difficult. This analysis of Maya leadership covers only that which is public knowledge, and involves two questions: Where are we today in relation to the original struggle of our ancestors? And where are we going today with modern Maya leadership? The movement is not homogenous and static, but dynamic and multifaceted, featuring efforts at revitalization at all levels of the Maya society in Guatemala, rural and urban. Spiritual revitalization efforts occur even in the most remote communities. There are revitalization movements in language and indigenous literature, in the forms of political and communal government in the communities, and in a growing interest in archeological sites and sites that are sacred to the Maya. The Maya movement has leaders at all levels, and this is a collective result of the efforts of men and women, young people, adults, and elders. The revitalization of culture is the task of the entire Maya people and their promoters at local, regional, national, and international levels.

Maya Leadership in the Context of Resistance

Historically, the Maya have expressed themselves and acted effectively when they have had space in which to develop themselves. For the past five hundred years, however, their actions have not been completely free manifestations of their potential, since their endeavors have been motivated by the need to respond to the domination to which they had been subjected. In other words, Maya leadership has expressed itself in restricted situations and developed fundamentally in a context of resistance and survival. Maya leaders have not been permitted to freely and completely express themselves in the pursuit of political and power positions in the same way as non-Maya leaders. As a result, the Maya leadership's mobility and expression can be called "resistance leadership." Our present emerging leadership is still in constant danger of being limited by the dominant elite and the persistent militarism in our country.

To advance further in the process of self-representation and ethnic affirmation in Guatemala, the Maya have developed several stages to their movement. One effective step is that of moving from the colonialist "Indian" identity and recovering the powerful and historical "Maya" identity (Montejo 1999a). By redefining their ethnic identity, Maya have changed their attitudes about themselves. They have gone from "Indian" leadership to "Maya" leadership. This process is necessary to reorient the movement toward the positive values arising from the hearts of the Maya themselves. The ability to call themselves Maya and to eliminate the imposed name "Indian," releases them from the poison of discrimination and racism in Guatemala. Renaming themselves and using the historical identity that belongs to the Maya culture has also produced a change in attitude among academics and the general public in Guatemala. The Maya concept is being used by Maya and non-Maya on a national level; and this Mayaness has invigorated the Maya presence in Guatemala and in the international arena. In self-identification, the Maya have also used powerful unifying symbols, ones that can be appreciated by the ladino population of the country (Otzoy 1999). These symbols include the use of the *Popol Vuh* and Mayan hieroglyphs and language (Warren and Jackson 2002). Some Maya, like Demetrio Cojtí, who insisted on using the term "Indian," are now recognizing the importance of using the term "Maya" as a generator of a liberating identity with historical depth. The transformation of individual and collective identity from Indian to Maya has created a regenerationist Maya identity, grown from the cultural roots of the Maya people in the *Mayab'* rather than conditioned by fundamentalist ideologies from the left or right.

The Prophetic Cycle of Time

In ethnohistoric texts we constantly find passages that insist on our retaking a new identity in our own land. In the *Popol Vuh* the first fathers advise all their descendants that they should maintain the memories of their ancestors.

> Oh, our children! We are going, we are returning; we leave you with healthy recommendations and wise advice. . . . We are going to begin the return, we have completed our mission, our days are finished. Think, then, of us, and do not erase us from your memory nor forget us. You will see your homes and your mountains again. Establish yourselves there, and so be it! Continue on your journey and you will see the place where we came from. (Recinos 1989:140)

These prophetic expressions of the indigenous peoples insist on the protagonist role that new generations must play at the close of this *Oxlanh B'aktun* (thirteen B'aktun) and the beginning of the new Maya millennium. The ancestors have always said that "one day our children will speak to the world." In this, Rigoberta Menchú leads the vanguard, as do other Maya writers who have published works now spread around the world (Sam Colop 1991; Ak'abal 2001; Gonzáles 1995; Montejo 1987, 1991, 2001).

The role of young leaders is expressed in the *Popol Vuh* through Hunajpu and Ixb'alamke when they defeat the lords of evil. The same occurs in *El Q'anil, Man of Lightning* (Montejo 1999b, 2001) when the Jakaltek hero Xhuwan Q'anil sacrifices his life in order to gain liberty for his people. *El Q'anil* also contains a prophetic reference to the arrival of cyclical time. According to the legend, the mysterious king who invited them to fight the enemy from the sea asked the lightning men not to kill all of the enemies.

> "Stop! Leave some seed of them.
> They are the owners of a great culture
> And fine manufacturers of beautiful silks."
> Xhuwan responded, "Have we come this far
> Not to finish off all of these demons?
> Alright, you are the king, and your will shall be done,
> But in *Oxlanh B'en,* when the war breaks out,
> We ourselves will come back as we are now
> And nobody else will act in our place.
> Then, we will finish off all of the enemy."
>
> (Montejo 2001:54)

The Maya movement and its leadership can be viewed within the Marxist theory of the struggle of the oppressed to change the power structures. However, the struggle of the Maya to shake off oppression is not new, but several centuries old. Although Marxist theory is viable, it does not explain why today's Maya, at the end of the millennium, are now revitalizing their culture and making it stronger than ever. The Maya have created this revitalization, not as a contribution or result of the guerrilla movement of our country, but as a response to the destruction of Maya cultural foundations by the Guatemalan army and, to a lesser degree, by the guerrillas. It seems evident that something stronger and deeper, perhaps the desire for survival, has mobilized the Maya people to represent themselves with this unprecedented strength. This revitalization force is a response to the prophetic time in which we are living, at the end of this fifth Maya millennium. This millennial or *b'aktunian* movement responds to the close of a great prophetic cycle, *Oxlanh B'aktun,* the great prophetic cycle of 400 years in the Maya calendar. For the Maya, this is not the close of the second millennium or 2000 years after Christ, but rather the close of the fifth millennium according to the ancient Maya calendar initiated in the mythical year that corresponds to 4113 BC.

If we review ethnohistorical books such as the *Popol Vuh,* the *Chilam Balam, El Q'anil,* and others, there are passages that give the people hope for a return to their roots at the close of the millennium. The messages in these books have given the Maya optimism for the struggle to achieve a better future for the indigenous peoples of the Mayab' region. In these messages can be seen the beliefs of the Maya people, the vision of their leaders for the future, and the rhetoric that should be fed by the messages of this prophetic time. The true leaders are those who frame their action within this cyclical time. Conversely, those leaders who are the spokespersons for foreign ideologies are not fully responding to the call for the resurgence of Maya culture. The Maya priests are, perhaps, the most genuine agents of this change and the leaders on the preparatory path toward a more just and less violent future in our country.

This b'aktunian theory responds to both the global and the cosmic meaning of the cyclical period of the thirteenth b'aktun, at the beginning of which we stand. We are not only seeking meaning or the interpretation of symbols; instead, this theory embodies the interrelation of human beings with the natural world and with the cosmos or supernatural environment. The b'aktun includes the global concept of time and the regeneration of life with new ideas and actions. In other words, the theoretical b'aktunian approach leads us to understand the effect of human ideas and actions on all that exists on the earth and their effects on the environment and the cosmos. These days we talk about the hole in the ozone layer and acid rain and the effects of global warming. Maya thought, in terms of interrelation, is a response to these prophetic cycles that remind us that we are human and that we depend on the earth and all that exists on it. These are not ideas from hippies or some members of esoteric, New Age religions. Interrelation is a universal law that watches over the right to life of all beings inhabiting the earth, including the forests and rivers murdered by deforestation and industrial pollution. It was recently reported that scientists, geneticists, and biologists at Harvard University discussed the development of a quasi-religious sentiment toward the environment in order to maintain balance and promote just and sensible development. This kind of human bond or kinship with other species is what biologist Edward O. Wilson (1986) calls "biophilia." This sentiment already exists in Maya b'aktun thinking.

The Maya revitalization at the end of the millenium is not a response to the fear of the so-called end of the world, which so many religions have tried impose upon us. Nor is it a product of indigenous superstition, but rather a

Traditional dance at the sanctuary of the Jakaltek Maya ancestor B'alun Q'ana', August 1998 (author's photo)

reaffirmation of our continuous presence on earth. Maya leadership until the 1960s was under the guidance of the *alkal txah,* or prayer-makers, who had the power to direct, both politically and religiously, the destiny of their communities. Their responsibility, or *cargo,* was to pray for the well-being of all of the children of the community and all of creation (La Farge and Byers 1931; Vogt 1969; Wilson 1995). In the same way, all living things, including animals, heroes, and ancestors, had their day according to the Maya calendar. Maya spiritual leaders, leaders of the people, were concerned with maintaining a respectful and appropriate relationship with nature and the supernatural beings through specific ceremonies. One result of this type of true leadership is that these leaders ended up poor at the end of their term, since they dedicated all of their time to the community's well-being and could not take advantage of the community's resources to gain illicit wealth while in power. The spirituality of the leader had to take precedent over all activities to be carried out. Beside his honesty and rectitude, the leader had to observe chastity and sexual abstention during his *cargo* (sacred office) in order to serve the people effectively (La Farge and Byers 1931; Vogt 1969). This practice is utopian, and it would be most difficult to carry out today, as is shown by the behavior of the highest authorities in the present government (2000–2004). In addition, many Maya now work, study, and lead organizations to earn a salary (a primary objective), to support their families, and to improve their social, political, and economic living conditions. The good of the community as a whole is not a primary concern for them.

The Maya movement has usually been analyzed and classified as a struggle of power between the dominant and the dominated. It is better understood as the continuous resistance of the Maya people against colonialism and internal neocolonialism. This is obviously a basic explanation of the movement, but not a unique one. The growth of the movement and the rise of Maya leadership on all levels correspond to something more complex and invoke the prophecies about the close of the millennium, here stated as the b'aktunian theory. Why is a resurgence of the Maya culture happening precisely at this time? One response could be that there are now more Maya scholars, but this is also a partial answer. Let us remember that this revitalization, occurring in the most remote Maya communities, is born of local leaders who are not intellectuals but rather traditionalists. We must go deeper in our investigation, to the plane of Maya causality and Maya thought.

Maya Leadership and the Revolutionary-Popular Movement

One of the frequent criticisms of the popular movement has been its militant or revolutionary tendencies. This revolutionary ideology, promoted by the Guatemalan guerrillas, served to raise the consciousness of the indigenous population regarding its need to join the revolutionary struggle in the country. Unfortunately, some of the actions of the guerrillas themselves were against the same people they wanted to redeem. The Marxist ideology promoted by the guerrillas was not fully accepted by the indigenous inhabitants, who resisted the displacement of their traditional leaders by the revolutionary ladino leadership imposed on them, leading to trouble, fear, and confusion in the Maya communities that were nonparticipants in the popular, proguerrilla movement. In Guatemala, the concept of militancy was always leftist and often violent. This militancy caused many Maya to respond to the revolutionary ideology that pushed them, in many cases, to "rise up" or take up arms and align themselves in the ranks of the Ejército Guerrillero de los Pobres (Guerrilla Army of the Poor) and the Organización Revolucionaria del Pueblo en Armas (Revolutionary Organization of the People in Arms). The Maya revolutionary militancy took place under ladino rather than Maya leadership. One hopes that the Maya people have learned a historic lesson from this: that ladino paternalism does not always respond to Maya needs and visions of the future, even when it is believed to be revolutionary.

Despite the manipulation of the Maya popular movement, there were also some positive outcomes. The experience acquired by Maya people was necessary in the context of a war in which the Maya were the focus of destruction. As a bloody and historical event, the alliance of some of the Maya sectors and the guerrilla movement is evidence of the achievements and failures of a people unprepared for armed struggle. One great problem of the leftist Maya militancy (Maya guerrillas) is reflected in the actions of their leaders who did not anticipate the consequences of their actions and exposed many of their followers to danger and death.

One aim of the revolutionary movement was to achieve a radical change within the system of government, giving the dispossessed greater access to the nation's resources. Not all Maya or their elders were in agreement or supported the armed struggle as a method to reach these revolutionary ideals. Maya leadership has always been diverse in its thoughts and its strategies of action. In Guatemala we can see four types of more visible Maya leadership: that of the militant leaders of the popular movement; that of the cultural, pan-Maya movement; that of the reactionary Maya who followed the "scorched earth" ideology and were organized in civil self-defense patrols; and that of the conservative and traditional Maya who did not take the part of or identify with either side of the conflict and silently tried to keep their social and cultural life apart from the conflict. These last have arisen lately as allies of pan-Mayanism, as in the movement of the *ajq'ij,* or Mayan priests. There are exceptions, however, to this trend since certain sectors of the spiritual leaders' movement have been part of the popular movement for some time.

Maya Leaders of Many Types

Overall, we can see three major political stances of Maya leadership: militants or revolutionaries, moderates or regenerationists, and conservatives or traditionalists. In this typology of leadership, differences are apparent in three constitutive elements: their beliefs or convictions, their methods, and their rhetoric. We have very little information about the general distribution of these three elements because the most prominent leaders, those who have been showcased by the media, are primarily the militants, whereas little attention has been given to leaders who serve as mayors or community authorities. These are also communal and traditional leaders, schoolteachers, catechists, promoters of the Catholic faith, healers, businesspeople, and the like, about whom even much less is known. The leftist leaders Rigoberta Menchú, Rosalina Tuyuc, Juan León, and the like receive strong international support from their allied groups and nongovernmental organizations (NGOs). But it is also necessary to focus on the grassroots, community leadership as well, since this has more impact on changing attitudes and local community action. We can also focus on the intellectual leaders who have influenced national and international public opinion. These people are a better model for the preparation of new Maya leaders who are more respectful of their people's ethnic and political diversity. These leaders are less well known because of their moderate and cautious positions. There are others who have a tendency toward political opportunism and an integrationist, neoliberal vision, such as those Maya leaders who have served in the previous ruling parties, the PAN and the FRG. These people occupy positions in the government and in Congress. Maya leadership is thus varied and diverse and does not fit into specific categories.

It is important to know about the ethnicity, class, and origins of leaders as well, because some Maya villages have better access to information and organizational and economic resources than others. Many Maya in the minority communities are concerned about the consequences of a situation where one or two majority ethnic groups, the K'iche' and Kaqchikel, monopolize the leadership of the entire Maya nation. And the question arises: Can any of the well-known Maya leaders be the representatives for all the Maya peoples of Guatemala?

The Maya middle-class sector is made up of several groups. One includes the intellectuals who live in the capital and who, after obtaining their academic degrees, have remained in the city to work. They have moved up in government institutions or in international organizations. Another group includes those Maya who, as a result of the influx of international economic aid to revolutionary and nonrevolutionary organizations, worked for these organizations and managed to raise their standard of living above that which they had before abandoning their communities to move to Guatemala's big cities. This phenomenon became evident during the 1980s and 1990s, especially among men and women without a university education who had figured strongly in the popular or leftist revolutionary political movements. And we must not forget that there are Maya who have always worked in the capital and who have improved their economic status without being tied to political and revolutionary organizations. The fourth group includes those who have taken advantage of international NGOs to develop projects financed by foreign institutions and embassies. Economically, this sector has made great advancement, and its field of action is urban as well as rural. The fifth group is that of Maya exiles who have contributed to the intellectual debate from their places of exile, especially those scholars concerned for peace and justice for the Maya people of Guatemala. The formation of this indigenous middle class is a recent event, but a very meaningful one. Another Maya middle-class sector is that of merchants, professionals, and politicians who have occupied positions in the government or have been in Congress. This group is small, perhaps only 10 percent of the Maya intellectual population.

It is within these groups that the most active and visible Maya leadership has arisen. For first time in the history of the country we have a great number of leaders, but in reality they have not had much impact. The competing agendas of personal advancement and the distancing from their home communities have meant that these people are not providing effective political or intellectual leadership. These Maya compete with middle-class ladinos in Guatemala, and this competition has increased. Some seek to share with the cleverer ladinos a piece of the economic pie generated by international donations, like the millions of dollars donated to Guatemala because of Hurricane Mitch or the money to promote the peace accords, which is being spent without any resulting social benefits. The ability of some Maya to be in the consumer world and to acquire social status separates them from the national reality lived by indigenous people in general. Some no longer send their children to public school, but rather to the private schools where the wealthy send their children. Since acquiring a good education is a distinguished goal, this would seem a great advance in the educational sense, but in the process these Maya students are being separated from the vast majority of Maya who do not have the same opportunities.

In some cases, individualistic rivalry has developed into class competition among the Maya themselves, and this weakens both the search for consensus and the effectiveness of Maya leaders. Quality leadership does not emanate from only one person. It is not the achievement of a lone individual or the product of fortuitous historical circumstances. Quality leadership comes from the spirit of collaboration, the service to the community that is part of the Maya cultural tradition. Maya leadership must be based on the traditions of the community and on ethical and moral ideals. Without this, our leaders will only be political or propaganda leaders, not unlike the ladino leaders who have always lied to the people during election campaigns.

The proliferation of Maya organizations are seen by some as healthy since there are many voices presenting ideas on what should be done, but it is difficult to reach consensus on the basic strategies to pursue. One possibility often mentioned is the formation of a Maya political party, which could be a step forward in raising political consciousness on voting rights and could mobilize a Maya voting constituency. In some ways this conflicts with the strategy of the construction of a multiethnic Guatemalan nationality. A Maya political party would have a difficult time overcoming the ideological barriers and political alliances currently existing among the Maya. Is there a leadership strategy that could mobilize all the Maya population to cooperate with this effort? The formation of the Ixim political party in 1970 and its consequent downfall and failure (as seen in its support of one of the bloodiest dictators of Guatemala, General Lucas García) is an experience and a lesson difficult to forget.

The divisions that arose among Maya groups supporting the left-wing parties (FDNG and URNG) also give evidence of the lack of direction and cohesion that a visionary and effective leadership should have. Only a Maya political party with leadership representatives from all twenty-one linguistic communities can produce better results. A more viable option, possibly achievable by 2010, is the creation of a political party with Maya and non-Maya leaders sharing equal political decision-making powers at the top levels. This course would aid in the unification (not assimilation) of national sectors to initiate projects in constructing a pluralist nationality. The solution to the racial conflict in South Africa is a good example of an alliance of interethnic leaders in order to put an end to racism and discrimination toward indigenous people formerly treated like second-class citizens. The problem will be in seeking political centralism and avoiding the aggressively militant impulses of the left wing. We must always seek a consensus on projects that can strengthen the unity of the Guatemalan people. In this case, the rights of the Maya people have not been recognized nor respected. The Maya people need leadership that watches over the security of the people. The experience of the Maya leadership in the popular and revolutionary movements who did not have major decision-making power is an example of leaders who committed the people without weighing the consequences. We must work with the ladinos who sympathize with the Maya cause since we need allies who reaffirm our millenary identity as Mayas and Guatemalans at the same time.

Public Intellectuals and Maya Leadership

During the 1990s, an important group of intellectual and academic leaders having greater visibility surfaced. These leaders have contributed to the search for productive strategies and work methodologies for the enhancement of Maya culture and an intellectual Maya renaissance on national and international levels. Their ideas and academic works in articles, books, and essays circulate among and are read by both Guatemalan nationals and foreigners. Their academic analyses and literature make them visible public intellectuals. Currently many Maya, both men and women, are preparing themselves in private and national universities around the country. They will add their talents and play an important role in a not-too-distant future.

Regional or local Maya leaders have worked and identified themselves with their grassroots communities. These leaders have been proposed in many cases for key positions in municipal or departmental governments through civic committees and community alliances. The most visible example of such an intellectual and political Maya leader is Rigoberto Quemé Chay, mayor of Quetzaltenango. Others have participated in party politics in order to occupy mayoral positions in their communities. Some of these leaders are more individualistic, and their goals have reflected more personal gain than community betterment for the people who supported them in their bid for office. Among these minor leaders there is corruption reflecting this lack of clarity in objectives and lack of responsiveness to the needs of the community. These mayors, some in office for a long time, have been in positions dependent on departmental and national power structures rather than support from their constituencies. They are always more responsive to party politics, becoming involved in those problems that lead to corruption and abuse of authority. In the case of Rigoberto Quemé, one can say that he is an open-minded leader and public intellectual. But despite his national image and pro-Maya agenda, many Maya were against him and instead stood with the official parties like the FRG that sought to obstruct his reelection as mayor of Quetzaltenango by alleging anomalies in the voting process. Despite the efforts of the FRG leaders in Quetzaltenango to stop him from taking power, Rigoberto Quemé Chay assumed the mayor's office for a second term. Currently the Comité Civico Xelju, Quemé's base organization, has split. One faction became the political party CASA, and it nominated Quemé as a presidential candidate for the general elections in November 2003. A lack of major support for his campaign forced him to drop out of the election.

Maya Political Leadership

The Maya leaders in the political sector have at times been the representatives or spokespersons for what their ladino party leaders or patrons wanted. The use of Maya identity among popular leaders, politicians, and intellectuals can be seen in the wearing of factory-made imitations of traditional dress to differentiate themselves from their ladino counterparts. These outfits are used only during political proselytizing, and once the wearers reach a certain level in government, they revert to a suit and tie. In the case of women, the use of traditional dress continues even when they are in high positions in governmental institutions or in Congress. Maya women have been more traditional in the use of their dress, and this can be seen in many Maya communities where men, obligated to work outside the community and often ridiculed there as "indios," gave up their traditional way of dressing decades ago.

The desire for political prominence among the current Maya leaders reveals several internal conflicts. The desire to establish a name for themselves in middle-class circles has promoted a certain level of acceptance and conformity toward the repressive Guatemalan system through which they have been able to climb to higher social, political, and economic status. These people have a personal rather than a communal vision, and this is revealed in their lack of seriousness and courage in not criticizing the devastating situation suffered by most indigenous people.

Judging by the pace at which indigenous organizations and their leaders work, it would seem that there is nothing urgent to be resolved or requiring any focus or special attention, since these groups want to do and to monopolize everything. The same individuals occupy positions in several indigenous organizations and NGOs in order to gain control of the information and the funds available. Perhaps this should make no difference, since countries in good faith want to donate their money and experiment with projects of all kinds. But even here, donating countries are selective. Spaniards give money to leftist organizations because they believe that this will repair the damage done by the conquest, the results of which still oppress the indigenous people. However, many of those who call themselves revolutionaries are as right-wing as those who govern us now. On the other hand, the United States gives its money to official organizations or international consortiums operating in Guatemala because it believes that this will strengthen the democracy that it previously helped truncate by supporting tyrannical and antipopular governments in the past. Other countries like the Netherlands have given their money directly to the

Maya themselves, organized in NGOs, but the funds were used up without any visible results from so many "miniprojects." Almost all of the projects fall into the hands of the same organizations, and we do not see needy communities receiving the benefits these programs should bring.

Maya leaders seem to be satisfied with this. No one is there to guide the others or to challenge the injustice that is still the lot of the indigenous majority and poor ladinos in marginal areas. Unfortunately, the strong voice of Rigoberta Menchú was extinguished little by little when she did not allow herself to be manipulated any longer. When she no longer danced to the URNG's tune, it withdrew its support. And so it seems that many of the current Maya political leaders are too interested in their socioeconomic status or are too hungry to refuse any offer of political position, even if it removes their ability to serve their people. Perhaps they are only acting as if they are challenging the system in public, especially in demonstrations where there is an indigenous majority, but when they are in a non-Maya context, they act in a way that is contrary to their own discourse.

Some also criticize Maya leaders who have been on tours abroad seeking support for the URNG and who no longer want to share with the people they lived with before. This is a criticism that the K'iche's have leveled at Rigoberta Menchú, who they say spends more time rubbing elbows with foreigners than with her own people. This criticism is not entirely realistic, since Menchú needs international support in order to continue her work seeking justice for those massacred by the Guatemalan army. For some national leaders, the humility that should characterize true leadership has vanished, and they prefer to associate with the foreigners who accompany them rather than to return to their communities; they have created their own NGOs and know how to get the most out of international funders.

The same thing has happened with Maya political leaders in governmental positions. Their lack of association or interaction with the grassroots population shows in their constant preoccupation with their social status and with preserving their image as rising bureaucrats. One of the greatest weaknesses of this group is that they do not see pan-Maya issues as their major priority. Their focus is on local or regional issues, and thus their national leadership is ineffective as well. There are no true, prophetic leaders for the Maya people in Guatemala who can guide the people with morality and righteousness, visionary leaders who can make decisions in consultation with the people rather than let others make the decisions for them.

New Tendencies in Maya Leadership

With the confusion following the dismantling of the guerrilla-led popular movement in Guatemala, the Maya people have now seen their own actions emerge and consolidate in two more visible forms: the formation of a group of more conservative Maya leaders, some of whom identify with political parties such as the FRG or the PAN, and the development of a Maya academic leadership of public intellectuals. The latter continue to critique the colonialist power structure, and their struggle is concentrated in the academic, political, and literary arenas, which provide a solid basis for the Maya movement. Maya public intellectuals have sought opportunities to study in different university fields in Guatemala and abroad. Higher education is pursued as the right instrument for liberating the Maya people from their negative image. These intellectuals have published books, novels, essays, and editorials, and have created artistic productions; in part, they are responsible for the resurgence of Maya culture on a national and international level.

The political tendency of Maya intellectuals oscillated first between the moderate left and centrists, and later between the neoconservatives and neoliberals. They are differentiated from popular leaders in that their political task is primarily developed in academia, writing, producing knowledge, and orienting cultural policies. One criticism of these public intellectuals is that they often work in international institutions (United Nations organizations like UNICEF and UNESCO, the United States Agency for International Development, and the like), and although they write for academic publication, they have no direct contact with the grassroots Maya communities. The local, regional, national, and even international bases must be joined to develop a more representative leadership. We need leaders with solid integrity and the ability to reason wisely, leaders who are seeking not only money but also solutions to the problems of poverty from which the country's indigenous majority suffers.

Maya leadership has to be developed on all levels, and the Maya leaders who have moved on different planes and taken action on these different levels have had a positive impact. Maya leadership will have to focus its attention on the communities where poverty, repression, and discrimination are palpable and are constantly expressed in social relations between Maya and non-Maya. Some leaders have been called to the international field by allied and revolutionary organizations, and they have responded to the interests of particular groups or certain ideologies. Their actions have transcended purely Maya concerns and have affected their own people as well as the general ladino population.

Primary school students in traditional Jakaltek Maya dress during the annual September 15 parade in Jacaltenango, September 2000 (author's photo)

Finally, education is also the road that leads to an informed and visionary leadership. The ladino elite knows this and has not facilitated access for indigenous people to higher education that could lead to internal self-determination. Young people should be able to see professionals as role models by which to orient their life and their future. We need well-prepared leaders who can truly be guides for our people and for future generations. Here, the words of Dr. Martin Luther King, Jr., one of the great African American leaders in the United States, are appropriate:

> God grant us good leaders. Times like these demand clear minds, strong hearts, true faith, and hands that are ready for action. Leaders that are not blinded and lost by the desire for power. Leaders that won't sell out, leaders who have opinions and wills. (quoted in West 1993:111)

These wise words need to be heard in Guatemala. The popular poll taken during the 1999 presidential campaign showed that the leaders conglomerated in the political organization COPMAGUA/URNG did not have the support of all the Maya, as they believed. They were unable to mobilize the voters in spite of the economic resources and support of international organizations. This failure raised questions about their capability and their lack of vision. Consequently, the conservative right closed the spaces left by their failure and consolidated power in the hands of the FRG party, led by Ríos Montt and President Alfonso Portillo. There followed a series of reprisals and acts of revenge against those who had tried to work for social justice and the clarification of the truth. The hostility and aggressiveness of the leaders and militants of the FRG party has now exposed them as among the most corrupt who have ever existed. In their hostility and military machismo, they have audaciously played with the Constitution as if it were a business contract, but they have not completely destroyed the aspirations of the Maya people to achieve social justice. Maya leaders should unify their voices so that the military conservatism of the past does not deprive us of the achievements reached through the peace accords. Those in power may want to read into the Maya movement the start of an ethnic war. Our proposals need to be clear and objective, planned and executed by the Maya themselves, in order to avoid confusion and misinterpretations.

Strategies for the Future

An aspect of the Maya movement that may be helpful in creating consensus between the Maya and non-Maya populations is discourse on deracialization. That is to say, the Maya need not be completely enclosed in their Mayaness, but can work to promote actions for unity and solidarity with their ladino counterparts. In questions of political proselytizing and seeking power, Maya leaders should use the strategy of deracialization, a conscious effort to avoid emphasizing their distinctive or particular ethnicity as something separate from their Guatemalan neighbors and without possibilities of unification. The Maya must not forget that mestizos also share Maya blood, even if they don't want to value that part of themselves. On the contrary, Maya leaders must emphasize issues that are of transracial or interethnic interest to gain the positions they seek in elections. Their messages and actions should represent the interests of their multiethnic constituency. This electoral political strategy can attract support from ladinos by emphasizing transracial political content that facilitates multiethnic coalitions. I believe that Maya must get involved in national politics in order to occupy government positions. Currently, important government positions are always allocated among friends and colleagues of the parties that win the electoral campaigns. Maya who are highly trained and sophisticated are not likely to be called to serve in government positions, since the winners distribute these jobs to supporters even if they are inept or ill prepared to carry out the tasks.

For a Maya leader to be effective on a national level in a government position, he or she needs to focus on the necessities of the Guatemalan people in general and not only on Maya issues. Ladinos, of course, have always proposed "national solutions" for all Guatemalans, but in reality these solutions have marginalized the majority Maya sector. Ladinos have always won elections in the past because Maya leaders, through lack of desire or opportunity, have not participated in these electoral contests. The few who have done so, like Rosalina Tuyuc or Quemé Chay, have achieved very good results. When the Maya are able to assert their electoral weight and political strength, they will have a great influence, and there will be real coalitions to initiate the foundations of a nation that is truly multiethnic.

This strategy of racial moderation should relegate the radical or fundamental substance of being Maya to the background for a while. It may be selling out if one transforms oneself into a "Madino" (Maya-ladino) from a hunger for power for oneself, but not if the goal is to place the Maya agenda in the foreground, equal with the ladino agenda. The national project is, above all, the construction of a multicultural nationality and a nation respectful of diversity. Currently, at the national level Maya leaders face the problem of defining an effective common strategy to bring about this unity in national diversity because they lack the resources to educate or raise the political consciousness of the Maya and ladino people to inaugurate such national plans and projects.

The question remains: Who are the representatives and voices of the Maya people? We know that the Maya leaders are many and represent different sectors and manifestations of the movement. We can also say that Rigoberta Menchú is a national and international figure who plays a role as a unifying leader. But when it comes to mobilizing the people for common goals, she has not been able to generate mass responses. There are many leaders who are considered influential in their communities and popular organizations, but their influence is not regional or national, and the majority of the Maya population does not know them. The Maya leadership, above all, has been manipulated and utilized in order to fulfill agendas that others order and direct. We need leaders who possess exceptional qualities in order to mobilize the population effectively.

African American leadership in the United States is a good example for us here. Many of their leaders received training for the Christian ministry. Their

great charisma and their concern for social justice were rooted in their theo-
logical training, and their policies have been broadly developed in the area of
civil rights. Extraordinary black athletes and artists also serve as role models for
black youth in the United States. They are better organized and have the benefit
of sectors of the press and mass media that have promoted and exploited their
image in sports and other forms of popular culture as actors, singers, athletes,
and comedians. This leads us to think that the mass media are very important for the promotion and visibility of leaders, at least in national politics in
Guatemala.

Good leadership, unity, and transparency are important values for enabling
people to call leaders to answer for their acts. They are indispensable for obtaining support and for reaching the group's and the community's objectives. Maya
leaders should pursue these basic values in preparing for and undertaking any
action. Their leadership should be popular among the Maya and attractive to
ladinos; it should be charismatic leadership that unifies ladinos and indigenous
people in a project for a pluralist nation.

The Maya movement must now find this type of collective leadership. The
national situation is once again turning difficult and inflexible in meeting the
need for cultural, political, economic, and social expression. The situation demands a unified and collective leadership: not one that seeks to assimilate
all groups under one certain ideology, but one that develops unified criteria
and action while conserving the autonomy of the participating groups. With
the unification of Maya leadership and its different voices and manifestations,
we can be more effective in the search for solutions to the problems that af-
flict Maya people. Only in this way will we be able to represent the interests
of the people rather than those of particular organizations. The main function of Maya leadership is to guide and offer strategic plans and assistance to
the communities in order to reach common objectives such as internal self-
determination. Maya leadership also must develop more effective lobbying
strategies that are directed and controlled by the Maya themselves. Collaborative leadership must be developed, greatly facilitating decision making and
agreements with national and international institutions for negotiating social,
political, economic, and cultural development. Collaborative leadership can
be achieved through organizing communication networks of all the organizations, transcending individual and private interests.

In other words, it is necessary to create a sense of community, making use
of traditional Maya strategies of equalizing criteria and seeking community

consensus. Perhaps a retreat can enable Maya leaders to get to know one another better, aiding them in developing more trust and communication among themselves and, as a consequence, constructing a stronger, more unified, and organized leadership. This methodology can increase the dialogue on the projects, goals, strategies, and dreams to be realized. Modern technology, reaching even the remotest villages, can assist in this dialogue. Various forms of this technology can be used immediately: regional television channels, buying time on radio programs to disseminate Maya culture and music, and a greater use of spaces in the regional and, when possible, national newspapers. Maya organizations also need to be connected through the Internet and e-mail. Finally, we must be more creative in the meetings that we hold, and not just hold congresses where reports are read about things that have not really been achieved. Ironically, more money is spent on these meetings than on bringing peace to the affected communities, since all the participants must be fed and luxurious accommodations in the capital must be paid for. The same people always attend, and the meetings are topped off with big dinner parties that are the main attraction for many.

Another strategy is to create communication networks with local and national foundations, banks, and state agencies for the purpose of carrying out local development initiatives. For this, we need more training and preparation in the use of information technology. The preparation of leaders is important. Local leaders must be creative and active in the search for resources and opportunities for their communities. When Maya leadership manages to unite its efforts and speak with a unified voice, we will be able to force the government of the moment to fulfill our demands and not push them aside as has happened so far. We must promote a real and informative analysis for the public on the current conditions of the Maya people's demands and evaluate the impact of Maya leadership in the national arena in order to improve its role and its contribution to the collective development of the country.

Finally, we must remember that Maya leaders have their origins in their specific communities and cultures, and they have to reflect the needs and aspirations of these communities. These Maya communities are repositories of a Maya essentialism that is also changeable. That is to say, we know that Maya communities exist, are historically constructed, share a common memory and history, and are now seeking their cultural, political, and economic emancipation. In Guatemala, we want to build a consensus between Mayas and non-Mayas in order to create an inclusive nation. Let the ladinos feel proud to share

Maya historical roots. Let them see contemporary Maya as not the caricature of the "ancient, classic Maya", but rather as the true descendants of these men and women who have constructed an extraordinary civilization that is living even now through its descendants. Let all Guatemalans feel proud of their past and their present since the current Maya will continue being Maya and recreating their culture with a vision of a better future.

CHAPTER 8

Maya Ways of Knowing

Modern Maya and the Elders

Oh, our sons! we are going, we are going away; sane advice and wise counsel we leave you. And you, also, who came from distant country, oh our wives!" they said to their women, and they bade farewell to each one. "We are going back to our town, there already in his place is Our Lord of the stags, to be seen there in the sky. We are going to begin our return, we have completed our mission [here], our days are ended. Think, then, of us, do not forget us. You shall see your homes and your mountains again; settle there, and so let it be!
—*Popol Vuh* (RECINOS, GOETZ, AND MORLEY 1983:204–205)

Introduction

In every native community of our continent, the elders have complained about the difficulties of performing their sacred rituals and of preserving native knowledge in the face of modernization. But even with the invasion of the modern world, the elders have managed to continue and to transform their identities within the dominant culture that has ruptured native worldviews and cosmologies. Despite the small spaces left for the expression of their own ways of life, they have managed to pass on their oral histories and help younger generations to root their identities in the land.

As a Jakaltek Maya, I have experienced the change, transformation, and revival of Maya culture in the highlands of Guatemala, and I recognize the important role of the elders in the sociocultural processes of continuous change and accommodation. Obviously, not all Maya value the teachings of elders. There are those who neglect the elders and consider their roles irrelevant (Sandoval 1992). Some elders are very concerned about our future, and they too understand that we Maya are linked to the outside world, so they have encouraged modern Maya to maintain their Mayaness against the forces that work to assimilate them. Our distinctive way of life has been inherited from our ancestors, and new generations of Maya have the responsibility to nourish and maintain it with whatever transformations are necessary for our survival in this highly technological and globalizing world.

In this chapter I discuss some of the issues that I believe are of vital importance for the continuous creation, recreation, and maintenance of the great Maya tradition. First, as a Maya, I have always considered my culture with respect. It is not just a "field of research" or the expression of an ancient world shattered into folkloric pieces. Second, it is necessary for modern Maya to revitalize and promote our culture for the future, and to do so we must understand the roots of our Maya traditions and show genuine interest and pride in them. Third, to leave our stamp on history for the future, we must take into account the teachings of the elders and build our strength from Maya ideology, politics, and epistemology.

In Maya culture, the elders are respected and consulted on such delicate issues as marriages, the sale of land, religious ceremonies, and communal histories (Salazar Tetzagüic 1992). Elders express concern about the ways Maya are linked to the outside world and the unequal social relationships their people have endured for centuries. The most important legend of the Jakaltek Maya, "El Q'anil, the man of lightning" (La Farge and Byers 1931; Montejo 1984, 1999b, 2001), illustrates the values of respect, communal solidarity, open-mindedness, and cultural identity. Other Maya parables distill the essence of the elders' knowledge and ways of teaching. This essay is, then, not just an anthropological analysis or interpretation of Maya culture, but the presentation of the dynamics of modern Maya life in the Cuchumatán highlands of Guatemala, described from an indigenous experiential or empirical perspective.

Oral Histories and the Elders

In 1950, Maya communities were still almost undisturbed by major technological innovations; they lacked roads, electricity, radio, telephones, TV, and the like. Maya communities relied almost completely on oral traditions to pass on their sacred beliefs and traditions to new generations. The Maya way of life during the first half of the twentieth century rested essentially on the concepts of respect and communal solidarity that gave Maya communities their distinctiveness and the means for their corporate survival (Farriss 1984; Lovell 1985; Cox de Collins 1980).

In the Cuchumatán towns of Jacaltenango, Santa Eulalia, Todos Santos, and Santiago Chimaltenango of western Guatemala, the maintenance and practice of Maya religion, which included the Year Bearer ceremony, was an important unifying force (La Farge and Byers 1931; Oakes 1951; Wagley 1949; Watanabe 1992). In 1929, Oliver La Farge marveled at how the ancient Year Bearer ceremony was still practiced among the Jakaltek and Q'anjob'al people he visited in the Cuchumatán highlands of Guatemala.

Unfortunately, a few years after La Farge's visit and the publication of his ethnography *The Year Bearer's People* in 1931, the Year Bearer ceremony came under intense attack by the ladino town authorities and the Catholic missionaries of the region. In Jacaltenango, the person held responsible for the eradication of the Year Bearer ceremony was Father Pablo Sommer, a Maryknoll priest who was considered an assiduous enemy of Maya culture by the community. During the years 1930 to 1950, many Maya priests, called *ajq'ij*, were punished for promoting what the ladino authorities and missionaries labeled a primitive and backward culture. La Farge mentioned the case of a Jakaltek man called Antil, an *Ahb'e* (diviner) whom La Farge interviewed for information on the Maya calendar.

> The man has twice been in jail, at times when Indians were civil Alcaldes, on complaint of witchcraft. He concluded from our note-taking that we had been sent by the President of Guatemala to spy on him, and was dead scared of being sent to prison, perhaps away at Quetzaltenango. (La Farge and Byers 1931:155)

The public ceremony of the Year Bearer was abolished in 1947, so my generation did not have the chance to witness and experience the ceremony as our parents did. But we continued to learn about it from the elders through the oral tradition. Thus, storytelling is considered most important for the transmission of traditional knowledge for the continuity of Maya culture.

The Storytelling Method

There are several techniques storytellers use to communicate with an audience. Among these discursive methods is the personalization of the stories as a way of inducing the listeners to be part of a direct experience of contact with their roots and heritage. For example, some storytellers start telling stories by insinuating that such an event occurred "here" in Xajla' (Jacaltenango), and it may occur again in the future since history follows a cyclical pattern.[1] The storyteller makes the event more personal and timeless, and the listener

Elders gathered for a storytelling evening in a refugee camp in Mexico (author's photo)

becomes linked to the place and the people who performed such incredible deeds. In a sense, storytelling provides the young people with the elements that are basic or primordial in maintaining their underlying Maya ethnic identity or Mayaness. Communal values are preached by the elders and expressed in everyday life through the repetition of stories, fables, myths, and legends that enhance the values of respect, communal solidarity, and the relation of humans with their environment. Thus, following the elders' and *principales*[2] teachings, we Maya find it useful to tell our stories to the world, not because we are "exotic" people with "strange" stories, but because Maya traditions are the expression of our Maya-logical world, one that has been fading away for the past five hundred years. The *Chilam Balam* makes reference to the elder's lamentations concerning this loss of Maya knowledge: "Should we not lament in our suffering, grieving for the loss of our maize and the destruction of our teachings concerning the universe of the earth and the universe of the heavens?" (Makemson 1951:4).

Among the elders I have been privileged to meet, I will describe with respect Señor Antun Luk.[3] He was one of those elders who did not hesitate to share with me his thoughts about our Maya heritage whenever I asked him to talk about it. Antun Luk was the most expert bonesetter in town. He would walk any distance to help anyone who asked him a favor, and he never charged for his service. He followed the tradition of serving the community because the gift of curing, according to him, was given by God, and a person with this inborn ability must serve the people without asking for a fee. I came to his house one day in 1975 when I had twisted my ankle playing soccer. He provided help, and ever since then we were very good friends. He visited my house frequently.

In January 1976, Antun Luk came to visit me as usual on a Sunday morning. He was concerned about the latest developments in Guatemala, particularly the announcement by President Kjell E. Laugerud García (1974–1978) that every able Guatemalan man must be ready to enlist in the army reserve in case Guatemala should declare war against England in defense of Belize, then a British colony seeking independence, but also a Guatemala-claimed territory.[4] Antun Luk did not know how to read or write, but he heard the news from other people who listened to the developments on the national radio station TGW. As a traditional bonesetter and a caring man, he understood that it was suicidal to declare war against one of the world's military superpowers without having matching weapons. He then mentioned the legend of El Q'anil, the Man of Lightning (see Montejo 1984, 1999b, 2001), a Jakaltek Maya hero who decided to give his own life in order to save his people and his community from destruction because of a war. This is how Antun Luk repeated to me his version of this legend, one that every Jakaltek person knows from childhood. As he retold the legend, he put special emphasis on the fact that the invaders fought from the sea with strange weapons, and our heroes defeated them by turning themselves into lightning. The legend is summarized below.

Q'anil: The Man of Lightning

One evening Jich Mam, our First Father, came forward in great majesty to tell the people of Xajla' the following news: "Brave sons of Xajla', I bring you a heavy heart and a strange story. Men have come to me from people far away who fight invaders hidden in the sea, who from that impossible battlefield destroy armies and raze whole villages with weapons no one has ever seen. Before long a whole people will have died. From their land these proud people have followed our name, the word of our courage a star guiding them. These men have brought us their hope and prayer, asking us to share the wealth of our hearts, honoring us with their confidence. We will go to them and to the bloody war that waits for us and we will return unbeaten."

Jich Mam chose the bravest and the strongest, but the sorcerers said that they were the best because they knew the darkest power that would stop the strange weapons of the invaders by the sea. "I shall become a wasp and sting them. I shall become a snake and sting them. I shall become a lion and tear out their throats," they said. The sorcerers went to the war and took with them two young men to be the carriers of their sleeping mats and jars. Then, the young porter Xhuwan became concerned about the faith of the sorcerers. He went to the lightning guardians in their sanctuaries on the hills around the town to ask for power. He visited several of these lightning men's sanctuaries, but only Q'anil acceded to his petition.

"Tomorrow my brothers will go to fight a war for a dying people far from here. Their messengers followed our fame to Xajla'. Their enemy fights only from the sea, protected by the waves and strange weapons. Our battalion that leaves in the morning is not of warriors but sorcerers. They can turn themselves into vicious beasts and strange pests, but what will they be on the beach but more targets for the invader's arms? We will all lose our lives by that sea, Father Q'anil," Xhuwan begged. "I want to save them. I want to prove the people of Xajla' cannot be beaten. I do not care if my blood runs on the sand or if I never return. Give me those powers I must have because tomorrow we leave with the morning star."

This is how Q'anil shared his powers of lightning with Xhuwan. On their way, the sorcerers ordered the two porters to fetch water, and this is when they discussed the danger of going to war with unmatched weapons. Xhuwan shared the power with the other porter and started to practice with the huge pine trees. But they did not reveal their secret to the sorcerers. They continued to walk for a long time until they reached that place of war.

When they arrived at the site of the battle, the sorcerers became fearful and wanted to go home. Then Xhuwan and the other lightning companions took care of the battle by turning themselves into thunderbolts. During the battle, the brother from Chiapas came to help them defeat the enemy. "I am your brother from Chiapas. In dreams I learned of your mission, and I am here to help. Allow me to act first." The elders tell us about that event in which our heroes transformed themselves into lightning. "Then the sky blazed with lightning, thunder exploded, and a crackling lightning bolt struck the sea, throwing back its waves and revealing the enemies. Xhuwan and his companion followed with fury. Again and again they unleashed their lightning bolts, pounding the bloodied waves of the sea."

Then the king who invited our fighters wanted to celebrate the victory with gifts to our heroes. But our warriors answered: "Do not think of us. We are thankful to have fought as promised. We ourselves think only of returning home." So our men turned back tributes and honors, preferring the peace of humility to all the world's feasts and celebrations.

On the way back to Xajla', Xhuwan and his companions told the rest: "You will return to Xajla' without us. We who used our power in that cruel slaughter can never live again among our people. We have promised never to return; not to Xaqla', not to our families. You must tell them that we are well and that the powers we used forbid us to return. We shall hide ourselves and our gold arrows in the great southern mountain of El Q'anil. We shall live with our father who gave us our power and look down on all Xajla'. When danger comes our banners shall fly in the clouds and our voices speak in the wind, day and night, year after year, always." All this the old ones know and have told us out of the aching memory of the past. And so they passed it to their children, and to their children's children, until it came to us who live today in Jacaltenango (Montejo 1984, 2001).[5]

Rooting our Identities

All Jakaltek children grow up knowing about the culture hero called Xhuwan Q'anil. This story is told to children by parents, grandparents, and the elders to establish at an early age a strong connection with the past. Recognizing that the Jakaltek share a common root and origin with the culture hero makes them proud of being connected to the ancient past and helps maintain unity and solidarity among the people. It is like saying: we are Jakalteks, and this is the legend of our people. In this way the Maya are connected to the land, because the landscape, the sacred geography, becomes the resting-place or sanctuary of the ancestors. Xajla'-Jacaltenango is surrounded in every direction by thunderbolts or guardian angels that protect the town from danger. The founding father protected his people by placing lightning bolts or guardians to defend them from the dangers of war: "Jich Mam, faithful to God's design, surrounded the settlement with the K'ues, the man-angels who are the thunder and lightning, our protectors every hour and day and every season of the year" (Montejo 1984:17).

This is how Q'anil, meaning the "yellow power or emanation," one of the most powerful lightning protectors, was placed at the southwestern part of the Jakaltek territory as a guardian by B'alunh Q'ana, the founding father who is also a Man of Lightning. Oliver La Farge recognized the importance of this legend and the difficulties of obtaining a full version of it. Briefly, La Farge said:

> A very interesting legend is that of Juan Mendoza [Xhuwan Q'anil], and one which we had some difficulty in obtaining. Shuwan Manel admitted frankly that he was afraid to tell it to us for fear of its hero who today inhabits the big hill that dominates the western view. (La Farge and Byers 1931:118)

Unfortunately, the Year Bearer ceremony and other religious practices—the main reasons for the religious gatherings of the major towns of the Cuchumatán highlands—were abolished during the decade of 1940–1950. These major religious ceremonies provided unity and solidarity among the people of the villages, and the attacks on them caused the elders to become more cautious in telling their stories to foreigners. As a consequence, the story of Q'anil became less relevant through the years until recently, when the revitalization of Maya culture in Guatemala revived it in the 1990s.

In 1975–1976, Juvenal Casaverde studied the politico-religious hierarchy among the Jakalteks and provided more systematic information about the nature and the attributes of the lightning guardians surrounding the town. According to Casaverde, Q'anil

> is one of the Jacaltec stock founding ancestors; he is a protector war deity; and he is one of the four Year Bearers of the traditional calendar. . . . The alcaldes rezadores of the stock Niman Conob' must regularly visit Q'anil's shrine, in relation with the traditional calendar, to perform rituals asking for his protection. (Casaverde 1976:33)

Despite the elimination of the Year Bearer ceremony as a communal celebration, the elders continued to go to the Q'anil sanctuary and ask protection for their children whenever they were drafted (most of the time, forcibly) for military service, far away in distant Guatemalan cities. This is why Antun Luk was particularly disturbed by the news about the possible military confrontation between Guatemala and England mentioned earlier. Although he did not understand international politics and the threat of a nuclear war between the superpowers during the 1960s and 1970s, the unmatched weapons and the poverty of the young Maya drafted forcibly to serve in the army were his major concern. The Maya people of these communities were also very concerned about the situation, and feared that thousands of people would die if such a war were to occur. Fearing massive destruction, the elders recalled the Q'anil legend and revived their faith in the ancestors and heroes. Antun Luk said that even if they couldn't handle the lightning bolts as in the legend, the children would be protected if Q'anil were remembered in his magnificence and asked for his protection.

According to the legend, whenever there is an imminent danger threatening the town, a yellow or red flag would appear at dusk on the peak of the Q'anil mountain, the volcano of war, signaling the presence and readiness of our mythical heroes to protect the town. One late afternoon during this time of high anxiety, a red nylon flag appeared at dusk on top of the Q'anil mountain. Someone wanted to make fun of the elders' beliefs and went up on top of the mountain to tie a red nylon banner on top of a tree. Obviously, the elders were very disgusted by the disrespectful attitude of young people toward their beliefs and traditions.

The conflict between Guatemala and Great Britain escalated at the end of January 1976. But during the early hours of February 4, 1976, an earthquake shook the land, causing the death of some 20,000 Guatemalans in just a few seconds. Again, Antun Luk came to visit me, and he said that God must have been angry at the world and at Guatemala in particular; that is why he had allowed the "world bearers" to remove the load on their backs, provoking the earthquake.[6] There was already much violence and many internal problems at home, and now the government was getting into further trouble by challenging a military superpower. Antun Luk, who claimed to be a descendant of Q'anil himself, said: "*K'anch'an anma meb'a' axkam ha'tik'a xhkamopaxoj tato ch'okoj hune howal ti'*" (Pity to the poor people since they will be the first to die if this war were to occur). He was referring to the Maya young men who are the first to be drafted, made to join the army, and sent to war.

It was uplifting to listen to the elder Antun Luk. He was part of the Maya political and religious *cargo* system abolished fifty years ago in Jacaltenango.[7] As a member of this cargo system, Antun Luk could recite by memory the ancient Maya sacred prayers in the traditional Mayan literary devices of couplets and triplets.[8]

Because of his knowledge, his understanding of the conflicts that have affected Maya life, and his sympathy with the suffering that Maya have endured in this ever-changing world, I asked him in 1981 what he thought about the current political situation in Guatemala. He said that this was a question to be asked of a politician and not of a traditional bonesetter. "[Ask] those who offer too many things to the communities during political campaigns and never fulfill their promises, just as Ríos Montt did," he said.[9] During his presidential campaign in 1974, General Ríos Montt came to the Cuchumatán communities and offered roads, schools, and potable water. He was defeated in that election attempt, but when he became president by a *coup d'etat* in 1982, he did not fulfill those promises. Instead, he implemented a scorched-earth policy and offered the survivors "Bullets and Beans," a policy of murder and genocide.[10] As a Maya peasant and traditional healer, Antun Luk did not want to deal with outside politics. His politics were rooted in communal life, caring for nature, and respecting the supernatural world. "We are related to the outside world," he said, "but not in a good way. We have been destroyed by those outsiders, and some bad ladinos only think of us as ignorant and backward people. Unfortunately we cannot handle the lightning in our hands and do not have another Q'anil who could lead us to freedom and get rid of this misery that we have endured for centuries."

During the violence of the early 1980s, the people in Jacaltenango were fortunate to have a native Catholic priest who worked hard to keep the people united during those difficult days of armed confrontation between the army and the guerrillas. The priest preached in the Popb'al Ti' language to the people during his Sunday sermons and used Maya anecdotes and parables to teach the people to value their culture. In an effort to explain outside politics, the priest used the ways of teaching of the elders and told the following story one Sunday during Mass:

> There was a boy who went to fetch firewood in the forest, and when he was tying up the firewood to be carried home, a group of furious wild pigs came running to attack him. Fearing for his life, the boy avoided the

danger by climbing a tree nearby. The wild pigs arrived, cronking their teeth, and they started to circle the tree, making a huge noise to scare the boy down. After a while, seeing that the boy was clinging to the tree with no intention of coming down, the wild pigs got tired and lay down at the foot of the tree to wait for the boy to descend. As time went by, the boy needed to pee desperately. Since he couldn't come down, he started to pee from the tree, wetting the head of one of the pigs. When the other pigs woke up, the smell irritated them, and they attacked the pig that had been urinated upon. The boy watched this happen from the tree and proceeded to urinate on all of the pigs waiting on the ground. Soon they all smelled so bad that they attacked each other, until some were dead and others ran off still fighting among themselves.

The priest explained that this is a parable of how we Maya have been living under alien rule and domination. "The Maya have always lived in communal life, and their social solidarity has been essential to the maintenance of their worldview and Maya traditions." The priest was careful not to get involved in the political situation, but from this message in the Mayan language people could draw their own conclusions. His words could refer to the violence that people were experiencing in the Cuchumatán highlands at that time when people were turning against each other. Perhaps we could say that "up there" the deceiving ladino military rulers have somebody urinating on their heads, and they get angry and destroy our culture. Or perhaps they have tried to turn us one against another. That was certainly true of the civil patrols and the soldiers who killed and massacred their own people. The soldiers and civil patrollers were indoctrinated with such brutality that they could kill their own relatives without remorse. "Up there" the military commanders who urinate on the heads of the soldiers made them mad, or even crazy, so that they could kill just as the Kaibiles, the army's most ruthless unit, did.

Maya Politics, Cosmology, and Epistemology

From these distinctive ways of explaining local politics in relation to the outside world, we can recognize that the elders have advocated for a politico-religious system that promotes respect for life and for a communalism in which every individual is important in the maintenance of the corporate community (Wolf 1957). This type of Maya polity finds major expression in the cargo system, the Maya politico-religious offices of which some part was accessible to every individual in the community (Cancian 1969; Vogt 1969).

In Maya politics, people in positions of power and authority are constantly reminded of their communal or public responsibilities. An excellent example is the election of a leader in the cargo system. The leader must be someone who has worked for his people and is recognized by the community. His authority is confirmed by the Maya political institution called *Lah-ti'*, a word meaning to compare discourses and come to a common consensus during a public assembly (Montejo 1993a:106).[11]

Generally, those who are elected and achieve the status of *principal* or *alkal txah,* the highest office in the modern Maya politico-religious hierarchy, are those who have given their time and service to the community.[12] Even after their time in office is over, they are expected to continue their communal service without individualism or personal interest. For example, among the Ixil, "after a person has served as *b'aal mertoma,* he then becomes a lifelong member of the elders (*principales*)" (Colby and Colby 1981:39–40). Antun Luk said that more frequently those who occupy this position end up being poor because they cannot use this civic-religious position to benefit themselves or to take advantage of others. The cargo office is a "burden" to be carried for the duration of your time in office, usually one year, which implies full-time service to the community without remuneration. If the elected *alkal txah* uses his position to enrich himself or to cause problems for his community, he is immediately thrown out and criticized and disgraced by the community. As Antun Luk spoke, I thought about the immense difference between Maya political systems and those of the corrupt rulers of Guatemala and Latin America.

The Maya system has worked to maintain cohesiveness and solidarity in the community and to nourish and maintain links with the natural and supernatural world. That is why we modern Maya, once again, are anxious to learn and preserve the elders' knowledge and to maintain our Maya worldviews and politics. This cosmic link and solidarity between humans and the natural and supernatural world is also expressed in Maya creation myths. According to the *Popol Vuh:*[13]

> Great were the descriptions and the account of how all the sky and earth were formed . . . how it was partitioned; and the measuring-cord was brought, and it was stretched in the sky and over the earth . . . by the Creator and the Maker, the Mother and Father of Life. (Recinos, Goetz, and Morley 1983:80)

This then is the link with the divinity that some elders who are prayer-makers want to maintain with their prayers and ceremonies. This is why the Maya say that they have been placed at the navel of earth, as do the Chamulas (Gossen 1984) or the Jakaltek, whose mythology placed them at the navel of sky. In the same way, the Yukatek Maya story of the *Kusansum* was prevalent until the Spanish invasion in the sixteenth century.[14] The Kusansum myth reinforced the cosmic link. According to Farriss, "the Mayans believed that a sacred umbilical cord, through which nourishment flowed in both directions, linked heaven and earth" (Farriss 1984:287). In other stories of the Yukatek Maya, the link has been called *Sak b'eh:* "it was a road suspended in the sky, and connected to the Maya centers of Uxmal, Tulum and Chichén Itzá" (Bricker 1981:166). But this link was ruptured by the Spanish conquest and the destruction of Maya sanctuaries and sacred places.

These ancient stories have continued in modern Maya oral traditions, and Maya recognize the importance given to the umbilical cord and the afterbirth, so that some modern Maya still perform rituals for their proper disposal. When a Maya child is born, the placenta is ritually buried in the ground at a specific place, usually near a water spring, a place holding special meaning for the Maya since it is where the individual is symbolically "planted" in the ground to root his or her Maya identity (Montejo 1990). In this way, Maya religious traditions root children to the land at the moment of birth, and it is hoped that the person will not become individualistic or selfish, but an integral part of the community, nature, and the universe.[15]

The persistence of religious belief systems among the Maya demonstrates that they have a different way of explaining their knowledge and representing the world around them. Maya ceremonies are also related to the ancient Maya calendar, a unifying element of the great Maya tradition that is also under the threat of disappearance; this, too, worries the elders. For example, among the Jakalteks the Maya calendar *b'isom tz'ayik,* the instrument for counting and recording the time *q'inal,* was almost totally destroyed in 1947. Following the ancient calendar, the names of the days, *q'inh,* were used for divination and for naming children after birth. To maintain the Mayas' sacred beliefs, the permanence of the their calendar is essential.[16]

But the modern world, and most Maya, depend on the Gregorian calendar for counting time. And the elders are afraid that the Maya calendar could disappear forever. Until the 1980s it was not used openly in the Cuchumatán region, but in response to the quincentenary commemoration, the elders decided to revive their hidden Maya rituals, and for the first time in modern history two hundred Maya priests from different linguistic communities congregated at the Maya sites of Zaculeu and Iximche in Guatemala to perform their ceremonies in public. Ceremonies were also performed by spiritual elders from different Maya ethnic groups when the members of the Academy of Mayan Languages of Guatemala took office in December 1992, "a solemn act during the transfer of the symbolic staff to the new board of directors of the Academia" (Sandoval 1992:31). In this way the silence imposed on us has been ruptured, and we have begun to perform our ceremonies without fear of being called *brujos*, or witches, but as Maya priests and experts in the ancient Maya calendar and sacred knowledge.

Maya revival is not easy in a country like Guatemala, where the countryside has been so heavily militarized. During my work as a schoolteacher in the Cuchumatán highlands for ten years, I witnessed the difficulties that the elders confronted in performing their ceremonies. In July 1982, when the civil patrol was formed in the Maya villages of northwestern Guatemala, the elders could not practice their religious ceremonies with the usual burning of candles and incense (*pom*) at night for fear of being accused of being guerrillas.

The attacks on the fundamentals of the Maya culture have been constant, but not everything is lost. The Maya are reviving and recreating their ceremonies, and they are telling the world that they are still alive after five centuries of denigration of their cultural heritage. Despite accusations of being *viejos superticiosos* (superstitious old men), the spiritual leaders and elders who perform Maya rituals have continued their mission of telling the world that Maya culture is not evil, but a different way of life that the West does not understand (Montejo 1993a). For example,

> when we Maya say that we respect nature, we are sincere, because we live what we say; we feel a unity with other living creatures on earth. It is not only that we are "close to nature" but that we recognize the value of life, and we respect others. The Maya cosmology and worldview are centered on communal practices in which all elements that promote life — cosmic elements (e.g., sun, wind), humans, and the environment — are interrelated. Our worldview also informs the politics of how we must act and react when this communalism is threatened by outside forces. (Montejo 1993a:104)

It has become necessary for Maya to know how this cosmic unity (human-natural-supernatural) is built and maintained. In the past, when a Maya farmer cleared a piece of land to plant corn, he talked to the trees. He asked permission of the "Giver of Life" to cut down the trees for the cornfield because he also needed to nourish himself and his family. The Maya world used to be different, and there was a true respect for life.[17] There are prayers and ceremonies that precede each activity in which the earth and life on it may be affected. Among the Yukatek Maya, the tortoise is believed to help men ask for rain during times of drought. That is why this animal is protected when Maya farmers prepare their lands for corn planting. When the bush is kindled at the time of burning, the pious agriculturalist does not fail to call out, "Save yourselves, tortoises! Here comes the fire!" (*Hoceneex acob, He cu tal le kake!*) (Redfield and Villa Rojas 1964:207).

Speaking from the K'iche' Maya tradition, Rigoberta Menchú has said that we Maya "ask pardon of Mother Earth when we cause a destruction on her face" (Menchú 1984b).[18] This appreciation and respect for life is the prime teaching of native people of our continent. Practicing his beliefs, the late patriarch of the Lacandon Maya of Chiapas, Mexico, Chan Kin cried desperately against the deforestation of the Lacandon jungle by loggers. Looking at the huge mahogany trees being felled, he was saddened, and reminded us that "the roots of all living creatures are linked. Every time a powerful tree falls, a star falls from the sky. Before cutting down a ceiba tree, permission should be asked to the lord of the forest, and to the lord of the stars" (Perera and Bruce 1982).

This philosophy of life, that "those who cut trees for pleasure shorten their own lives" (Montejo 1991:62), is constantly expressed in the daily activity of native people. But it is difficult to continue the teachings of the ancestors and elders if there is oppression in every moment of our lives. Our ways of teaching and learning are not recognized as viable ways. To have a dialogue with a tree may sound absurd to Western rationality, but humanity's link to nature and the supernatural world has been very important in Maya beliefs and rituals.[19] In other words, the Maya have their own knowledge system, a particular way of expressing their worldviews from different epistemological grounds. But how can the Maya continue with their cultural beliefs and sacred knowledge in relation to earth if their land has been taken for the expansion of coffee plantations and cattle ranches? In Guatemala, Maya small farmers cannot live without land. For indigenous people, "the land is the property of the ancestors and people live on it without owning it" (Bunzel 1981:52). The landscape serves as a sanctuary for religious rituals and offerings to God and all his manifestations. That is why "on the top of the highest mountains we render cult to the absolute

Being, that is why the volcanoes, the mountains, and the highest hills occupy a privileged place in our Maya rituals" (Matul 1989).

Thus, the major dream and desire of a Maya small farmer is to have a piece of land to cultivate his corn, the metaphor for humans, because corn is life itself and corn has an important place in Maya culture. Unfortunately, encroachment on communal lands has forced Mayas to stop performing some essential religious ceremonies. It becomes difficult for a small farmer to get involved in ceremonies of planting and harvesting if he is a landless peasant.[20] During the scorched-earth policy of Ríos Montt in 1982, hundreds of villages and cornfields were burned, and the inhabitants of many isolated villages were forced into exile by the Guatemalan army (Montejo 1987, 1999a; Manz 1988; Carmack 1988; Falla 1992).

Histories of the Maya people are communal histories, and the philosophy that has guided their lives stems from their religious beliefs and cosmology. A Maya priest has said that the "spirituality of the Maya is life itself" (Cutzal Mijango 1990:4). This life is expressed in communal ways. Having participated in communal works in my town, I have come to understand and value this Maya way of life. One of the forms of Maya social organization that has helped to maintain Maya identities is the form of communal work called *Wayab'*, part of a larger Maya theory of corporate survival that I will call *Komontat*.[21] When the army established barracks in the Cuchumatán highlands during the war, it became impossible to continue these communal activities. Whenever men and women came together for communal purposes, they were suspected of organizing and making plans against the government (Manz 1988).

As in ancient times, the destruction of Maya villages was also prophesized by the elders in the Cuchumatán highlands (Montejo 1990). I remember in 1965 when an elderly man called Kaxh Manel commented to a group of people gathered as usual in the corridor of his house to listen to his stories. There were no roads in the region, and no car had yet entered the town at that time. The people asked for a road, and a dirt road was constructed communally with the help of a Maryknoll missionary. The town then became linked to the rest of the country. As modernization came to the region, the elders were also concerned about the price that the people would have to pay for such conveniences. This is when Kaxh Manel said, "Don't be joyful when the first car comes to town, instead, be sorrowful, since it will be the sign of tragedy and sadness in our lands." Indeed, when the road system, the *Transversal del Norte*, was built during 1980–1981 in northwestern Guatemala, army patrols entered Maya communities, bringing morally unacceptable social problems and behaviors such as rape, kidnapping, torture, and killings.

This is what happened in the community of El Limonar on January 5, 1981. The men in the community were constructing the house of one of the villagers in their accustomed communal way when the army arrived. The soldiers surrounded the village where the men were singing and giving thanks to God after finishing their communal work. The soldiers raped the women and ordered the sixteen captured men to kneel, and in this position they shot them in the head (Montejo and Akab' 1992).

In this period of the disrupted town life, individual Mayas began to receive dreams from the ancestors, who gave advice on how to defend and protect their children. In 1980 even before the counterinsurgency war reached its most extreme levels, some people recounted their dreams to me. The elders dreamed that our ancestors passed through the sky in a procession headed toward Mexico. Others dreamed that the patron saints abandoned their chapels and crossed the border into Mexico (Montejo and Akab' 1992; Montejo 1999a). These dreams of the elders proved true when Maya villages were bombed and burned during what the army called "Black August" in 1982, producing one million displaced Guatemalans, among them the 46,000 UN-registered refugees who went to seek safety in Chiapas, Mexico, carrying with them the wooden images of their patron saints.[22]

Conclusion

In Guatemala, despite the systematic destruction of native cultures, the revival of Maya ethnic identity has become very strong, and there are interethnic movements for the recreation and redefinition of a pan-Maya identity. These efforts deepen the roots of our Maya heritage and reaffirm our presence, which is stronger than ever. The revival of Maya cultures is inevitable, despite the efforts of some sectors of the Guatemalan elite to uproot the Maya from their sacred beliefs and knowledge. For this reason native values and politics are important for the construction and maintenance of native people's worldviews.

Maya political movements have developed in a restricted way, rupturing the established non-Maya frameworks, names, and images created for native inhabitants. This is a continuous task. If we are to promote our values and worldview, we have to eliminate the denigrating images that were imposed on us and reaffirm our Maya identity (Montejo 1993a:110).

For the past five hundred years, the Maya have been neglected and persecuted instead of being allowed to freely express their creativity and promote
their Mayaness. The complaints and lamentations of the elders concerning the
destruction of Maya knowledge were stated in the books of the *Chilam Balam*
as follows:

> We complain in great sorrow, in loud voices . . . and death. Our grief is
> torment. We are pierced with a great longing to read the books of wood
> and the writings on stone, now in ruins. They contain the seven well-
> springs of life! They were burned before our eyes at the well. At noon-day
> we lament our perpetual burdens. (Makemson 1951:5)

Against this "perpetual burden" and aggression, native people of the continent
are building an indigenous internationalism for the purpose of getting rid of
the denigrating images and representations that have portrayed not only Maya
but all native peoples negatively. With the recharging of our Maya cultural traditions and the emergence of a Maya unity with plural identity, we are ensuring
that the voices of our ancestors and elders are becoming louder and louder
again. We must struggle to maintain our life where our placentas have been
planted, since the land is essential for our lives and provides our communal
spirituality.

Finally, it is my hope that we learn to value and recognize indigenous knowledge expressed by the elders when they explain Maya beliefs and spirituality,
with emphasis on values such as the respect that links humans, nature, and
the supernatural world. By knowing and valuing these ways of life, we will
understand the suffering that indigenous people have endured for the past
five centuries. The major concern of Guatemalan Maya at present is their cultural survival in a world that has encroached upon their worldview, not only
with exploitation, but with ethnocidal wars that keep them apart from their
dreams of creating and recreating a pan-Maya ethnic identity. We hope that
Maya culture may be practiced without restrictions, as has been prophesied by
the *Chilam Balam*:

> As soon as they have departed we will no longer need to speak exceed-
> ingly softly when we cast our lots. And in the day there will be no more
> violent disputes. Our good fortune will unite us. We will be able to look
> at ourselves in the mirror without sadness. We will amuse ourselves once
> more when that day comes. (Makemson 1951:8)

At present, the modern Maya are engaged in the revitalization of Maya culture, and we are optimistic that we will secure our place in history for the next centuries. Meanwhile, the teachings of the elders must continue, and modern Maya must draw their strength from their wise words. In 1982, Antun Luk communicated to me his hope for the continuity of our Maya religious traditions. "Hopefully our ways will be continued in the future if our sons and daughters retake our paths" (*Oxoqwal xhtoh st'inhb'akoj sb'a yala' tatoh xtxum sb'a sk'ul k'ahole, kutz'ine*). We modern Maya are responsible for this task of cultural recreation and revitalization of Maya culture. If in the past "Maya have been seen as insignificant, now we have to fight for our rights as significant people with a millenarian history" (Montejo 1993a:108).

CHAPTER 9

Leadership and Maya Intellectuality

To be a Maya intellectual is in many ways to isolate oneself from the world and inevitably move in epistemological circles revolving around books and the production of knowledge. These circles are often closed and marginalized since many people care more about their daily lives in their communities than they do about feasible cultural models for the future. By definition, the work requires academic preparation, a formidable goal, especially since access to higher university education has been very difficult for Mayas to obtain. It is necessary for intellectuals to move within the capitalist world of print and publication, with all its attendant technology, including the Internet, in order to convey the thoughts one generates from a critical and analytical position within the academic world. Even at lower educational levels we see how necessary it is for students, schoolteachers, or university students to master the challenges of knowledge represented on paper or in computers and to prepare themselves for the demands that modern technology and globalization bring.

Beyond the production of knowledge, Maya intellectuals have many functions in the daily life of their people, their culture, and their nation. Because they serve as a bridge between two cultures, they must be in constant association with both Maya and ladino people, and in that position they are able to promote a better understanding of Maya culture. Maya intellectuals also report on ethnic issues and ethnic conflict from an ideological and political perspective. Some intellectuals of Maya origin decline the role of spokesperson for their childhood culture and, making themselves comfortable in their academic world or their professional work, forget any obligation they might have to their people.

Many Maya intellectuals are unknown because few have opted to produce knowledge and speak out from the depth of their culture. The reasons for becoming a Maya intellectual are very diverse, but at the core is the individual's need to advance and to have a platform for expressing creative thought. It has been difficult for Maya intellectuals to find opportunities to join Guatemalan intellectuals. Ladinos have more educational opportunities, and especially more economic opportunities, whereas Mayas have had to fight hard to realize their dreams of good academic training. During the 1960s and 1970s, the Escuelas Normales, the Instituto Indígena Santiago, the Instituto Indígena Nuestra Señora del Socorro, the Seminario Mayor, and the Seminario Menor de San José, Sololá, served as educational platforms for readying the first indigenous intellectuals to attend the national University of San Carlos of Guatemala or private institutions such as Francisco Marroquín University or Rafael Landívar University.

During these decades, few Maya from western Guatemala had access to university educations. The greatest obstacle was economic, since the universities operated only in large cities, primarily the capital and Quetzaltenango. Maya who lived (and still live) in proximity to these cities had greater access to education. During these years, some of the currently important Maya leaders, Dr. Alfredo Tay Coyoy, the *licenciado* Manuel de Jesús Salazar, and Dr. Demetrio Cojtí, received their educations. During the next decade, another generation of Maya intellectuals, men and women including licenciada Otilia Lux, Dr. Enrique Sam Colop, Dr. Irma Otzoy, licenciado Rigoberto Quemé Chay, anthropologist and journalist Estuardo Zapeta, licenciado Francisco Morales Santos, licenciado Gaspar González, the poet Humberto Ak'abal, and this author, received their educations. Most of these intellectuals have attained national and international visibility, publishing important academic and literary works.

A belief, still commonly held among ladinos, is that Maya, or "Indians" as they are still called, cannot reach higher goals in education. The Maya men and women mentioned above have broken through that denigrating limitation. Indigenous people are thought to be good only for the *mecapal* (the carrying strap worn around the forehead for transporting heavy loads on one's back) and not for intellectual and academic activities. Many young Maya intellectuals have taken advantage of scholarship programs offered by international institutions such as the Maya Educational Foundation and the United States Agency for International Development. The United States embassy in Guatemala has also offered scholarships so that some Maya can study abroad, follow different careers, or obtain masters degrees in the capital. There is now a broader opening in education for those who dream of reaching advanced academic degrees, thanks to educational support from these and other international institutions.

One problem facing these Maya intellectuals is the lack of indigenous and academic publishing agencies where they can express themselves freely. Many have published in university magazines and in newspapers, but very few have managed to publish books or academic essays. These barriers to visible Maya academic production are due to limited resources for publication, and Maya intellectuals always struggle to find spaces in print or to publish their work and make their thoughts known to national and international readers.

Maya intellectuals are also distanced from their home communities. Academic work and intellectual activities take place in urban and university settings, and through emigration to these places they lose some contact with their communities. We should also note that their work often has little impact on these communities because the work is often abstract or theoretical and seeks to influence broader, national audiences and events. Reaching these audiences and events, in turn, requires the social status and prestige obtained only through higher university education.

Maya intellectuals often face the criticism that by assimilating and using Western sciences and academic fields, they are playing within the very system that has oppressed the Maya. The hard sciences — physics, chemistry, math, biology, and genetics — are clearly expressions of the thought and the universal laws under which the Western world operates. Mayas must master these disciplines. We cannot afford to be unaware of new research and developments in the physical and social sciences or in the humanities. But we also want to bring indigenous knowledge to light and incorporate its insights into the knowledge shared by the world. During the Maya classic period, the accumulated Maya wisdom gave rise to high expressions of architecture, mathematics, philosophy, hieroglyphics, and art. Almost all this wisdom, collected in hieroglyphic texts and codices, was destroyed during the conquest or burned by the monks who converted the Maya to Christianity by force. The reclamation and reconstruction of this wisdom are topics that Maya intellectuals need to discuss as part of the mandate for the Maya university they wish to establish in Guatemala.

Thus, for Maya intellectuals to be successful in their university careers they must respond equally to the necessities of academic requirements and to the maintenance of their connections with the Maya culture itself. We cannot, as Maya intellectuals, separate ourselves from the social, political, economic, or cultural reality of our country; nor can we isolate ourselves from the modern intellectual world and parochialize ourselves completely. There are positive values, wisdom, and experience in both worldviews, Maya and Western. One task of Maya intellectuals is to bring to light, develop, and share with the world the remaining local Maya knowledge inherited from the ancestors.

Maya leaders have many tasks ahead of them. There has never been much space or time for them to engage in dialogue among themselves and establish the priorities of their communities, culture, and nation. Politics offers one way to do this, although the corruption that abounds even in the highest spheres of government makes this option highly suspect. Another way is to accept work that serves all Guatemalans while simultaneously generating knowledge that benefits our people and the different manifestations of Maya culture.

Other options are not so helpful for promoting Maya culture. Maya intellectuals who are inclined toward evangelizing and studying the Bible work not to elevate their culture but rather to extinguish the Maya spirituality generated by the *ajq'ij* or Maya priests. Instead, they promote various forms of Protestant and Catholic religious fundamentalism. The religious movement Acción Católica, Catholic Action, had a similar effect in the 1960s when it displaced the authority of elders and *principales* who practiced the traditional form of politico-religious leadership, thus hastening the end of the Maya knowledge inherent in those offices (Arias 1990).

In spite of the cultural richness of Maya people in Guatemala, the expressions of the Maya literary tradition and academic productions by the Maya themselves are small in number. Some Maya intellectuals still depend on ladino intellectuals or foreign scholars to speak and write their ethnographies and local histories. This is not the fault of the Maya intellectuals, but rather of the system that limits the possibilities of advancement to positions where the production of academic or literary works is rewarded. Indeed, when more than 60 percent of the adult Maya cannot read, and when those who can read scarcely have time for it, there is hardly a growing audience clamoring for more literature.

At the start of this new millennium, many barriers still curtail Maya excellence in education, particularly at the higher levels. Economic and social constraints force people to settle for short academic careers, and many Maya choose the fields of teaching and bilingual education because the educational pathway to them is shorter. Often the schools and teacher-training institutes are of poor quality: teachers without academic training are often the voluntary educators of others. The absence of teaching materials and research centers, including libraries for the teaching colleges, increases the problem. During the 1980s the Guatemalan army rampage eliminated many Maya leaders. Elementary schoolteachers were especially targeted for persecution since they were considered intellectuals who, the army believed, helped the guerrillas convince the population to join the revolutionary movement in the rural areas (Montejo 1987; Perera 1993). This campaign set rural education among Maya children back at least ten years. Among educational institutions, there remains a sense of abandonment by the government, and thus our national education has always been mediocre. With the advances in technology and computer science in other parts of the world, we lag even further behind those countries that consider education a priority for the advancement of their people.

Myths about Maya Intellectuality

Many people would find it surprising to talk about Maya intellectuals. Guatemala's racism makes it difficult to talk about Maya who competed successfully with non-Maya for intellectual positions. Even some Maya would say that it is just bragging to speak of Maya intellectuals. But Maya intellectuals exist, and some are quite exceptional. From the time of the conquest, indigenous people have been conditioned to positions of servitude and mental deficiency, and the non-Maya have insisted that the *criollos* or *mestizos* are the only *personas de razón* (people of reason). Indigenous people have always been perceived as incapable of thinking or reasoning like real human beings.

The endemic cultural racism in Guatemala has caused Maya intellectuals to suffer from continued discrimination, even when they have obtained a university education. This is especially true for women who wear traditional dress. Only ladinos with higher education can understand the level of education that some Maya have attained, but most ladinos are without this level of education, and they cannot imagine — or wish to recognize — this achievement on the part of Mayas. In the general Guatemalan culture, the suit, or *tacuche,* and tie are the social markers of the intellectual and scholar. But if Mayas, even those with doctorates, show up in traditional dress, the clothing they normally use, they are not considered intellectuals but rather Indians or campesinos. This artificial perception accords intellectuality only to those who are dressed according to the stereotype.

Academic institutions, universities, and research centers have always been managed by non-Maya, and some believe that Maya are incapable of such tasks. Racism is expressed in classrooms and in social relations among students and professors. "Indians" may have their dreams of success, but they cannot reach the pinnacle of the academic world, since this is reserved exclusively for intelligent people, people who reason logically. Some prefer that indigenous people be subjects of study rather than researchers, intellectuals, or scholars. This type of racism always puts Mayas on the defensive to avoid being categorized as inferior. Mayas must always struggle to get our actions and productions approved by publishers, who are always white people, not indigenous people. This unequal power relationship places Maya leaders and intellectuals in a negative position since it does not allow the Maya to act and think freely. This conditioning is colonialist; others make decisions for the Maya, who act like puppets instead of real actors. Maya leaders and intellectuals are the recipients of contempt and devaluation under the guise of sponsorship or aid.

Not all Maya intellectuals need support for their thinking and actions. There are many who are not conditioned by reductionist pressure from the right or left. The few Maya intellectuals who serve as models for the new cultures and generations have many commitments to their communities. These intellectuals, because they are few, play many roles — educators, researchers, critics, poets, writers, and politicians, all at the same time. Maya leaders and intellectuals are often immersed in political activism and the pursuit of cultural, political, educational, and economic vindication for the Maya people. These numerous roles take time and concentration away from other deeper tasks such as the creation of knowledge and wisdom, long the most appreciated value of the Maya culture.

All Maya intellectuals have received a Western education and are placed within the non-Maya, Western academic world. To graduate, we must respond to the educational parameters established by these universities and fulfill the requirements established by administrative bodies and university professors. Many traditional Maya intellectuals have great knowledge without the credentials to be accepted by university authorities in intellectual positions. They have knowledge of the Maya calendar, agriculture, traditional medicine, or ritual understanding, and they are leaders of their people and communities, but are not considered producers of knowledge.

The few Maya intellectuals in key academic positions cannot accomplish as much as they would like because they are so few. Contingents of Maya scholars should find places in all the social sciences and humanities in order to influence Guatemalan state policy. Maya intellectuals are defensive because the non-Maya majority makes decisions and occupies spaces closed to the Maya. Always being on the defensive saps energy by placing the person in a constant struggle with a system where jobs are never secure.

The Revolutionary Movement and Maya Intellectuality

One problem in Guatemala has been the uneven intervention of human-rights organizations in revolutionary political movements. These human-rights organizations, focused on class struggle, have excluded Maya intellectuals from their work in order to concentrate on militant revolutionary figures or activists. From the mid-1980s until the signing of the peace accords in 1996, these groups gave tremendous support to Rigoberta Menchú. They worked for the resolution of the Myrna Mack case and with Jennifer Harbury to solve the disappearance of her husband, the guerrilla leader Everado. They supported the work of the Council of Ethnic Communities Ranujel Junam (CERJ), the group working to make participation in the civil patrol voluntary.

Many Maya widows and leaders who were not aligned with these leftist groups received no support. They were unable to present their demands in court or receive international solidarity. This compartmentalization of Maya leadership has not helped the Maya themselves. If we look around Guatemala, we can see that there has not been much benefit from the deaths of thousands of our brothers and sisters who allied themselves with the guerrillas. Some Maya intellectuals were more cautious, and dedicated themselves to writing and promoting Maya culture. It was safer to promote the values of Maya culture rather than throw oneself against the military forces and rise up in an unorganized and hopeless revolution. Although the revolutionary leftists contributed to the silencing and selective elimination of those who were critical to their agenda, guerrilla actions cannot be compared with those of the Guatemalan army, which silenced indigenous people with great massacres, ethnocide, and genocide. Perhaps it was the scope of these massive violations of human rights that caused the human-rights activists and solidarity organizations to focus their support on those leftist groups that represented the only organized resistance against violence in Guatemala at that time.

I do not want to say Maya resistance supported by non-Mayas was bad or without benefits, but Maya resistance has existed for centuries and has done so without putting the majority of the population at risk. I believe that non-Maya intellectuals and ladinos who support the Maya cause of social, economic, and cultural vindication should work together and consult together on an appropriate vision for this country. Perhaps progressive, visionary, non-Maya intellectuals should collaborate with Maya intellectuals to generate an academic platform more inclusive of Maya who are pursuing education as a tool for a better future.

Maya intellectuals who allied with the guerrillas did not become anything more than organizers and spokespersons for the tasks established by a central ladino command. They did not obtain space for their creativity, and their role in the revolution did not have any further transcendence, except in two instances: Rigoberta Menchú's oral recordings that were transformed into her book, *I, Rigoberta Menchú,* and the writings of Luis de Lión, a major literary figure during the armed conflict. Known during the 1970s for his newspaper articles, he was disappeared by the army in 1984. His novel *El tiempo principia en Xibalba* was published after his death in 1985.

Other Maya leaders, intellectuals, poets, or writers who might have emerged from the militant leadership in the revolution are not known. The reason is that Marxism, the imported revolutionary ideology that some attempted to sell to the Maya, was never accepted. The Maya have their own native ideology that has flourished when the culture was in danger of disappearing. Although the guerrilla cause, that of liberating the people, was valid, the methods and means used did not convince the great majority of indigenous people, and the support for which the guerrillas had hoped did not materialize. Of course, those who joined the revolutionary movement were the Maya who had the least academic preparation; they could be absorbed and manipulated easily by the ladino revolutionary leaders. During the guerrilla war in Guatemala, we did not see any Maya guerilla's intellectual work in the treaties or writings of the ladino leaders of these movements. The ladino leaders held the hegemony of the command, and the Maya intellectuals in the movement were limited to acting or reacting within this Marxist-Leninist line of thinking. At least during the 1960s and 1970s, it was the ladino revolutionaries who generated the criticisms of the capitalist system they were trying to revolutionize. They prepared the policies and strategies of the revolution, and they asked the Maya to be only followers. In my opinion, and as I observed the situation in the western highlands during the late 1970s, the Marxists considered the indigenous Maya to be stubborn, weak people who needed to become revolutionaries.

However, we must recognize that the revolutionary movement helped the indigenous inhabitants be more critical and better able to analyze the motives behind their situation of neocolonial domination and control. National problems previously known only by urban ladinos were brought to awareness at local or regional levels. Maya people learned about the central government structure and its institutions that serve only the privileged class. There was more direct, although violent, contact between the dominator and the dominated sectors. This helped indigenous people open their eyes and reflect on their condition as poor and marginalized people in a nation that is rich in natural resources. In other words, the revolutionary movement politcized the masses, and since then indigenous discourse has been not only local, but also articulated on a national and international level.

In spite of these contributions, the revolutionary models experienced by the Maya have not responded to the needs of the indigenous communities. Maya intellectuals need to reactivate their ancestors' forms of political organization and begin to think critically about the current situation. This vital link between contemporary Maya people and their communities has been difficult to achieve for several reasons. Maya intellectuals, with their different economic, political and, intellectual status, are more isolated from their communities and are often faced with resentment and even envy when they approach their communities wanting to do something positive. In indigenous communities, opportunities are more limited and competitive, and people are more easily frustrated. Intellectuals should return and work at the grassroots level, even though they may have to withstand the criticism, rumors, and envy of those who stayed home and fell behind.

Ultimately, Maya intellectuals have an important role to play at this political juncture. More Maya intellectuals are needed to cover all possible disciplines. The idea is to recreate Maya culture and project it toward the future, but not to isolate it from the rest of the country or the outside world. Maya intellectuals need to be more creative and to produce both literary and academic writing. A people whose self-expression is alive is a people with the possibility of shining in the future. It is not enough to have good ideas and remain asleep, dreaming about the future—we must act. The romanticism and nostalgia through which others view our cultures are not helpful either. Maya have the possibility of re-writing their history, representing themselves as they want to be seen, and this is a permanent challenge to the Maya intellectuals of today and tomorrow.

Political Intellectuals and the Maya Movement

The politics of the Maya movement in Guatemala has not been studied in depth. Some anthropologists have written about what they considered a global Maya movement or pan-Maya movement (Montejo 1997; Warren 1998a; Fisher and Brown 1996). Pan-Mayanism embodies the possibility that different Maya cultures, whether in Guatemala, Belize, Mexico, or the United States, can initiate relationships for mutual understanding and protection of their cultural patrimony, the Maya culture. Few theoretical studies have been developed to account for this new modality, the manifestation of a transcommunal, transnational, Maya ethnic movement. We know a great deal about political leaders like Rigoberta Menchú, but not much about the intellectual leaders who are generating political and theoretical plans for the advancement and strengthening of Maya culture.

Very few Maya have worked in intellectual fields, writing or promoting treatises against the racism and colonialism from which we Maya have yet to escape (Cojti Cuxil 1994; Montejo 1999a; Zapeta 1999; Sam Colop 1991). From a theoretical and academic point of view, Maya have not produced works of the category of Edward Said's *Orientalism* (1979). There is still no ethnographic current or tradition in criticism of the colonialism and neocolonialism Guatemala has experienced. Thus, intellectually, we still have not left behind the Western colonialism that we are experiencing, and therefore we cannot speak of a postcolonial period within Maya studies. Maya intellectuals are still learning to master what should be the criticism of the social sciences, especially anthropology, epigraphy, and archeology. What are the role and the future of anthropology and Maya studies in Guatemala? The Maya intellectual voice is still not heard in these debates, unlike in India or other regions of the world where native intellectual voices are strong and decisive.

This lack of presence demonstrates that the Maya need to work harder in Guatemala to promote their ideals of peace, justice, and reconciliation and to make their voices heard. Maya intellectuals have the social responsibility to assume their mission in this revitalization process as voices and builders of the future of Maya culture. Since Maya intellectuals must develop and work within the capitalist system operating in Guatemala, the reproduction of discourse or writing often reinforces the ideology of capitalist domination. Many still are not ready to use their Mayan language to produce literature or create academic concepts derived from their own Maya cosmovision. Those who do come primarily from campesino or working-class bases, and they bring to their work a better understanding of the constant struggle of the marginalized Maya people. They have no commitment to the elite, and the Maya intellectuals who come from these social strata generally have a clear vision of what they want for their people and their nation. These people are also ready to sacrifice more of their time and offer their work for the well-being of all, and they collaborate decisively in the construction of a better national future. From this group will arise the leaders that Antonio Gramsci (1973) calls "organic intellectuals."

Maya intellectuals must always maintain this culture of the Maya people's resistance while they act as catalysts for positive changes in their culture. They must be leaders who propose rather than conform or surrender. They must propose specific goals and help people reach their liberation through education (Freire 1985). This is very difficult because Maya intellectuals tend to move in more abstract, theoretical, and propositional planes, and not in mass movements and civil disobediences. Further, Maya intellectuals find some doors closed to their ideas in their own communities, and many are not appreciated by their own people or in the academic institutions in which they work. For the Maya academic field to flourish, Maya intellectuals must struggle twice as hard, even rowing against the current. It is not an easy task to write for important publishing houses. Even obtaining a prestigious university position is competitive and exhausting work, and Maya academics must always face the preferential treatment of foreigners who specialize in indigenous cultures and who make a living by speaking for the Maya.

Organic and public Maya intellectuals should dedicate themselves more to the practice of their ideals in helping resolve national problems and not so much in only talking about them. The true Maya intellectual must move between theory and practice, because the two complement each other and serve to propose premeditated and precise actions as opposed to overexcited or adventurous actions. Maya intellectuals must continue producing art, literature, and academic works so that their voices and their presence can impact national discourse. Perhaps the unification of all Maya intellectuals could be one first step. Then we should seek solidarity with the ladinos who appreciate Maya culture and value indigenous intellectuality. It is certainly necessary for Maya intellectuals to continue linking Maya communities and peoples throughout the country. This means promoting pan-Mayanism and the solidarity, brotherhood, and collective struggle of all Maya peoples of Guatemala. It means remaining in communication with the Maya of other countries and those who have settled in Mexico, the United States, and Canada as refugees from the armed violence of the 1970s and 1980s. What we are seeking is solidarity among all our people and a better understanding between Mayas and ladinos. The goal is to attain peace and social justice for the Maya and to generate the social, political, economic, and cultural transformations that we hope can unify all Guatemalans.

Indigenous Rights, Security, and Democracy in the Americas

The Guatemalan Situation

Introduction

The struggle of indigenous people for their rights and self-determination, and the polemics that this basic issue represents for those who historically have dominated them, dates back to the Spanish conquest of the early sixteenth century. Early advocates for indigenous rights and freedom, including Bartolomé de Las Casas, have long insisted that indigenous people are humans and that their basic and natural rights must be respected (Hanke 1974). Unfortunately, racist and biologically based theories of alleged indigenous inferiority prevailed, and more dangerous identities and images were imposed on indigenous people. These images have ranged from the passive images and stereotypes of Indians as a backward drag on their nation-states, to those of Indians as "time bombs" and threats to national and international security.

After the collapse of the Soviet Union and the fragmentation of Yugoslavia, political and economic strategists of the Americas have seen ethnicity as a force powerful enough to change violently the familiar geography and view of the world. When nation-states reject the multiplicity of cultures in their territory and impose the homogenizing view of their elites, struggle and violent conflicts develop when the demands of indigenous people are denied. For the minority in power, the ruling class, fear about the collapse of the existing nation-state is reasonable as long as they continue their monopoly of power and violent repression of indigenous populations. As ethnic conflicts and internal political violence increase on regional levels, some geographers have predicted that many more nation-states will develop in the twenty-first century, all forged, "some violently and some by agreement[,] from the territory and peoples of existing states" (Nagengast 1994:110). For this reason, the human rights and self-determination of indigenous people are essential issues to be discussed at this moment when the nation-states of the Americas are envisioning an alliance for sustainable development, trade, and the strengthening of democracy in the region.[1]

Respect for the rights of indigenous people is the basic premise for real peace, social justice, and democracy in the Americas. Currently, a pan-Indian movement across the Americas has developed for the purpose of articulating their demands on a hemispheric scale. The recognition of their rights as original inhabitants of this continent and their rights for self-determination is the central issue that mobilizes indigenous people. How do these demands affect the security of the indigenous and nonindigenous people as well as the survival of the nation-states in Latin America? These are questions to be discussed in an effort to search for all possible answers to the current national and regional conflicts in Latin America (e.g., Guatemala, Chiapas). It is hoped that policy makers will take into account the need for dialogue with indigenous people and will respond positively to their demands. Indigenous and nonindigenous people need to dialogue, debate, and come to a consensus on the most effective ways of dealing with the violence and the human-rights abuses that have persisted for centuries.

It is time to listen and give serious attention to the plight of indigenous people, to consider their demands seriously in order to build a real nationalism within the framework of peace and social justice. We indigenous people have historical identities and deep cultural roots in this continent, yet we have not been allowed to be an integral part of our nationalities. In other words, there will be no national unity if the marginalization of the great majority of the indigenous populations persists. It is important to recognize that the stability of nation-states in the Americas for the next century depends on governments' ability to deal effectively with the legitimate demands of indigenous people. This includes their demands for land, education, free expression, and the practice of their cultural traditions — essentially, their self-determination.

Indigenous Rights: A Brief Historical Background

The violation of indigenous rights in the Americas began with the Spanish conquest of the early sixteenth century. Although some early advocates for indigenous rights managed to ameliorate some of the prevailing hardships, any real solution to the problems of dispossession and subjugation was postponed for centuries. The images and stereotypes of indigenous people imposed during those early years of colonization have persisted deeply in the mind of the dominators. One of these early views was expressed by Francisco López de Gómara, who wrote that indigenous people were "stupid, wild, insensate asses, prone to 'novelties,' drunkenness, vice, and fickleness, that, in short, they were the worst people God ever made" (Hanke 1974:124). This view justified the colonists' appropriation of the land and resources of indigenous people. These stereotypes became so ingrained and persisted so long that they were used to inure indigenous people to forced labor and treatment as beasts without human rights or dignity. In the case of Guatemala, during the first half of the twentieth century the abuses against indigenous people were legalized by the government through the *mandamientos* and the law against vagrancy.[2]

Through the course of time, the justification for the abrogation of indigenous rights changed to suit the current situation. At the end of the twentieth century, negative views of the Maya included the belief that they were prone to violence, evidenced by their supposed alliance with the guerrillas; thus, the Maya constituted a danger to the hegemony of the elite. Consequently, the caretakers of our national security, the army, in their disrespect for human rights, became the enemy of the people. The army's justification for massacres of Maya communities was related to their lack of understanding of the culture and history of the people that they destroyed. The tendency of the state has been to suppress any opposition to the elite view of the world and nationalism. In the case of Guatemala and Mexico, indigenous people have been seen as troublemakers not willing to acquiesce to that elite view, so they have been subjected to violent attacks by these national armies.

Frequently, indigenous people have been classified by their governments as either "passive Indians" or as "violent ethnic groups," categories into which most Maya communities in Guatemala were sorted during the armed violence of the early 1980s. For example, the Ixil Maya historically were seen as resistant to change and rebellious by nature. Because of their supposed violent nature, special military strategies were implemented in the Ixil Maya communities to bring them under control (Cifuentes 1982). An account by an ex-soldier of an attack against an Ixil community in northern Guatemala reported that the commander in charge explained to his soldiers before an attack that

it's because these miserable people are guerrillas, communists and we have to kill them. If we don't burn their asses now, they will hurt us later. Besides, these people shouldn't live anymore. They are savages, they live in the jungle. Not like in Guatemala City and in Xela where you have good people; these miserable people should be swept from the face of earth. (Montejo 1993a:329)

In Guatemala, then, indigenous people continue to be seen as uncivilized and as a threat to national security and unity. The state was the major violator of the individual and collective security of its own people. The Guatemalan government created a sense of insecurity that added to the intransigent attitude of the guerrillas, who have themselves inflicted fear in indigenous communities and contributed to the nation's violent life and instability. It is difficult, however, to accuse indigenous people of disloyalty to their country. As Guatemalan citizens, they have been very respectful of their elected authorities. Historically there are examples of the effective participation of indigenous people in the construction of nationality whenever they have been provided with the space to promote their cultures. This strong support of indigenous people was relevant during the liberal and conservative projects of nation-state building in Latin America after independence from Spain. Indigenous people considered Rafael Carrera to be a protector of their cultures, land, and autonomy. For this reason, the Maya of western Guatemala — Jakaltek-, Q'anjob'al-, Chuj-, and Mam-speaking Maya — continue to refer to Carrera as "our President." So, "at least in theory, the Conservative approach offered the Indians protection from excessive exploitation and thereby permitted their cultural survival" (Woodward 1990:67).

Another example of Maya concern for national security, and a demonstration of their loyalty to Guatemala, became evident in 1975. At that time President Kjell Eugenio Laugerud Garcia announced to the nation that Guatemala was about to engage in a war against Great Britain for Belize.[3] Despite their own insecurity at that time, when they heard that an external conflict was attempted against the security of the nation, Maya people were prompt to enlist to defend the country. In other words, in the event of international threat, the Maya do constitute a unity with all other Guatemalans, so they are "Guatemalans" ready to defend their nation against external aggression. In the face of imminent danger, and knowing that the troops were composed mainly of Mayas, the elders in Maya villages in western Guatemala organized themselves and went to pray at their sacred sites for the protection of all Guatemalan soldiers. The prayers and ceremonies were performed on behalf of everyone, not only for the Maya. This collective concern showed that the Maya are not selfish, but concerned for the life and security of all Guatemalans in general. For this reason, it is sad to see that what the Maya received for their loyalty to the nation was repression and the continuous abuse of their human rights.

Historically then, repression and ethnocide against indigenous people has been justified as the response to what has been called the "irrational" uprisings of indigenous people who do not want to accommodate themselves within civilized nation-states. Indigenous people are blamed as rebellious when they struggle for their survival against the systematic destruction of their ways of life. State-sponsored repression, guerrilla warfare, and the racist treatment of the indigenous people by the ladino-mestizo or nonindigenous population in general has provoked the massive abuse and denial of human rights.

Indigenous Rights: The Demands for Self-Determination

The demands of indigenous people for their rights to be respected on this continent began with their early contact with Europeans. Since then, indigenous leaders have questioned the authority of those who have violently dispossessed them of their lands. The religious and political power of the pope and the king as they extended their dominion to the New World was the first direct blow to the earliest indigenous rights and self-determination. They questioned the expropriation of their lands even while being forced to give up their freedom and liberty to foreigners, as is illustrated in the following anecdote. In 1519, Fernández de Enciso documented the reaction of the *cacique* of Cenú in Panama who insisted that an interpreter explain the *requerimiento* to him.[4] The cacique commented:

> The part about there being one god who ruled heaven and earth he approved; as for the pope who gave away lands that he didn't own, he must have been drunk; and a king who asked for and acquired such a gift must have been crazy. (Hanke 1974:37)

The dispossession of indigenous people was so painful that Bartolomé de Las Casas became one of the first Europeans to defend indigenous rights and freedom. To pursue his ideals of liberating the Indians, Las Casas sold his own *encomienda* and used the proceeds to defend indigenous people in Spanish courts. "To Las Casas, Indian uprising against Spanish domination served the just defense of the Indians' liberty, and to attempt to crush those uprisings was unjust war" (Friede and Keen 1971:478). But to other Europeans, the struggles of indigenous people to have their rights respected and to have the freedom to decide for themselves was seen as a subversive act, and the repression against them for demanding their rights was considered "just" and necessary for maintaining national security and stability from colonial times to the present.

Because struggles within nation-states have become so unbalanced against indigenous people, pitting small, often unarmed groups against national military forces, indigenous people have turned to the international arena for greater support in pressing their governments to comply with their demands. "Indigenous organizations have consistently framed their demands in terms of self-determination, recognizing that this claim has a basis in international law" (Van Cott 1994:13). This is why indigenous people have seen the United Nations Declaration on the Rights of Indigenous People as the essential document for demanding their rights. The UN supports and "affirms the fundamental importance of the right of self-determination of all peoples, by virtue of which they freely determine their political status and freely pursue their economic, social, and cultural development" (*Cultural Survival Quarterly* 1993:65).

Self-determination by indigenous people means the revival of their cultural identities and traditions, which have been largely overlooked or even destroyed by outside pressures and interference. During the twentieth century, "self-determination of this kind has been lost in the push for progress in most parts of the tribal world" (Bodley 1990:152). By demanding their rights, indigenous people destroy the myth of the "passive Indian," becoming dynamic actors in the construction of their future. Indigenous people, who were predicted to disappear by the end of the twentieth century, are now making their presence felt more strongly than ever. And for this reason they are now considered a threat to national security and "democracy" in the Americas. If self-determination is achieved by the indigenous people, they will begin again to strengthen their local self-governmental authorities such as the "elders' council," the *principales* in Maya communities. During the 1960s, these indigenous organizations were the focus of attacks by groups like Catholic Action which attempted to remove all indigenous elements from Catholic worship practices (Arias 1990).

In the current debates on indigenous rights, some people consider self-determination a threat to national stability and security and do not see it as a part of people's human rights. "Others are convinced that self-determination is the essence of human rights. . . . Self-determination for every people; for every nationality, a state" (Nagengast 1994:125). These two views are played out in a number of arenas—political, economic, territorial, and cultural—and competing forces find reasons to deny those elements of self-determination that would limit existing power arrangements.

Here, I want to speak for self-determination as the right of indigenous people to freely express themselves by using their knowledge systems and cultural values, i.e., for self-determination in a cultural sense. In this view, self-determination is not a radical position or a movement for "self-isolation." It implies strong cooperation between indigenous and nonindigenous people to achieve the recovery and recreation of their histories and traditions. The end result of codifying indigenous values and knowledge systems is to be shared with the entire national community in an effort to develop a more inclusive educational system. In Guatemala, a major goal is to liberate the minds of all Guatemalan children from the established stereotypes and cartoon images of indigenous people on which the racist discrimination and the unequal social relationships between Maya and non-Maya are based. It is, then, important to take Maya knowledge seriously and use it to enhance the richness and diversity of the Guatemalan nation.

One problem during the 1980s and early 1990s was the radicalization of human-rights discourses by some human-rights activists, including some indigenous leaders. This radicalization, a result of the violent armed conflict during the early 1980s, was a factor in the controversy over self-determination. Today some indigenous leaders still follow ideologies of confrontation and do not act within the Maya ideals of dialogue and *aq'ank'ulal,* or peaceful resolutions. Other leaders are too local in their approaches, and their viewpoints are more parochial and less inclusive of all the different Maya and non-Maya perspectives in Guatemala. The appropriation of indigenous demands by politically polarized groups has also created consternation among policy makers and authorities. Some demands made during the preliminary discussions leading up to the Guatemala peace accords were presented in such a radicalized way that they were vitiated with "populist" and left-leaning rhetoric. Often, indigenous leaders followed radical strategies by openly challenging governments without leaving space for rationalization, dialogue, and consensus building. Radical presentations of demands with no space for negotiation have created a resistance from nation-states, fueling their paranoia and refusal to accept and approve the genuine demands of indigenous people for cultural self-determination.

Indigenous Rights: Security and Democracy

The forced enclosure of indigenous people within their "village universe" and the practice of elitist groups in defining and deciding indigenous status with policies that enforce racist approaches to their cultures are being changed. These same policies of control and domination have forced indigenous people to organize themselves internationally in an effort to secure their individual and collective rights. Indigenous people have widened their view of the world, and they are engaged in a pan-Indian movement of self-determination across the Americas (Varese 1988). We no longer think of indigenous people as enclosed communities with narrow visions of their national life and future. In the past, the Western world had a monopoly over the way indigenous people in the Americas were represented. Today, indigenous people are more sophisticated, and they have overcome enormous cultural and geographic distances, reaching into the heart of great industrialized nations once beyond their knowledge. Now it is not surprising to see that while American or European tourists contemplate Tikal in Guatemala, a Jakaltek Maya or a Mapuche Indian may be visiting the United Nations in New York City. The media, supersonic transportation, communication, and technology have both expanded and shrunk the world.

International communication and solidarity have become, then, major factors in pressing governments to comply with the demands of their indigenous populations. Or,

> as a result of subsequent activism by minorities and indigenous people, the international community has been forced to recognize some rights of minorities to internal self-determination, that is within the boundaries of existing states. (Nagengast 1994:127)

Some states are challenging these indigenous rights movements for self-determination as unconstitutional. They argue for this illegitimacy based on their national constitutions, but most national constitutions in the Americas were developed without the participation of, or without even considering the existence of, their internal indigenous people and cultures (Trask 1993). Other countries have taken a more culturally relativistic approach to human rights by saying, "Let us deal with our own problems." During the 1980s, military officers of the Guatemalan army responded to questions from North Americans about human-rights abuses by saying, "Let us deal with our problem, and do not preach social justice to us because you, too, have gotten rid of the indigenous people in your own country."[5]

While some governments refuse to enter into dialogue with their indigenous people and do not want to recognize their demands, others are already accommodating indigenous demands in their political constitutions. "The parliament of Norway established in 1987 the Sami Advisory Assembly to preserve the lifestyle and culture of their indigenous people" (Benedito 1994). In

Canada, the Inuit have pressed successfully for land claims and political control over their vast aboriginal territory they call Nunavut (Lobo and Talbott 2001). And the legislative reforms and restructuring of the Bolivian constitution in the 1990s opened many channels for self-determination on the community and regional level by indigenous groups (Healy and Paulson 2000:2).

During the past two decades, indigenous people, through such organized bodies as the World Council of Indigenous People, recognized by the United Nations as an observer nongovernmental organization, have been proposing changes in their treatment by their governments. But many national governments have refused to consider indigenous demands as legitimate. Instead, their demands are seen as disruptive to national stability and sovereignty. This rejection has forced indigenous people to become more politicized. In Guatemala during the 1960s and 1970s, many indigenous people began to question their powerless position in Guatemalan national life. Maya peasants learned their rights as Guatemalan citizens and analyzed the Guatemalan Constitution. According to Arturo Arias, these leaders "studied the Guatemalan Constitution in order to know what it said and to contrast what was written with reality. This, in turn, raised the issue of human rights and the discussion became more explicitly political" (Arias 1990:241).

The conflicts that disrupt national security do not originate with indigenous people. Instead, powerful elites create such insecurities by denying the rights of indigenous people. In Guatemala, the creation of an environment of rejection and conflict provided space for more radical groups with alien ideologies to enter Maya villages and claim as theirs the suffering and neglect that the Maya had borne for centuries.[6] The paternalistic attitudes of the radical groups also undermined the security and self-determination of indigenous people. During the past armed conflict, indigenous people were used as armed combatants by both sides, and yet on neither side was there any real interest in Maya culture and self-determination. This became evident when the Maya were excluded from participating directly in the peace negotiations, even though these negotiations had direct implications for their lives and future.

The same state that denies indigenous rights provides space and justification for the current political conflicts and uprisings. Some experts on Latin America now argue that "the hemisphere may be entering an era of violent Indian conflicts" (Balmaceda 1994:29). The Zapatista uprising in Chiapas was the starting point for indigenous uprisings throughout Mexico. Peru and Colombia face simmering indigenous conflicts. Armed conflicts often develop when all other channels for communication and negotiation are blocked. Nevertheless, I do not believe that armed confrontation is the right method for achieving the demands of indigenous people.

Democracy will be a reality in Latin America when the silenced indigenous populations are given the opportunity to participate in the active life of their nations as members of civil society. In Guatemala, the army and government must allow more participation by civilian society in internal security policies. The debate over the extent of civilian versus military controls has taken place even within the military. "Even the armed forces are increasingly divided over the question of their role in society and the extent to which they should allow civilians to exercise effective political power" (Millett 1991:65). The Guatemalan army's chief strategist, General Hector Gramajo, has argued that Guatemala as a state has essentially two major preoccupations, "the protection of the individual, and to guarantee the general well-being of all Guatemalans" (Gramajo 1989).

Ironically, the Guatemalan army was the greatest violator of these two charges during the counterinsurgency war. Since 1954, the climate in Guatemala has been one of terror. The selective killing of individuals in the 1970s escalated into major massacres of indigenous communities and massive violations of human rights in the 1980s. The peace negotiations, the peace accords, and the establishment of a civilian face on the government eased the terror somewhat in the 1990s, but by the turn of the millennium, individual killings, death threats, and a nonfunctioning system of justice have increased the terror factor again. Gramajo's thesis for "national stability" says that peace in Guatemala can be achieved with a balanced relationship between the political, economic, social, and military forces in the nation (Gramajo 1989). He suggests that two major actions should be taken to achieve this national stability. The first is "to change existing stereotypes of other sectors for recognition and tolerance (tolerance of diversity and multiculturalism). The second is that the respect and obedience to the National Constitution and other laws is vital for the maintenance of peace and the progress of Guatemala" (Gramajo 1989:51).

Gramajo is right, but to achieve the goal of national stability, changes must start with the army itself. The peace accords stressed the reduction of the national budget for defense in order to balance its power with that of other civilian institutions. But this had never happened, until 2004 when the army was reduced by over 40 percent. Despite this reduction, the army has not lost its power and authority, and it is gaining control once again of the political spaces opened by civil society and indigenous people after the signing of the accords.

The Guatemalan government delayed ratifying Covenant 169 of the International Labor Organization (ILO) until 1997. The past two governments, under presidents Alvaro Arzú and Alfonso Portillo, argued that the covenant was unconstitutional or that it wasn't necessary, because its protections of indigenous rights were already guaranteed in the Guatemalan Constitution. But international pressure and indigenous protest within Guatemala brought the issue to a successful conclusion. The implementation of Covenant 169 is now more important then ever, since the national referendum for changing the Constitution to include the indigenous rights reforms, mandated by the peace accords, failed.

Indigenous people are seen as a threat and danger to the nation-states when their struggles for self-determination are linked to drug traffickers and guerrilla warfare. That is why some political analysts have referred to indigenous demands for human rights as part of what they have called the new "world disorder." Ethnic conflicts, whether in Chechnya, the former Yugoslavia, or Northern Ireland, have become one of the worst fears of nation-states. In Guatemala a report from the mid-1990s stated that, "military officers privately voice fears that a 34-year-old Marxist-led insurrection might turn into a powerful Indian-rights movement if conditions don't improve for the marginalized indigenous majority" (Balmaceda 1994:29). Fears of indigenous demands prompted the military to dismiss them as separatist movements in what some critics of the army have called "a military ethno-hysteria" (Zapeta 1994). In other words, "these military sectors [the older, more conservative wing of the Guatemalan army] see any indigenous political progress as a national security threat" (Zapeta 1994:12). One thing was certain, indigenous people were fed up with both the URNG guerrillas and the Guatemalan army. It is necessary to distinguish the indigenous movement from guerrilla activities, since these accusations do not help to resolve the sources of violence in Guatemala.

Some international human-rights organizations may have prorevolutionary biases, but the pressure that they can put on governments to clarify past atrocities seems effective. Jennifer Harbury, with the support of former U.S. Senator Robert Torricelli, forced the United States government to release documents about the CIA and its complicity with the Guatemalan army in the killing of the American citizen Michael DeVine and the guerrilla combatant Efraín Bámaca (Weiner 1995). The concepts of security and democracy are thrown in doubt in this case. Violations of human rights not only come in response to local or regional issues, but can be commanded by international pressure and the interests of superpowers such as the United States, a longtime supporter of military dictatorships in Latin America. The disclosure of these CIA strategies in Central America (Jonas 2000) should now trigger major campaigns to deny immunity to those human-rights violators and to hold them accountable for their crimes so that such atrocities can not occur again.[7]

Participating heads of state at the Summit of the Americas in Florida in March 1995 agreed to recognize indigenous cultures without prejudice or discrimination. In doing so, they committed themselves to recognizing the self-determination of their heterogeneous and diverse cultures and to promoting democratic societies that respected human rights and protected cultural diversity, pluralism, the rights of minorities, and the promotion of peace in and between nations. So that this is not just an exercise in words, the commitment should provide support and solutions to the claims and demands of each country's indigenous population. Indigenous demands for self-determination are not threats to national security or dangers to national and territorial unity. Indigenous people existed before modern nation-states came into being (Churchill 1999). It is more often the case that the state itself has been the threat to the security and survival of indigenous people. We must recognize that "no single issue affects the survival of indigenous peoples as much as the state appropriation of the resources, in particular land, that indigenous peoples require if they are to survive as recognizable societies" (Clay 1993:64).

The possibility for permanent peace in Guatemala rests on serious consideration of the cultural concerns and peaceful demands of its indigenous people. As an unnamed indigenous leader from the Kalahari Desert said, "We have much to offer the rest of the world. We are deeply committed to the future of our children and grandchildren, and we wish to leave to them a healthy environment that we have long treated with respect" (Hitchcock 1994:12). Self-determination pursued by indigenous people is not selfish, nor is it based on egotistic desire; it is the way of life that indigenous people want to create and decide for themselves, while at the same time sharing it with the rest of the world.

Indigenous Rights: Strategies for Cooperation

The major strategy for cooperation between indigenous people and their nation-states should be based on an inclusive, multicultural, and intercultural educational system. General knowledge of the indigenous cultures must be well founded and free of prejudice and discrimination, and the educational system must effectively reach the nonindigenous population so as to eliminate their entrenched, stereotypical ideas about indigenous people being "inferior." Indigenous values and traditions must be added to textbooks for the benefit of both indigenous and nonindigenous people. Indigenous people must become more than representatives of archaic cultures used as folkloric patrimony. They must become human beings with human needs and feelings, people in search of peace, freedom, and social justice. Formal and systematic education is also necessary for indigenous people so that they can know their rights, recognize external pressures, and discern appropriate responses when confronted with external ideologies that tend to draw them into political and armed conflicts. In Guatemala, a massive program of literacy and numeracy for adults is needed, in addition to the proper resources for the education of indigenous children who live in remote areas. The preservation and promotion of indigenous languages and cultures also requires additional technological and communication assistance.

As applied to Guatemala, these strategies of cooperation between indigenous and nonindigenous people include the following:

1. It is necessary to organize working groups of Maya academics in order to create and concretize Maya knowledge that can be placed in the national educational curricula (Tay Coyoy, in Adams 1994).

2. The Ministries of Education and Culture need major reforms, and both should coordinate efforts to enhance multicultural and intercultural education in Guatemala. The uniqueness of the Guatemalan nation-state is based on the diversity of its culture, and this same cultural heritage can be used to educate Guatemalans themselves, becoming more than a resource to attract tourists. All Guatemalans must learn about the ancient roots of Maya culture and appreciate the diverse ways of being Maya in Guatemala today.

3. Maya children and young people must have access to formal education at all levels. This education, combined with the free and unprejudiced expression of their traditional ways of teaching and knowing, will enable them to make decisions about their future. Knowing their own culture and that of the larger society will decrease the likelihood of their being manipulated by external forces. An educational process like this can truly pave the way toward self-determination for the Maya.

4. If we want a pluralistic nation-state, indigenous people must be allowed and encouraged to hold high office, both appointed and elected. Maya leaders must respond to the needs of their Maya communities rather than be manipulated by the ideology of various political parties, whose rhetoric is only in evidence during political campaigns.[8]

5. The dichotomous Indian-ladino conflict, one that has characterized ethnic relations in many countries of the Americas, must end. The resources of the nation belong to all and should rightfully be shared among all members of the society. These resources are not the patrimony of only one group, or of the most powerful. If we are to persist as a unified, multicultural nation-state, this dichotomy must be broken.

6. We must strengthen the local power of the people in order to make the nation-state a diverse system (Ochoa García 1993). People in their own communities and regions know how to organize their lives. They must participate in discussions of their problems to find solutions to them. Maya communities use the *lah-ti'* (dialogue and consensus), an indigenous procedure for decision making to benefit their villages. There is a need to strengthen indigenous forms of decision making and to support the resulting Maya consensus on specific courses of action.

7. One mechanism to help achieve the above is the inauguration of an institution for the coordination of national projects and development for indigenous people. A Bureau of Maya Affairs could be composed of representatives of the twenty-one Mayan linguistic communities in Guatemala. In this organization, indigenous people would have a national institution to coordinate programs and channel development resources for and by indigenous people.

Conclusion

National security begins with respect and protection of the cultures that compose the nation. Until now, indigenous cultures have been seen as alien in their own territories. Indigenous people must at last feel that they belong fully to the nation-state so that they can coexist with other ethnic groups. Their work, knowledge, and creativity can enhance the Guatemalan nation. In the past forty years we have lived a nightmare that has distanced all of Guatemala from our national dream of unity and solidarity. We have come to recognize that neither the political parties, the authorities, the army, nor the guerrillas can provide solutions to Guatemala's problems if the indigenous population is impeded from directly participating in the search for those solutions.

The geopolitics of the region must not follow Cold War, East-West strategies, but recognize instead that indigenous people have been here for centuries. Indigenous cultures are a great asset to humanity. As Rigoberta Menchú (1995:5) has written, "We must understand that the presence of indigenous people in a country is not necessarily a synonym of conflict; instead, it is a source of the richness of national identity and the symbol of an integral development of humanity."

We should not be afraid of the terms *autonomy* and *self-determination*. Indigenous people need to take charge of their own institutions so that they can collaborate among themselves and contribute more effectively to the building of national unity and equality. Indigenous people need a real space in their nation and need to be treated as equals of the nonindigenous population. We cannot continue to see both groups as antagonistic; rather, they must be complementary in the creation of a multicultural nation-state, a priority for all citizens of that nation. While indigenous people struggle and await that day to come, hopefully soon, the prayers of the ancestors are being repeated with more insistence by modern Maya priests, as they pray for a new dawn for their descendants.

Look at us! Hear us! Do not leave us, oh, God, who art in heaven and on earth, Heart of heaven, Heart of Earth! Give us our descendants, our succession, as long as the sun shall move and there shall be light. Let it dawn; let the day come! Give us many good roads, flat roads! May the people have peace, much peace, and may they be happy; and give us good life and useful existence! (from the *Popol Vuh;* Recinos, Goetz, and Morley 1983)

CHAPTER 11

The Twenty-first Century and the Future of the Maya in Guatemala

For the Maya, as for all indigenous peoples of the continent, the supposed celebration of the quincentenary (1492–1992) was a wake-up call for those who had been sleeping until then to organize a cultural and militant resistance against the celebration held in the colonized countries. The opposition of indigenous leaders was so strong that they managed to avert a euphoric, unthinking celebration of genocide in the Americas. At the same time, however, the term "500 years" was abused to the point of ridiculousness, and many arguments became empty. In these discourses, both Maya and ladino leaders of the popular movement spoke of the 500 years as a purely romantic event without any historic depth. Unfortunately, Maya memories of the Spanish invasion of this continent are gone, and except for the ethnohistoric accounts written in Mayan after the conquest, we have no clear memory of the violent events of the conquest. Very few Maya stories and mythical accounts refer to the invasion known as the conquest of Guatemala in our country's history books. Our children can only recite whatever is written in the official history textbooks promoted in Guatemala.

Even during the invasion of the Maya territory, Spanish chroniclers had their doubts about each other's texts. Bernal Díaz de Castillo, having decided that he had the unique authority to tell the "truth" about the events of the invasion of Mexico and Guatemala, wrote the *True History of the Conquest of Mexico*. By calling his work a true history, Díaz del Castillo insisted that the other versions were not official, authentic, or true. We are fortunate to have those few ethnohistorical documents written by the Maya themselves in their own languages that narrate the fatal events of 1524. Those stories, our version of that history and of these five hundred years since, continue to be an accumulated chronicle of five centuries of suffering.

At the beginning of this present millennium, the Maya are weakened and badly organized, both politically and economically. Our collective amnesia continues to blindfold us and stifle our understanding of the magnitude of the original genocide. How can we effectively understand the pain of our ancestors if we do not agree on past events? Perhaps the Spanish invasion is already an event of the past, one now being erased from our minds. But the massacres of the 1970s and 1980s again opened these unhealed historical wounds. The cries of the fallen once again disturb our sleep, and once again we see a river of blood and tears in the streets and paths of our villages. We are conscious of this, but we have kept silent. What has happened to us, the Maya? Why do we keep this "memory of silence" for which Monsignor Gerardi gave his life? It is sad to think that the holocaust experienced by the Maya of the devastated communities is unknown to the ladinos of Guatemala's cities. A friend, a professor at a private university in the capital, commented to me, "It's sad to see the ladino people, even students and professors, who don't know the magnitude of the genocide that took place in the rural communities of Guatemala."

If we diminish these bloody events and justify these massacres as necessary to "pacify" the indigenous people who supported the guerrillas, and if we say that it was their own fault for getting involved in these problems, we obscure the true sense of the counterinsurgency war and its calculated and premeditated elimination of entire Maya communities. Further, it was only in Maya communities that civil patrols were organized, whereas more privileged ladino communities and people in the urban areas were exempted. Is this not yet another example of the racism that the Guatemalan indigenous people have experienced for centuries? Of the several thousand people murdered, the majority never knew why they were killed and never knew who the guerrillas were or what they were doing. Colonel Francisco Gordillo Martínez commented on this scorched-earth strategy in the film *When the Mountains Tremble* (1984). Paraphrasing the words of Mao Tse-tung, Colonel Gordillo said, "The people are to the guerrilla as water is to a fish. The fish without water will die, and the guerrilla without the people will also die." Thus, indigenous and civilian people were seen as support for the guerrillas, and the army proceeded to commit massacres in which thousands of innocent people were killed, including children, women, and the elderly, as in the Finca San Francisco Nentón (Falla 1992), where 302 people died, including newborn babies.

In order to destroy the support for the guerrillas, this military doctrine gave not the slightest consideration to the fundamental rights of the Guatemalans who were killed. For military strategists and officials, the lives of indigenous people had no value, or at least not a value comparable to those of ladinos. If a military official died in combat with the guerrillas, the repression against the civilian indigenous population was even harsher. Destruction and genocide were the legacy of a government that reached extremes of immorality, chaos, and disregard for human rights. Such was the case during the de facto government of General Efraín Ríos Montt (1982–1983) and that of General Romeo Lucas García before him.

Similarly, the guerrillas, who had a mainly bourgeois and ladino leadership, often used the indigenous population as cannon fodder. They sought various ways of involving the Maya in this war, a war that suddenly presented itself in many indigenous villages. In some regions the guerrillas had more time to convince people and prepare the terrain in their favor, but in the end the guerrillas also caused damaged to the indigenous communities because they contributed to the spread of fear and mistrust among the inhabitants by "meting out justice" or selectively assassinating those who were not in favor of the war.

It is difficult for the ladino population to understand the true meaning and reasons behind these massacres because the indigenous people have always been considered backwards and destined to vanish. The Maya have been called "dirty, backward, stupid Indians," and thus although genocidal policies have been implemented against them, the perpetrators of these crimes have enjoyed immunity from prosecution.

In this sense, the reasoning of the ideologues of liberation theology is appropriate when they say that the poor should not be blamed for their problems, but rather the system and the government should be seen as worse sinners for committing these crimes and violating the human rights of their citizens. Indigenous people are not to blame for their state of subjugation, but rather they have been conditioned to exist within the reduced space in which they are permitted to live. We must remember that the usurpation of indigenous land and the forced labor to which indigenous people were subjected during the dictatorships of Justo Rufino Barrios, Manuel Estrada Cabrera, and Jorge Ubico caused the majority to fall into extreme poverty. We can say the same about the results of the armed conflict that ravaged the country. The fact that the brunt of the repression has fallen on the indigenous population corresponds to the discrimination and racism that exists against them. The military saw indigenous people as inferior beings and wanted to show them that if they "got involved with this kind of idiocy" (the guerrillas) they would be easily tortured and eliminated (Montejo 1999a). To the army, indigenous people are still seen as a burden or "problem" for the Guatemalan state.

This, then, is the most explicit form of racism and marginalization suffered by the majority indigenous population. The Maya are not the cause of the nation's backwardness; on the contrary, it is their way of life and their ethical and moral values that could resolve many of the problems of violence and criminality that are buffeting the country. But because racism in Guatemala is invisible to ladinos, they have always had the power and the authority to insist that this is the "Indian problem." Saying that indigenous people — rather than the system that exploits them or the army that eliminates them — are the problem is a comfortable way to hide the true ideology and discrimination that the powerful use to make themselves feel righteous, even while they trample their own principles of nationalism, peace, justice, liberty, and democracy.

How to Live Together Peacefully in Guatemala

Given the chaos we have experienced since the war, including the remilitarization of the country, it is difficult to think of a single path to the solution of our problems and the creation of a vision and positive image of Guatemala. To cure and heal the national wounds caused by the fratricidal war that centered on the army and the guerrillas, it is urgent and necessary to recognize our values as a people and our values as a millennia-old culture. To this task, Maya culture can bring life, presence, and a positive image to Guatemala. We must create a common history that can sustain our identities over time, place, and space. Something must be learned from the pain and suffering of the Maya people. We cannot simply ask the widows, orphans, and other survivors of the armed conflict to forget their loved ones who were massacred and disappeared. We must listen to the collective voice of those who were assassinated, whose blood cries out for justice from the clandestine graveyards, and offer fair retribution for the affected communities. It is very easy to ask the indigenous people to forget: we are a people who have historically been silenced by force. If the majority of victims had been ladino, justice and retribution would have been swift. Who will speak for the thousands of Guatemalans who were massacred yet had nothing to do with the guerrillas or the army's "scorched earth"?

Our government should focus its attention on the necessities and deficiencies of public services in education, health care, and community development. The superhighways of the southern coast are important for the development of this region, but so are the construction of schools and education for our young people, who will be the intellectual treasure of the future of this country. Even more important, we must attend to rural areas and promote social assistance and education for the regions devastated by the armed conflict. There are villages that cannot be easily reached because they lack roads. Rural farmers need to transport their products to local or regional markets, and their contribution to the national economy should be recognized. We must raise the quality of life for all Guatemalans and not just a few. The Guatemalan government has always placed a much lower priority on the issues of indigenous people, ultimately leaving them abandoned and without support.

As an example, Jacaltenango, a large town since pre-Hispanic times (its Mayan name *Xajla and Niman Konhob'* means "Great Village"), does not have sufficient drinking water; its streets have almost impassable potholes; the telephone system is still precarious; and a good access road is needed. Existing roads, initiated and maintained by residents during the armed conflict, are now difficult to travel on. Despite this neglect, rural towns like Jacaltenango are intensely productive. Perhaps the government thinks that it does not need to worry about them, since they have always made do with what they can manage. Fortunately, the people of Jacaltenango see education as the future, the way to raise their standard of living, even if each government in turn has failed to make the education of the indigenous population a priority. The heads of Guatemalan educational and cultural institutions have not experienced the limitations of life in rural areas. Every year we lose ground in the struggle to bring positive, pertinent education to our children. And each year they are becoming more entranced by electronic games; by the movies of Bruce Lee, Chuck Norris, Sylvester Stallone, and Arnold Schwarzenegger; and by pornography on the Internet. We are losing our values of respect and solidarity, our traditional methods of education, and the oral tradition, the source of knowledge for our people.

In rural areas, small producers, merchants, and educators need support to pursue lives equitable to national progress. Joint programs could be carried out, combining the strengths of the communities, private initiatives, labor organizations, and the government itself. Although we recognize its contribution, the private sector should not be put on a golden altar alone while rural farmers and small indigenous merchants are left to wallow through the mud. These people bring life to the informal economy and the local markets. We have to break away from the dogma that the large landowners and corporations are the only ones who move the nation and that the rural farmers, indigenous people, and the poor are those that paralyze and obstruct progress. Everyone collaborates and is part of the productive gears that move the nation.

In order to get the country rolling on the road toward justice and peace, we need to generate new leadership among the Maya. We have seen during the war and postwar years that leaders who kept themselves afloat by hanging on to others were not effective. We need true leaders who are not opportunists and do not seek momentary fame in order to satisfy personal and egotistical needs. We need leaders with a vision for the future, who give priority to national issues but also extend their vision to the global and transnational world; leaders who make the values of the past palpable and integrate them into the present in order to revitalize them; leaders who know and work within the legal framework of human rights; leaders who can state and demonstrate with facts that there is space for creativity in an environment of peace and social justice.

We need leaders who do not propel the people into confrontation but rather into unification based on egalitarianism. This is the leadership that is needed and the kind that we should maintain and support, leaders who can link the two societies, Maya and ladino, in the reconstruction of the country, in dialogue and nonviolence. These leaders must have a grassroots connection and must serve their communities and be transparent in their actions. Leaders must be able to sit down with their communities and give an exact account of their actions. We need true leaders who work for the well-being and advancement of our peoples, leaders who can lead us along the paths of the twenty-first century with clear ideas of democracy and solidarity.

If we do not manage to balance the power of the Maya with the non-Maya, we will have the misfortune of seeing our people more and more divided, and we will fall into ethnic conflict, which should be avoided at all costs. We do not wish a violent future for our children. We need to prepare ourselves for the future — not an easy task if we do not construct and share resources for creating a nation that is truly unique and just. All Guatemalans are called to contribute to this change, framed within an experience of peace, democracy, and solidarity. This is the historic challenge for all our generation, all Maya and non-Maya people of Guatemala together.

The Maya Future and the National Issue

The strategists who planned and carried out the war in Guatemala and who decided the fate of thousands of Guatemalans continue unpunished, and some have even returned to power. Those already back in power, like Efraín Ríos Montt, are seeking means to invalidate the peace accords. These military leaders have never concerned themselves with understanding the indigenous people of Guatemala in any way other than as a cheap labor force. Neither the government and army nor the URNG can convince the Maya that the past is only history and that we must simply wash our hands of the bloody events and forget what happened. The politics of forgetfulness can only construct an uncertain and dangerous future for Guatemalans. It aims to forget the lessons of the past as if they were not important to the construction of a more just future, shared by the different ethnic groups within our national territory. We cannot, therefore, forget a past that has been bloody for the Maya. We cannot forget that no one has answered for the crimes committed against the unarmed civilian population. Can it be that the 200,000 Guatemalans who were killed during the thirty-six years of armed conflict are only numbers and do not mean anything?

There is pain, suffering, and extreme poverty for the many in Guatemala, and happiness, pleasure, and wealth for a few. Some of these few who have the power to kill and decide the fate of their countrymen live freely because they enjoy immunity for their criminal acts. We cannot dream of a true nationalism here as long as the enemy is one's own brother, countryman, or compatriot. We recognize in Guatemala's present government (FRG) a modern and astute neocolonialism that surreptitiously replicates the colonialism of the past in an updated, internal, neoliberal version. The ideology of oppression against the indigenous peoples of Guatemala still corresponds to the past racist treatment of the Maya by the criollos and ladinos in the colonial and independence periods (Adams 1990). At the present time, we still need international solidarity organizations monitoring and mediating for indigenous people in Guatemala so that we can fight for true justice and democracy.

Fortunately, some thinkers addressing Guatemala's future truly wish to see the rights of the country's indigenous peoples respected. Some suggest a structural revision of Guatemalan nationalism (Smith 1990). We suggest, we ask, that government institutions and officials pay attention to Guatemala's majority sector. Maya people are the numeric majority but a minority in terms of participation or control of power.

Others see the current Maya movement as a potential cause of violent national ethnic conflict (Hale 1996). According to these ideologues, permitting indigenous people to enjoy their rights fully would give them too much power. The Maya could then turn the country upside down and begin persecuting the ladino public. This is, of course, absurd. It is one of the ideas used to keep the Maya from defining themselves and becoming the masters of their own actions and the builders of their own destiny and future.

Other outside observers insist that Mayas must work harder to abandon their ancestral traditions in order to succeed in this modern world. These people recognize the backward situation in which the Maya live, but rather than blaming the governments that have neglected them for centuries, they instead blame the Maya as responsible for their backwardness and poverty. In both cases, people continue to talk about assimilating indigenous people into ladino mainstream society, which would lead to the extermination of the living Maya culture in this country.

We need Maya leaders who can create programs for the consolidation of Maya thought and worldviews for national use in unification. For this we need to give the Maya people a "first opportunity" for a true commitment to their people and the opportunity for self-representation and self-determination. We need to have Mayas in positions of power and in government cabinets as ministers and vice-ministers in the fields of education, culture, agriculture, and environment and in its embassies because Guatemala is a multicultural and multilingual nation. For example, in the Ministry of Culture we need to have Maya who are respectful of their cultural roots and who can procure the repatriation of the national patrimony that has been dispersed to museums and collections around the world; Maya who would thus conserve the richness of our historic past. This ancestral Maya culture gives our current nationalism roots, and this unifies the multiethnic population of the country. Globally, Guatemala is a distinctive country because of the richness and diversity of its indigenous culture, and Guatemalans must become a dignified people, respectful and protective of its national patrimony. Therefore, the future of Guatemala concerns all Guatemalans, and we Maya cannot depend on a handful of ladino strategists who attain power and who have always decided our future. We know that their decisions have never favored Maya people; on the contrary, they have always gone against or forgotten the Maya.

Isolating the Maya from discussions and debates regarding the reconstruction of the country will only delay the process of democratic justice and liberty that we hope for. The Maya must have a presence, and their contributions must figure in the center of national projects of reconciliation and reparations to those communities affected by the armed conflict. To do this we need to promote reconciliation and unification in all the different sectors of the country, and all must have the same rights and obligations that our national constitution provides.

Since the period 2000 to 2003, there has been an epidemic of violence and corruption throughout the country, a national, urban sickness contaminating even the municipal institutions in rural areas. All government institutions have been cracking under the immorality of some of their leaders; education, culture, religion, politics, and the economy have been separated from the primordial human values of respect, transparency, solidarity, and human sensitivity.

It is time to return to promoting these basic values in Guatemalan communities, and Maya communities could contribute by our example, our support, and our respect for life. Unfortunately, there needs to be reconciliation within Maya communities as well. These values are being lost in the indigenous communities because, especially during the time of the civil patrols, army-imposed fear and espionage shredded community integration and respect. The process of reconciliation must also contain responsible solutions to the problems that have conditioned the Maya to stagnation and poverty.

Finally, many speak of the problems that indigenous people have experienced—the poverty and the violation of individual and collective rights—as something that is purely circumstantial. That is, they speak of the problems but do not delve into their roots or into a conscious search for their solutions. Mayas must demand solutions that fulfill the peace accords and correspond to constitutional rights. All Guatemalans will benefit from recognizing and utilizing the indigenous capital, culture, and Mayan languages as a shared patrimony, and as a guarantee of a just coexistence for all in the new Guatemalan nation we all dream of and imagine (Anderson 1990).

The Situation at Present

The document made public by the Commission of Historical Clarification (Comisión para el Esclaramiento Histórico de Guatemala; CEH), *Guatemala: Memory of Silence,* became a real testimony to the world that the massacres committed by the Guatemalan government and army and some by the URNG guerrillas reached levels of genocide. The report describes the armed conflict starting between 1958 and 1962 and ending with the signing of the peace accords under the government of President Alvaro Arzú in 1996. The report stated that from 1961 to 1985 the army developed strategies to rid the country of an internal enemy: the subversives, or guerrillas. Their national policy of terror and massacres claimed the lives of 200,000 Guatemalans, many of them Maya, during this thirty-six-year war. Of the victims, 83.3 percent were indigenous people from Maya communities and 16.5 percent came from the ladino population (CEH 1999).

The CEH, which functioned as the Guatemalan truth commission, interviewed survivors of this holocaust and confirmed that those responsible for the violations of human rights were the army and the guerrillas. To provide justice for the victims, the CEH presented recommendations and urged the Guatemalan government to commit to their implementation. But just as with the peace accords, the Guatemalan government has been reluctant to implement any recommendations to facilitate justice and reconciliation. The CEH also commented on the support of the United States and Cuba for opposite sides of the conflict, and during his visit to Guatemala in March 1999, President Clinton acknowledged the connection of the United States to this armed conflict and he asked "forgiveness" for the damage done.

The Arzú government was also faced with the assassination of Bishop Juan Gerardi Conedera, which diminished even further the hopes for a permanent peace in Guatemala. Despite, or perhaps because of, evidence that pointed to the army's involvement in this murder, the investigations were continuously obstructed and postponed. The lack of justice and the failure of President Arzú to bring the murderers to trial demonstrated once more that the army continues to maintain its power and the privilege of acting with impunity. Although the U.S. Federal Bureau of Investigation offered assistance with the investigation and the DNA tests that could identify the killers, its offer of help was ignored. Despite President Portillo's promise to find those who were responsible for the crime and bring them to justice, that process has been delayed, denied, obstructed, and reduced to a mockery and a sham. For Myrna Mack, the anthropologist assassinated in 1983, the actual killer, Noel Beteta, an ex-agent of the Presidential Guard, was sentenced to twenty-five years in prison. In 2002, two army officers, General Edgar Godoy Gaitan and Colonel Juan Oliva Carrera, were sentenced to thirty years in prison for being the intellectual authors of the crime. But in May 2003, these two men were released from prison on a technicality (*Siglo Veintiuno*, May 8, 2003). These cases demonstrate the utter collapse of the law in Guatemala and the inability of the courts to function in an impartial way. Those who committed crimes and massacres in the past continue untouched by the law, and immunity exists for those with power and connections.

New evidence of kidnapping and torture carried out by the army with the knowledge of the CIA was revealed in Washington, DC, by Kate Doyle of the National Security Archives and her team of researchers. They have made public recently declassified secret documents, including a Guatemalan army list of 183 individuals who were disappeared during the armed conflict (*Prensa Libre*, May 23, 1999). The army log also contained the photographs of those individuals, and these were made public on the Internet. The Human Rights Office of the Catholic Church met with family members of the disappeared and the Grupo de Apoyo Mutuo (GAM; Mutual Support Group) and decided to follow up on the investigation. Nevertheless, despite this new and compelling evidence, the army has denied any participation (*Prensa Libre,* May 26, 1999). What is needed now is a genuine change in the judicial system and decentralization of power.

To carry out the implementation of the peace accords, the Guatemalan government called for a popular referendum on May 16, 1999, to vote on some recommended changes to the Guatemalan Constitution. Unfortunately, the outcome of this referendum was resoundingly negative on the part of those who voted. This "no" vote was a step backward and threw any hopes for constitutional reform into the garbage. There were many reasons why the Guatemalan population voted against the constitutional reform. Indigenous people lacked information and understanding of the content and import of the reforms. The major Guatemalan newspapers promoted the "no" response. The extreme right argued that these changes to the Constitution would give the Maya too much power over the ladino population, insinuating that the Maya might even ask for autonomy and split the country into little, autonomous nation-states. Another factor was the role of COPMAGUA, the indigenous umbrella organization with strong political ties to the former guerrilla groups. Most Guatemalans, Maya and non-Maya alike, were tired of the armed conflict and did not want to deal with COPMAGUA, which they saw as a messenger of the Guatemalan National Revolutionary Unity (URNG), now reformed into a political party. The indigenous population also needed to be educated in civics so that they could recognize that voting, no longer a mandatory act commanded by the army, is a necessity and a fundamental right of each citizen.

In the presidential election of 1999, the Guatemalan Republican Front (FRG), the right-wing party headed by General Ríos Montt, was the winner. People questioned why the Maya voted for the genocidal Ríos Montt and his presidential candidate, Alfonso Portillo. There were no easy answers to this question. First, the previous ruling party, Partido de Avanzada Nacional (PAN), had privatized national assets and institutions, such as the national telephone system (GUATEL), and President Arzú was accused of being too arrogant, developing a negative and confrontational relationship with the national media. Despite PAN's achievements, such as the construction of major highways and roads, the people continued to suffer poverty and the lack of economic opportunities in the countryside.

But the question remained: Why did the Maya vote for Ríos Montt and his candidate Alfonso Portillo? It was truly surprising that in some places where the massacres had been more intense, as in El Quiché, the Maya voted strongly for Ríos Montt's party. I conducted a few interviews with Mayas in western Guatemala after the election, and their answers indicated that local issues rather than national ones were important. The Indian mayors in some Maya communities were very corrupt, especially those who belonged to the official PAN party. For this reason, the Maya voted to get rid of the local authorities, and their votes did not necessarily indicate support for the party to which the challengers belonged. The media and the multiple surveys taken claimed that Portillo was ahead in the polls, and this strongly influenced the voters. According to some indigenous people, they were afraid that if they didn't vote for the FRG, Ríos Montt would take reprisals against them. Accordingly, they thought it was better to support the bad one, so that he would not kill you as he had during his scorched-earth campaign in 1982.

In many of these communities, the former heads of the civil patrols monitored the voting at the election tables, influencing and intimidating the voters. Rather than suffer more at the hands of the civil patrols and from military repression, they voted for the FRG, which, in any case, seemed to be the clear leader in the elections. On the other hand, it was also difficult to vote for the URNG political party. It had demonstrated many problems in the campaign and had a record of weakness during the negotiations. The Maya had little confidence in voting for this party. Thus, the reasons why the Maya voted for Ríos Montt's party were fear, intimidation, and the lack of powerful or compelling alternatives.

After Portillo became president, the national situation took a brief positive turn. He initiated some major changes by calling attention to his "pluralistic" government and bringing representatives of different factions to his cabinet. He named to his cabinet two Maya who had criticized the FRG and opposed Ríos Montt, even denouncing him as an assassin: the vice-minister of education, Demetrio Cojtí, and the minister of culture, Otilia Lux de Cotí. Maya criticism of Lux de Cotí was especially severe, because despite serving as a member of the CEH, which condemned the massacres of thousands of Maya, she accepted a position in the Portillo government. The Maya remembered that during the presentation of reports by the CEH, Lux de Cotí gave a very mild response to the massacres, and she called for reconciliation and for "forgetting" the past, just as the army wanted. In this position she was sympathetic to the needs of the FRG, which then was seeking the presidency in order to cover up human rights abuses and unexplained massacres. The same strategy was used by the PRI in Mexico, since indigenous leaders seem to be easy to co-opt when offered political positions, even by those they criticize.

In November 2003 Guatemala again entered the season of presidential elections, and the political parties again tried to be nice to indigenous organizations in an effort to win their votes. This time, the difference was that there were three Maya parties, and one of them, Partido CASA, nominated Rigoberto Quemé Chay as a presidential candidate. President Portillo had not been able to fulfill his promises. His government had been chastened by the United States and criticized by the European Union for its corruption, its inability to control crime or prosecute criminals, and its reluctance to move forward with the implementation of the peace accords, all issues for which international funders had committed resources and on which the ordinary people of Guatemala, Maya and ladino alike, had based their hopes for real peace and lasting justice.

Another major event was the indictment presented by Rigoberta Menchú in Spain against the army officers responsible for massacres in Guatemala. This action is perhaps one of the most effective she has taken since she received the Nobel Peace Prize in 1992. Her written indictment "Justicia Universal para el Genocidio en Guatemala" (Universal Justice for Genocide in Guatemala) was accepted by the National Audience of Spain in December 1999. The major abusers of human rights and genocide listed in her indictment are General Efraín Ríos Montt, General Oscar Humberto Mejía Víctores, General Fernando Romeo Lucas García, General Angel Aníbal Guevara Rodríguez, Colonel German Chupina Barahona, former police officer Pedro García Arredondo, and General Benedicto Lucas García. Her indictment focused on the killing of her father, who was burned alive in the Spanish embassy, the killing of her mother and brother, and the killing of twelve Catholic priests and lay Christian leaders, mainly during the regime of Romeo Lucas García. This action took the Guatemalan army by surprise. Ríos Montt, the former president of the Congress in Guatemala, understands that he risks being taken prisoner and held for trial if he travels abroad, as happened to General Pinochet of Chile.

Meanwhile, Maya organizations continue in their struggle to make themselves visible and carry out their work for achieving peace and justice in Guatemala. A few Maya politicians with seats in Congress may not be able to accomplish much; they are surrounded by astute individuals, including a former head of state, Vinicio Cerezo. To keep up with Maya issues and not become radicalized once more from the left or right, the Maya must now unify their efforts, make alliances, and speak with one voice on common issues.

Reparations is one important issue for Maya leaders. During the Arzú government, attempts were made to create a law for reparations and assistance to the victims of the internal violence. The international community was willing to support such a program and even to provide financial assistance. Although the law for reparations was never completed, the Maya Commission for Peace and Reconciliation has initiated efforts to bring reparations to Maya communities. They believe that reparations should be planned and implemented by the Maya themselves so that resources properly reach the affected communities. The Portillo government, unfortunately, promised compensation only to the civil patrollers, who contributed to the fight against the guerrilla forces and, in some cases, participated in the massacres. Most human rights groups saw this payment to the civil patrollers as an inappropriate attempt to buy votes and reward FRG supporters prior to the fall elections.

The government has shown its willingness to ignore and obstruct the full implementation of the peace accords, but the Maya people are now better organized, and they will make every effort to see that their rights and identities are respected. They are urging the government to comply with the recommendations of the CEH and initiate reparations laws to benefit not only the present Maya and ladino populations in rural communities but future generations as well.

The FRG government did not give any attention to the peace accords, but instead created more instability and poverty in the nation through misuse of the nation's resources and blatant corruption at all levels of government. Guatemalans once again went to the polls and cast their votes in November 2003, hoping for a real change and a better role for Maya intellectuals and leaders in a new government. Unfortunately, the political parties that they supported — the FRG and the Unidad Nacional de la Esperanza (UNE; National Unity for Hope) — did not win the elections. The winner was Oscar Berger.

A Maya-Ladino Dialogue as a Strategy for Peace

One of the best ways to achieve peace and human solidarity in Guatemala would be through serious dialogues between Mayas and ladinos. Several previous experiments with this process have opened some doors, but it has been difficult to reach a consensus among people, ethnic groups, and even internally among Maya and ladino groups. Diverse opinions and projects do not necessarily coincide, even if they are aimed at the same goal. Despite the problems, it is important that meetings and dialogues between these communities continue and be supported so that together we can start this journey of dialogue in search of unity and solidarity between and among Mayas and ladinos. We need to work with young leaders so that they can contribute to the democratization and the strengthening of the fragile peace that we now experience in Guatemala. We cannot deny that the relationships between Maya and ladino have been unequal until now. Certainly, not all ladinos consider the indigenous people as inferior human beings, but neither has there been a strong effort on the part of ladinos to end the rejection and neglect of the Maya people by previous governments. Sincere and serious dialogue between Mayas and ladinos has not yet taken place in our country, because we have always seen the "other" with fear and contempt. The antagonism and confrontation characteristic of Maya-ladino relationships has hindered the development of any national project that would benefit all Guatemalans.

For centuries we have seen and endured the racial divisions in our communities, and now we are experiencing the result of this unequal relationship. Both groups have come to realize the existence of this division and antagonism, and although the problem may be obvious, the answer is not. Despite several attempts, there has been no real communication or dialogue among ourselves. The Maya have organized meetings before, and there are meetings in the most luxurious hotels almost every week. But what has been missing is a real desire to sit down and discuss with the right people the problems that we have in common, problems that affect all Guatemalans.

Speaking with sincerity to one another about our common problems will work as a positive therapy that could lead us to develop a better interethnic relationship that respects our diversity. Certainly, a dialogue or words alone are not sufficient: we need actions, as well, to cure this malaise. Through joint introspection we may be able to generate a strong force of unity, respect, and cooperation for the welfare of our nation. We, the Maya, must recognize the need to change the mentality of those who think of themselves only as victims and as a dominated people, and counter those who want to romanticize the past and return there in order to avoid the world of contradictions in which we now live. But such an idyllic place does not exist.

As I write this, I recognize that nobody likes to be criticized, so we have to do it in a constructive way. This is a mental exercise or therapy that will help us locate those little monsters of racism and discrimination that we all carry inside ourselves without realizing it. Although this is the case for Mayas, it is especially so for ladinos. We all need to search sincerely for an opportunity for dialogue so that we can find solutions to our lack of understanding of one another.

Finally, let me assert that the problems of class antagonism and of political ideologies, whether from the right or left, have caused much damage, even

Maya-ladino dialogue, Quetzaltenango, 2000 (author's photos)

pushing us into an internal and fratricidal war. A dialogue is an important way to get to understand one another as we work for a Guatemalan nation that is new, democratic, and respectful of human rights. This is a challenge not only for Maya leaders, but also for the ladinos and the Guatemalan people in general. The century that we are entering is already tense, and we will need to consult each other in order to survive as a nation in the twenty-first century. A Guatemala that is a bilingual and pluricultural nation—not only in name, but in fact—will respect, value, and promote the country's ethnic diversity. It is beautiful to dream that this new millennium could be the millennium of the Maya, secure within a new Guatemala.[1]

NOTES

Chapter 2

1. Since 1992, the public celebration of Maya ceremonies by these experts in the ancient Maya calendar has spread to the entire Mayan-speaking area, including Belize and Chiapas.

2. Beginning in January 1993, the refugees in UN-supervised camps in Mexico started to return to Guatemala in a collective and organized manner. The first group of 2,800 returnees was established in a new community that they called "January 29th Victory" in northern Guatemala.

3. The Zapatista uprising in Chiapas in 1994 brought public attention to the neglect that the Maya of Chiapas face and raised the consciousness of the Guatemalan Maya regarding the discrimination and brutality their Chiapan relatives experienced at the hands of Mexican military and paramilitary groups.

4. The formation of Maya elitist and hegemonic groups in Guatemala, as in the case of the Kaqchikeles and K'iche', has become evident. This differentiation is the result of unequal access to educational opportunities, which are denied especially to Maya in the smaller, remoter, or more peripheral linguistic communities. This situation has been criticized recently. See the article by Estheiman Amaya, "El Nuevo Imperio de los Kaqchikeles" in *El Regional* (September 2–8, 1994) and in *Rutzijol*, "Selección de noticias acerca del pueblo Maya" (September 1–5, 1994), Chimaltenango, Guatemala.

Chapter 3

1. Since texts have multiple meanings, this is my personal reading of one third-grade textbook; another reader may carry out a different reading and reach a different deconstructive result, depending on his or her cultural, social, and political background. But, because this textbook has a dominant message, my analysis tries to show that the images of the Maya represented in the text are not natural, but ideologically constructed.

2. More than 4,500 Indians were tortured during the three months of the Inquisition, and an official inquiry later established that 158 had died during or as a direct result of the interrogations (Clendinnen 1987:76).

3. The Ixil Maya are one the twenty-two Maya ethnic groups living in the northern highland region of Guatemala. The Ixiles were also one of the Maya ethnic groups most affected by the army violence during the early 1980s.

4. Oliver La Farge (1931) is among the early-twentieth-century ethnographers

who recognized this social injustice against the Maya on the plantations (*fincas*). In *The Year Bearer's People* (1931), La Farge commented that

> [h]owever the labor may be obtained, the system is most demoralizing.... Some owners of *fincas* do attempt to make things decent, providing the Indians with proper lodgings, dealing justly with them and watching over their welfare. Some of the best of these are the Germans. Others rob and cheat the Indian in every way they possibly can and take little or no care of him. (La Farge and Byers 1931:81–82)

5. Since the signing of the peace accords, a program of bilingual education promoted by the Ministry of Education through the Maya-guided program PRONADE is promoting bilingualism and helping secure the teaching of Mayan languages to young children.

6. I will not characterize the whole of Morley's work as wrong or bad since all research is relative to the particular historical moment in which it is undertaken. Morley did come to appreciate highly the ancient Maya culture, calling it, ethnocentrically, "the most brilliant civilization of the New World" (Morley 1983:17).

7. Contemporary scholars of the Maya defend their field by saying that Morley was neither an anthropologist nor an archaeologist, and thus does not represent the field. It is unfortunate, then, that during his lifetime he was one of the best-known scholars, and his work was tremendously popular, even among these newer academic researchers. His ideas have endured in the popular mind and created the ideas and images that many still hold about the Maya.

8. In the section on the Maya pantheon and cosmology in his book *The Ancient Maya,* Morley is eager to demonstrate that the Maya can be credited with worshiping hundreds of gods, thus perpetuating the image of idolatry first created by the conquistadors and early missionaries like Landa.

9. Morley and others failed to distinguish between gods and the highly esteemed gifts from a monotheistic God, gifts that were personified in glyphs. A more thorough study of Maya culture fails to substantiate this conflation of categories.

10. It is important to clarify that not every child in Guatemala receives the same deficient education. Families with disposable income have had always the choice of educating their children in private schools with private teachers, and these private schools follow a curriculum similar to that found in the United States. Other wealthy parents send their children abroad to receive a "better" education, a symbol of status and social prestige. Educated in this way, the children

of the rich grow up alienated from the reality of their own country and become accustomed to the more luxurious lifestyle of highly industrialized nations.

11. As a primary school teacher in Guatemala until 1982, I was also submerged in this cultural amnesia. Schoolteachers must buy their own textbooks; except in private schools, children do not receive copies of books for individual use. Most learning consists of rote recitation by pupils. Most schoolteachers are not well prepared, not given appropriate training, and not taught anything about Maya history. Teachers take the information in textbooks as the "truth" and repeat it as gospel to their pupils without ever thinking that they are being used to perpetuate the same cultural amnesia in the children's minds.

12. The quetzal is the national bird of Guatemala, the symbol of liberty. Atanasio Tzul is a K'iche' Maya who opposed royal taxes and directed a rebellion against Spanish officials in 1820.

13. A recent project at the Centro de Investigaciones Regionales de Mesoamerica (CIRMA), directed by Dr. Richard Adams with the help of some Guatemalan historians, has as its goal the writing of updated and corrected social-studies textbooks. The series includes textbooks written by non-Maya historians and anthropologists for use at primary, secondary, and even university levels. One part of this project is a series of local ethnographies and histories to which both Maya and non-Maya have contributed. The United States Agency for International Development funded the textbook series, which is now being printed in Guatemala.

14. The presence of the Tlaxcaltecas is recognized, but their role is minimized, since the textbook relates that "Los indios que vinieron de México *acompañado* a Alvarado, le llamaban Quauhtemallán a estas tierras" (The Indians who came from Mexico *accompanying* Alvarado called this land Quauhtemallán; Cortés 1990:24, emphasis added). ("Quauhtemallán" means "place of abundant trees or woods.") The book acknowledges the Tlaxcalteca warriors only as "companions" of Alvarado, without mentioning their role in the conquest.

Chapter 4

1. The Chagnon-Tierney controversy over the Yanomami Indians of Venezuela, as portrayed in *Darkness in El Dorado: How Scientists and Journalists Devastated the Amazon,* is a good example of this continued misrepresentation of indigenous people in anthropology.

2. The *Popol Wuj,* the *Anales de los Kaqchikeles,* and the *Título de Totonicapán* are ethnohistorical documents written in Mayan languages by indigenous writers after the Spanish conquest of Guatemala in 1524.

3. The captains of war and Spanish lords were rewarded with *encomiendas,*

royal grants that gave them full title to the land and the labor of the Indian serfs living on the land. These became the great Spanish estates of the New World.

4. The Frente Democrático Nueva Guatemala (FDNG) was a political party organized by Rosalina Tuyuc, the head of the widows organization CONAVIGUA. The FDNG nominated Tuyuc, and she became one of the first women appointed to the Guatemalan Congress. This party lost its support and became extinct after the elections in 1999.

Chapter 5

1. President Arzú (1995–2000) presided over the signing of the peace accords. He was succeeded by Alfonso Portillo (2000–2004), who was followed by the current president, Oscar Berger (2004–2008).

Chapter 8

1. The original Mayan name of this town was *Xajla'*, but the Nahuatl-speaking allies of Pedro de Alvarado (Aztecs and Tlaxcaltecs) renamed it Xacaltenango (Jacaltenango) during the invasion of Guatemala in 1524.

2. The *principales* are the elders of the community who have served in the cargo-system hierarchy of politico-religious offices. Since they are the most knowledgeable and their service to the community has given them sacred standing, their role has become that of advisors and guides to the people.

3. Antun Luk (may he rest in peace) died in 1983, one year after I went into exile. I did have the chance to see him after we talked about *El Q'anil: The Man of Lightning* in November 1982, but he wanted me to return to my town and stay with my people.

4. During the struggle of Belize (then known as British Honduras) for independence from England and Guatemala, General Kjell Eugenio Laugerud García wanted to keep that country as an integral part of Guatemala, as he claimed it had been historically. In the struggle, England threatened to destroy the Guatemalan army if it attempted to thwart the decision of Belize to be independent.

5. An expanded edition of *Q'anil: The Man of Lightning* with the Mayan text was published by University of Arizona Press (Montejo 2001).

6. According to Jakaltek mythology, the four bearers carry the earth, and earthquakes are produced when they remove the porter's strap to rest their foreheads. Another elder, Mat Tiyes, has said that one of bearers constantly inquires about his birthday, but God does not tell him the date to avoid making him too excited, which would cause him to shift his load violently and cause earthquakes.

7. *Cargo* was a system of civic-religious offices in Maya communities. Men moved up to more responsible religious and political offices as they grew older.

Cargo offices should be performed with religious commitment and as a genuine service to the community.

8. This Mayan literary device, called *ninhq'omb'al,* is used particularly in sacred songs and prayers.

9. Ríos Montt was the presidential candidate for the Christian Democratic Party of Guatemala in 1974. His loss in that election is generally attributed to fraudulent vote counting. After becoming president by a coup d'état in 1982, he presided over the bloodiest phase of the counterinsurgency war. In 1999, Ríos Montt's political party, the Frente Republicano Guatemalteco (FRG), won the elections, and Ríos Montt became president of the Guatemalan Congress.

10. During Ríos Montt's short term in office, some 440 Maya villages were razed, and one million people were displaced.

11. Lah-ti' is a Maya political and democratic way of electing community leaders. At a communal meeting, all are encouraged to voice their concerns and reach consensus. (*Lah* = equal, *ti'* = mouth).

12. In Jacaltenango, this is the highest level in the hierarchy of the cargo system. The *alkal txah* is the prayer-maker, or head of the civic-religious Mayan ceremonies.

13. Scholars have named this K'iche' Maya ethnohistorical document the *Popol Vuh.* Recently, K'iche' Mayan speakers have renamed it *Pop Wuj.* It is also named differently in other Mayan languages; for example, *Popb'al Hum* in Popb'al Ti', the Jakaltek Mayan language.

14. From the Yukatek Mayan language, *kusansum* means a rope that gives life, the symbol of the umbilical cord.

15. The syncretization of traditional Maya beliefs with tenets of Christian doctrine occurred over five centuries, resulting in a dynamic and complex worldview and system of faith.

16. The Maya regular calendar, composed of 18 months of 20 days, plus 5 sacred days, made up a year, *hab'il,* of 365 days.

17. Young Maya in most Maya communities do not faithfully observe these traditional forms of knowledge and respect for other living beings.

18. This statement is from the film about Rigoberta Menchú, "When the Mountains Tremble" (Skylight Pictures, New York, 1984).

19. Recent experiments by U.S. and Japanese scientists have shown that plants have "feelings." Plants respond differently to the intensity of sounds directed toward them. They say that plants grow if you say nice things to them, as was demonstrated by the waves emitted by the plants registered in the spectrographs.

20. Landlessness particularly marked the Maya refugees in Mexico who struggled to survive in an alien territory from 1982 until 1996.

21. *Wayab'* is a Maya concept of mutuality, the communal and moral responsibility of caring for the survival of each member of the community through mutual help. *Komontat* is a Maya theory of cosmic unity, a philosophy of life based on the consensus of communalism.

22. On January 20, 1993, the first repatriation or *retorno* took place when 2,800 refugees returned to northern Guatemala to build a new community, which they called "Victoria 20 de Enero." Over the next ten years a majority of the refugees returned to Guatemala, but some accepted the conditions of the Mexican government for remaining in Chiapas.

Chapter 10

General note: An earlier version of this chapter was presented at the conference "Security in the Post-Summit Americas" sponsored by the North-South Center of the University of Miami, the National Defense University's Institute for National Strategic Studies, and the Fondation canadienne pour les Amériques (FOCAL; Canadian Foundation for the Americas) in the session, "Indigenous Rights and Security Issues in the Americas" Washington, D.C., March 30–31, 1995.

1. Summit of the Americas, declaration of principles: "Partnership for Development and Prosperity: Democracy, Free Trade and Sustainable Development in the Americas" (Miami, Dec. 1994).

2. The vagrancy law declared that "every Indian who was not the titled owner of a certain amount of agricultural land was a vagrant and was required to work certain number of days a year on the fincas, usually the coffee farms" (Adams 1990:142).

3. At that time, Guatemala reclaimed Belize as part of its territory that had been usurped by Great Britain during the early colonial period.

4. The *requerimiento* was a statement read to indigenous people by the Spaniards ordering them to submit peacefully to Spanish rule. When that order was not obeyed, the Spaniards used the refusal to justify warfare and the subsequent enslavement of indigenous people.

5. This is depicted in the film *When the Mountains Tremble* (Skylight Pictures, New York, 1984).

6. In Guatemala, the two primary groups working in Maya communities were the guerrilla organizations the Ejército Guerrillero de los Pobres (EGP) and the Organización del Pueblo en Armas (ORPA), both of which operated under the umbrella organization Unidad Revolucionaria Nacional Guatemalteca (URNG).

7. Several court cases have been filed with the Organization of American States and in Guatemala to try the perpetrators of the massacres in the 1980s

for genocide. Many of the most fearful human-rights abuses at this time are the threats made against the participants (witnesses, lawyers, judges) in these cases.

8. Recent governments have seen more Maya faces in appointed offices: Otilia Lux in the Ministry of Culture and Demetrio Cojtí in the Vice-Ministry of Education. There are a few others in Congress, generally affiliated with political parties that otherwise care nothing about Maya concerns.

Chapter 11

1. This final section was adopted from remarks made at the forum "Diálogo Maya-Ladino," which took place in Guatemala City, November 2000.

SELECTED BIBLIOGRAPHY

Adams, Richard N. 1960. "Social Change in Guatemala and U.S. Policy." In *Social Change in Latin America Today*. New York: Vintage Books.

———. 1990. "Ethnic Images and Strategies in 1944." In *Guatemalan Indians and the State, 1540–1988*, edited by Carol A. Smith, 141–162. Austin: Univ. of Texas Press.

———. 1994. "A Report on the Political Status of the Guatemalan Maya." In *Indigenous Peoples and Democracy in Latin America*, edited by Donna Lee Van Cott, 155–186. New York: St. Martin's Press.

Ak'abal, Humberto. 2001. *Ajkem Tzij/Tejedor de Palabras*. Guatemala: Editorial Cholsamaj.

Alvarado, Pedro de. 1924. *An Account of the Conquest of Guatemala in 1524 by Pedro de Alvarado*, edited by Sedley J. Mackie. New York: The Cortes Society.

Anderson, Benedict. 1990. *Imagined Communities: Reflections on the Origin and Spread of Nationalism*. London: Verso.

Arias, Arturo. 1990. "Changing Indian Identity: Guatemala's Violent Transition to Modernity." In *Guatemalan Indians and the State, 1540–1988*, edited by Carol A. Smith, 230–257. Austin: Univ. of Texas Press.

———, ed. 2001. *The Rigoberta Menchú Controversy*. Minneapolis: Univ. of Minnesota Press.

Argüelles, José. 1987. *The Mayan Factor: Path Beyond Technology*. Santa Fe, N.Mex.: Bear and Company.

Asad, Talal, ed. 1973. *Anthropology and the Colonial Encounter*. Atlantic Highlands, N.J.: Humanities Press.

Asturias, Miguel Angel. 1977. *Sociología Guatemalteca: El Problema Social del Indio/Guatemalan Sociology: The Social Problem of the Indian*. Reprint of the 1923 Spanish edition. Tempe: Arizona State Univ. Press.

Balmaceda, Liz. 1994. "Amid Reunion, a Vast Gulf on Human Rights." *Miami Herald*, Dec. 3, sec. A, 29.

Barrera Vásquez, Alfredo. 1963. *El libro de los libros del Chilam Balam*. 2nd ed. Mexico: Fondo de Cultura Económica.

Barthes, Roland. 1989. *Mythologies*. Translated by Annette Lavers. New York: Noonday Press.

Belsey, Catherine. 1985. *Critical Practice*. London and New York: Methuen.

Benedito, R. Medina. 1994. "The Emerging International Standard on Indigenous Peoples' Rights: Issues and Implications for Missionizing in Third World Countries." Paper presented at the annual meeting of the American Anthropological Association, Atlanta, Ga.

Bodley, John H. 1990. *Victims of Progress*. 3rd ed. Mountain View, Calif.: Mayfield.

Bricker, Victoria R. 1981. *The Indian Christ, The Indian King: The Historical Substrate of Maya Myth and Ritual*. Austin: Univ. of Texas Press.

Brintnall, Douglas E. 1979. *Revolt against the Dead: The Modernization of a Mayan Community in the Highlands of Guatemala*. New York and London: Gordon and Breach.

Bunzel, Ruth. 1981. *Chichicastenango*. Translation of the 1952 English edition. Guatemala City: Editorial José de Pineda Ibarra, Ministerio de Educación.

Burgos-Debray, Elizabeth, ed. 1983. *Me Llamo Rigoberta Menchú y Así Me Nació la Conciencia*. Barcelona: Ediciones Argos Vergara, S.A.

Burns, Allan F. 1993. *Maya in Exile: Guatemalans in Florida*. Philadelphia: Temple Univ. Press.

Burt, Jo-Marie, and Fred Rosen. 1999. "Truth-Telling and Memory in Postwar Guatemala: An Interview with Rigoberta Menchú." *NACLA: Report on the Americas* 32(5): 6–10.

Campbell, Lyle, and Terrence Kaufman. 1985. "Mayan Linguistics: Where Are We Now?" *Annual Review of Anthropology* 14:187–198.

Cancián, Frank. 1969. *Economics and Prestige in a Maya Community: The Religious Cargo System in Zinacantan*. Stanford, Calif.: Stanford Univ. Press.

Canclini, Nestor García. 1984. *Las Culturas Populares en el Capitalismo*. Segunda Edición. México: Editorial Nueva Imagen.

———. 1985. "Cultura Nacional y Culturas Populares: Bases teórico-metodológicas para la investigación." Unpublished manuscript.

Carlsen, Robert. 1997. *The War for the Heart and Soul of a Highland Maya Town*. Austin: Univ. of Texas Press.

Carmack, Robert M. 1979. *Historia Social de los Quichés*. Seminario de Integración Social. Guatemala City: Editorial José de Pineda Ibarra, Ministerio de Educación.

———. 1988. "Quiche-Maya Culture in the Context of the Guatemalan Revolutionary Movement." Paper presented at the conference "Maya Culture, Past and Present," State Univ. of New York, Albany.

Casaus Arzú, Marta. 1992. *Guatemala: Linaje y Racismo*. Guatemala: FLACSO.

Casaverde, Juvenal. 1976. "Jacaltec Social and Political Structure." PhD diss., Univ. of Rochester. Ann Arbor, Mich.: Univ. Microfilms International.

Castañeda, Quetzil. 1996. *In the Museum of Maya Culture: Touring Chichen Itzá.* Minneapolis: Univ. of Minnesota Press.

CEH (Comisión para el Esclaramiento Histórico de Guatemala). 1999. *Guatemala: Memoria de Silencio.* Washington, D.C.: American Association for the Advancement of Science.

Chávez, Adrián Inés. 1979. *Pop Wuj.* Mexico: Ediciones de la Casa Chata, Centro de Investigaciones del INAH.

Churchill, Ward. 1999. "The Tragedy and the Travesty: The Subversion of Indigenous Sovereignty in North America." In *Contemporary Native American Political Issues,* edited by Troy Johnson. Walnut Creek, Calif.: Altamira Press.

Cifuentes, H. Juan Fernando (Capitán de Navio). 1982. "Apreciación de Asuntos Civiles (G-5) para el Area Ixil." *Revista Militar* (Guatemala: Centro de Estudios Militares [CEM]) Sept.–Dec.

Clay, Jason W. 1993. "Looking Back to Go Forward: Predicting and Preventing Human Rights Violations." In *State of the Peoples: A Global Human Rights Report on Societies in Danger,* edited by Marc S. Miller. Boston: Beacon Press.

Clendinnen, Inga. 1987. *Ambivalent Conquests: Mayas and Spaniards in Yucatán, 1517–1938.* Cambridge: Cambridge University Press.

Clifford, James. 1988. *The Predicament of Culture: Twentieth-Century Ethnography, Literature, and Art.* Cambridge, Mass.: Harvard Univ. Press.

Clifford, James, and George E. Marcus, eds. 1986. *Writing Culture: The Poetics and Politics of Ethnography.* Berkeley and Los Angeles: Univ. of California Press.

Cojtí Cuxil, Demetrio. 1994. *Políticas para la Reivindicación de los Mayas de Hoy: Fundamento de los Derechos Específicos del Pueblo Maya.* Guatemala: Editorial Cholsamaj.

———. 1996. "The Politics of Maya Revindication." In *Maya Cultural Activism in Guatemala,* edited by Edward Fischer and R. McKenna Brown, 19–50. Austin: Univ. of Texas Press.

Colby, Benjamin N., and Lore M. Colby. 1981. *The Daykeeper: The Life and Discourse of an Ixil Diviner.* Cambridge, Mass.: Harvard Univ. Press.

Contreras, Daniel J. 1951. *Una Rebelión Indígena en el Partido de Totonicapán en 1820: El Indio y la Independencia.* Guatemala: Imprenta Universitaria.

Cook, Garrett W. 2000. *Renewing the Maya World: Expressive Culture in a Highland Town.* Austin: Univ. of Texas Press.

Cortés, Elsy de. 1990. *Estudios Sociales, 3er Grado: Historia Geografía y Cooperativismo, Colección ESFUERZO.* Guatemala City: Tipografía Santa Lucía.

Cox de Collins, Anne. 1980. "Colonial Jacaltenango, Guatemala: The Formation of a Corporate Community." PhD diss., Tulane Univ. Ann Arbor, Mich.: Univ. Microfilms International.

Culbert, T. Patrick, ed. 1973. *The Classic Maya Collapse*. School of American Research Advanced Seminar Series. Albuquerque: Univ. of New Mexico Press.

Cultural Survival Quarterly. 1993. "UN Draft Declaration on the Rights of Indigenous People." In *Cultural Survival*. Cambridge: Cultural Survival Publications.

Cutzal Mijango, Salvador. 1990. "Creo en un Dios Pobre." *Noticias Aliadas* (México), Oct. 4.

Davis, Shelton, and Julie Hodson. 1982. *Witnesses to Political Violence in Guatemala: The Suppression of a Rural Development Movement*. Impact Audit No. 2. Boston: Oxfam America.

Demarest, Arthur. 1992. "Ideology in Ancient Maya Cultural Evolution: The Dynamics of Galactic Politics." In *Ideology and Pre-Columbian Civilizations*, edited by Arthur A. Demarest and Geoffrey W. Conrad, 135–157. School of American Research Advanced Seminar Series. Santa Fe, N.Mex.: School of American Research Press.

Earle, Duncan. 1988. "Mayas Aiding Mayas: Guatemalan Refugees in Chiapas, Mexico." In *Harvest of Violence: The Maya Indians and the Guatemalan Crisis*, edited by Robert M. Carmack. Norman: Univ. of Oklahoma Press.

Esquit Choy, Alberto, and Víctor Gálvez Borrell. 1997. *The Mayan Movement Today: Issues of Indigenous Culture and Development in Guatemala*. Guatemala: FLACSO.

Estrada Monroy, Agustin. 1973. *Empiezan las historias de los indios de esta provincia de Guatemala*. Guatemala: Editorial José de Pineda Ibarra.

Falla, Ricardo. 1992. *Masacres de la Selva: Ixcán Guatemala (1975–1982)*. Editorial Universitaria, Coleccion 500 Años, Vol. 1. Guatemala: Universidad de San Carlos de Guatemala.

———. 1994. *Massacres in the Jungle: Ixcan, Guatemala, 1975–1982*. Boulder, Colo.: Westview Press.

Farriss, Nancy. 1984. *Maya Society under Colonial Rule: The Collective Enterprise of Survival*. Princeton, N.J.: Princeton Univ. Press.

Fergusson, Erna. 1949. *Guatemala*. New York: Knopf.

Fisher, Edward F., and R. McKenna Brown, eds. 1996. *Maya Cultural Activism in Guatemala*. Austin: Univ. of Texas Press.

Freidel, David. 1986. "Maya Warfare: An Example of Peer Polity Interaction." In *Peer Polity Interaction and the Development of Sociopolitical Complexity*, edited by Colin Renfrew and John F. Cherry, 93–108. New York: Cambridge Univ. Press.

Freire, Paulo. 1985. *The Politics of Education: Culture, Power, and Liberation.* South Hadley, Mass.: Bergin and Garvey.

Friede, Juan, and Benjamin Keen. 1971. *Bartolomé de Las Casas in History.* De-Kalb: Northern Illinois Univ. Press.

Galeano, Eduardo. 1999. "Disparen sobre Rigoberta." *La Jornada* (México), January 16.

———. 2001. "Let's Shoot Rigoberta." In *The Rigoberta Menchú Controversy,* edited by Arturo Arias, 99–102. Minneapolis: Univ. of Minnesota Press.

García Escobar, Carlos René. 1999. "Antropólogos gringos vs. antropólogos chapines." Distributed via e-mail by aeu@centramerica.com, March 18.

Gates, William, trans. 1978. *Yucatan before and after the Conquest.* New York: Dover Publications.

Gillin, John P. 1960. "Some Signposts for Policy." In *Social Change in Latin America Today.* New York: Vintage Books.

Gonzáles, Gaspar Pedro. 1995. *A Mayan Life.* Elaine Elliot, trans. Rancho Palos Vertes: Yax Te' Press.

Gossen, Gary H. 1984. *Chamulas in the World of the Sun: Time and Space in a Maya Oral Tradition.* Prospect Heights, Ill.: Waveland Press.

———. 1986. "Mesoamerican Ideas as a Foundation for Regional Synthesis." In *Symbol and Meaning beyond the Closed Community: Essays in Mesoamerican Ideas,* Gary H. Gossen, ed. Albany: State Univ. of New York Press, Institute for Mesoamerican Studies.

———. 1999. *Telling Maya Tales: Tzotzil Identities in Modern Mexico.* New York: Routledge.

Gramajo, Hector A. 1989. "Tesis de la Estabilidad Nacional." *Editorial del Ejército* (EDE) Octubre. Guatemala, C.A.

Gramsci, Antonio. 1973. *Letters from Prison.* New York: Harper and Row.

Grandin, Greg. 2000. *The Blood of Guatemala: A History of Race and Nation.* Durham: Duke Univ. Press.

Grandin, Greg, and Francisco Goldman. 1999. "Bitter Fruit for Rigoberta." *The Nation,* February 8.

Guzmán Böckler, Carlos. 1979. "Prólogo" to Adrián I. Chávez, *Pop Wuj,* 7–27. México: Ediciones se la Casa Chata, Centro de Investigaciones del INAH.

Hale, Charles A. 1996. "Mestizaje, Hybridity, and the Cultural Politics of Difference in Postrevolutionary Central America." *Journal of Latin American Anthropology* 2(1):34–61.

———. 1999 "Travel Warning: Elite Appropriations of Hybridity and Other

Progressive-Sounding Discourses in Highland Guatemala." *Journal of American Folklore* 112(445):297–315.

Handy, Jim. 1984. *Gift of the Devil: A History of Guatemala.* Toronto: Between the Lines Press.

———. 1994. *Revolution in the Countryside: Rural Conflict and Agrarian Reform in Guatemala, 1944–1954.* Chapel Hill: Univ. of North Carolina Press.

Hanke, Lewis. 1974. *All Mankind Is One.* DeKalb: Northern Illinois Univ. Press.

Hart, Jeffrey. "A Classic of Lies." *Independent Voice* (Dixon, California), February 17, 1999.

Healy, Kevin, and Susan Paulson. 2000. "Political Economies of Identity in Bolivia, 1952–1998." *Journal of Latin American Anthropology* 5(2):2–19.

Hill, Robert M., and John Monaghan. 1987. *Continuities in Highland Maya Social Organization: Ethnohistory in Sacapulas, Guatemala.* Philadelphia: Univ. of Pennsylvania Press.

Hitchcock, Robert K. 1994. "Seeking Sustainable Strategies: The Politics of Resource Rights among Kalahari Bushmen." Paper presented at the Annual Meeting of the American Anthropological Association, Atlanta, Georgia.

Hobsbawm, Eric. 1988. "Introduction: Inventing Traditions." In *The Invention of Tradition,* Eric Hobsbawm and Terence Ranger, eds. Cambridge: Cambridge Univ. Press.

Horowitz, David. 1999. "I, Rigoberta Menchú, Liar." *Salon Magazine,* http://www.salon.com/col/horo/1999/01/nc_11horo2.html

Jane, Cecil. 1988. *The Four Voyages of Columbus.* New York: Dover Publications.

Jonas, Susanne. 2000. *Of Centaurs and Doves: Guatemala's Peace Process.* Boulder, Colo.: Westview Press.

Justeson, John, ed. 1985. *The Foreign Impact on Lowland Mayan Language and Script.* publication No. 53, Middle American Research Institute. New Orleans, La.: Tulane Univ.

Kaltsmith, Alfred. 1998. "El testimonio de Rigoberta Menchú." *Siglo Veintiuno* (Guatemala), July 12.

Krupat, Arnold. 1992. *Ethnocriticism, Ethnography, History, Literature.* Berkeley and Los Angeles: Univ. of California Press.

La Farge, Oliver, and Douglas Byers. 1931. *The Year Bearer's People.* Middle American Research Series. Publication No.3, New Orleans: Tulane Univ.

Landa, Diego de. 1982. *Relación de las cosas de Yucatán.* México: Editorial Porrúa.

———. 1983. *Relación de las Cosas de Yucatán.* Mérida, Yucatán, México: Ediciones Dante.

Las Casas, Bartolomé de. 1989. *Brevísima relación de la destrucción de las Indias.* Madrid: Ediciones Cátedra.

León-Portilla, Miguel. 1974. *El Reverso de la Conquista.* México: Editorial Joaquín Mortiz.

Leventhal, Richard. 1987. Personal communication: Graduate seminar, State Univ. of New York, Albany.

Liano, Dante. 1999. "Respuesta a Stoll." Distributed via e-mail, January 29.

Lión, Luis de. 1985. *El tiempo principia en Xibalba.* Guatemala: Editorial Serviprensa Centroamericana.

Lobo, Susan, and Steve Talbott, eds. 2001. *Native American Voices: A Reader.* Upper Saddle River, N.J.: Prentice Hall.

Loucky, James, and Marilyn M. Moors, eds. 2000. *The Maya Diaspora: Guatemalan Roots, New American Lives.* Philadelphia: Temple Univ. Press.

Lovell, W. George. 1985. *Conquest and Survival in Colonial Guatemala: A Historical Geography of the Cuchumatan Highlands, 1500–1821.* Kingston and Montreal: McGill/Queen's Univ. Press.

Lucero, Lisa J. 2002. "The Collapse of the Classic Maya: A Case for the Role of Water Control." *American Anthropologist* 104(3):814–826.

Lutz, Christopher H., and Karen Dakin. 1996. *Nuestro pesar, nuestra aflicción: tunetuliniliz, tucucuca.* México and Guatemala: Universidad Nacional Autónoma de México y Centro de Investigaciones Regionales de Mesoamérica.

Lutz, Christopher H., and W. George Lovell. 1988. "Core and Periphery in Colonial Guatemala." In *Guatemala Indians and the State, 1540–1988,* Carol A. Smith, ed., 35–51. Austin: Univ. of Texas Press.

Makemson, Maud W. 1951. *The Book of the Jaguar Priest: A Translation of the Book of Chilam Balam of Tizimin.* New York: Henry Schuman.

Manz, Beatriz. 1988. *Refugees of a Hidden War: The Aftermath of Counterinsurgency in Guatemala.* Albany: State Univ. of New York Press.

Marcus, George E. 1986. "Contemporary Problems of Ethnography in the Modern World System." In *Writing Culture: The Poetics and Politics of Ethnography,* James Clifford and George Marcus, eds. Berkeley and Los Angeles: Univ. of California Press.

Marcus, George E., and Michael M. Fisher. 1986. *Anthropology as Cultural Critique: An Experimental Moment in the Human Sciences.* Chicago: Univ. of Chicago Press.

Matul Morales, Daniel E. 1989. "Estamos Vivos: Reafirmación de la Cultura Maya." *Nueva Sociedad* (Caracas, Venezuela) 99.

Mediz Bolio, Antonio. 1941. *Libro de Chilam Balam de Chumayel.* Mexico City: Ediciones de la Universidad Autónoma de México.

Menchú, Rigoberta, with Elisabeth Burgos-Debray. 1985. *Me llamo Rigoberta Menchú y así me nació la conciencia.* México D.F.: Siglo XXI.

Menchú, Rigoberta. 1984a. *I, Rigoberta Menchú: An Indian Woman in Guatemala.* New York: Verso.

———. 1984b. Interview in *When the Mountains Tremble,* directed by Pamela Yates and Tom Sigel. New York: Skylight Pictures.

———. 1995. "Discurso de la Premio Nobel de la Paz." Quincuagésimo Primer Período de Sesiones de la Commisión de Derechos Humanos. Geneva, Switzerland.

———. 1999. "Menchú no perdona." *Prensa Libre* (Guatemala), April 29.

Messer, Ellen. 1993. "Anthropology and Human Rights." *Annual Review of Anthropology* 22:231.

Millet, Richard L. 1991. "Unequal Partners: Relations between the Government and the Military." In *The Next Steps in Central America,* Bruce L. R. Smith, ed,. Brookings Dialogues on Public Policy. Washington: Brookings Institution.

Montejo, Víctor D. 1984. *El Q'anil: The Man of Lightning.* Carrboro, N.C.: Signal Books.

———. 1987. *Testimony: Death of a Guatemalan Village.* Willimantic, Conn.: Curbstone Press.

———. 1990. "The Elders Dreamed of Fire: Religion and Repression in the Guatemalan Highlands." *Challenge* 1(3). EPICA, Washington, D.C.

———. 1991. *The Bird Who Cleans the World and Other Maya Fables.* Willimantic, Conn.: Curbstone Press.

———. 1993a. "The Dynamics of Cultural Resistance and Transformations: The Case of Guatemalan-Mayan Refugees in Mexico." PhD diss., Univ. of Connecticut. Ann Arbor, Mich.: Univ. Microfilms International.

———. 1993b. "Tying Up the Bundle and the Katuns of Dishonor: Maya Worldview and Politics." *American Indian Culture and Research Journal* 17:103–114.

———. 1997. "Pan-Mayanismo: La pluriformidad de la cultura maya y el proceso de autorrepresentación de los mayas." *Mesoamérica* 18(33):93–123.

———. 1999a. *Voices from Exile: Violence and Survival in Modern Maya History.* Norman: Univ. of Oklahoma Press.

———. 1999b. *Q'anil: el Hombre Rayo/Komam Q'anil: Ya' K'uh Winaj.* Rancho Palos Verdes, Calif.: Yax Te' Press.

———. 2001. *Q'anil: Man of Lightning.* Tucson: Univ. of Arizona Press.

Montejo, Víctor D., and Q'anil Akab'. 1992. *Brevísima Relación Testimonial de la Continua Destrucción del Mayab' (Guatemala),* Providence, R.I.: Guatemala Scholars Network.

Montes, César. Date unknown. Article in *Siglo XXI.*

Mooney, James. 1965. *The Ghost-Dance Religion and the Sioux Outbreak of 1890.* Chicago: Univ. of Chicago Press.

Morales, Mario Roberto. 1996. *Fundamentalismo Maya.* Guatemala: Periódico Siglo Veintiuno.

———. 1998. *La articulación de las diferencias o el síndrome de Maximón.* Guatemala: FLACSO.

Morley, Sylvanus G. 1983. *La Civilización Maya.* México: Fondo de Cultura Económica.

Morley, Sylvanus G., and George Brainerd. 1983. *The Ancient Maya.* Stanford, Calif.: Stanford Univ. Press.

Mulhare, Eileen M. 1999. "Respuesta a Galeano." Distributed by e-mail, Colgate Univ., February 4.

Nagel, Joane. 1996. *American Indian Ethnic Renewal: Red Power and the Resurgence of Identity and Culture.* New York: Oxford Univ. Press.

Nagengast, Carole. 1994. "Violence, Terror, and the Crisis of the State." *Annual Review of Anthropology* 23:109–36.

Nelson, Diane. 1999a. "Rigoberta Menchú: Is Truth Stranger Than Testimonial?" *Anthropology News* 40(4).

———. 1999b. *A Finger in the Wound: Body Politics in Quincentennial Guatemala.* Berkeley and Los Angeles: Univ. of California Press.

Nwafor, Azinna. 1973. "Liberation and Pan-Africanism." *The Monthly Review* 26(6):12–28.

Oakes, Maud. 1951. *The Two Crosses of Todos Santos.* Bollingen Series 27. Princeton, N.J.: Princeton Univ. Press.

Ochoa García, Carlos. 1993. *Los contextos actuales del poder local: Gobernabilidad y municipalismo.* Guatemala: Palabras del Venado, Friedrich Ebert Colección.

Otzoy, Irma. 1996. "Maya Clothing and Identity." In *Maya Cultural Activism in Guatemala,* Edward R. Fischer and R. McKenna Brown, eds. Austin: Univ. of Texas Press.

———. 1999. "Tecun Uman: From Nationalism to Maya Resistance." PhD. Dissertation, Special Collection, Shields Library, Univ. of California, Davis.

Peeler, John A. 1998. "Social Justice and the New Indigenous Politics: An Analysis of Guatemala and the Central Andes." Paper presented at the Latin American Studies Association Congress, Chicago, September 24–26.

Pellizi, Francesco. 1988. "To Seek Refuge: Nation and Ethnicity in Exile." In *Ethnicities and Nations: Processes of Interethnic Relations in Latin America, South-*

east Asia, and the Pacific, Remo Guideri, Francesco Pellizzi, and Stanley J. Tambiah, eds. Austin: Rothko Chapel Books and Univ. of Texas Press.

Perera, Víctor. 1993. *Unfinished Conquest: The Guatemalan Tragedy.* Berkeley and Los Angeles: Univ. of California Press.

Perera, Víctor, and Robert D. Bruce. 1982. *Los Ultimos Señores de Palenque: Los Lacandones Herederos de los Mayas.* Barcelona: Editorial Argos Vergara.

Petrich, Perla, ed. 1998. *Literatura Oral de los Pueblos del Lago Atitlán.* Casa de Estudios de los Pueblos del Lago Atitlán. Guatemala: Editorial Nawal Wuj.

Prescott, William H. 1934. *The Conquest of Mexico.* New York: The Junior Literary Guild.

Recinos, Adrián. 1978. *El Popol Vuh: Las antiguas historias del Quiché.* Novena Edición. San José, Costa Rica: Editorial Universitaria Centroamericana.

———. 1980. *Memorial de Sololá, Anales de los Cakchiqueles, Título de los Señores de Totonicapán.* México: Fondo de Cultura Económica.

Recinos, Adrián, Delia Goetz, and Sylvanus G. Morley. 1983. *Popol Vuh: The Sacred Book of the Ancient Quiche Maya.* Norman: Univ. of Oklahoma Press.

Redfield, Robert. 1950. *A Village That Chose Progress.* Chicago: Univ. of Chicago Press.

Redfield, Robert, and Alfonso Villa Rojas. 1964. *Chan Kom: A Maya Village.* Chicago: Univ. of Chicago Press.

Reed, Nelson. 1964. *The Caste War of Yucatán.* Stanford, Calif.: Stanford Univ. Press.

REMHI (Proyecto Interdiocesano de Recuperación de la Memoria Histórica). 1998. *Guatemala: Nunca mas.* Guatemala: Oficina de Derechos Humanos del Arzobispado de Guatemala (ODHA),

Riding, Alan. 1985. *Distant Neighbors: A Portrait of the Mexicans.* New York: Knopf.

Rodriguez Guaján, Demetrio (Raxché). 1989. *Cultura maya y políticas de desarrollo.* Guatemala: COCADI.

Said, Edward W. 1979. *Orientalism.* New York: Vintage Books.

Salazar Tetzagüic, Manuel de Jesús. 1992. "La comunidad maya y los ancianos." *Rutzijol,* "Selección Quincenal de Noticias Acerca del Pueblo Maya." Chimaltenango, Guatemala: Centro Maya Saqb'e.

Salazar Tetzagüic, Manuel de Jesús, et al. 1995. *Universidad Maya de Guatemala: Diseño Curricular.* Guatemala: Editorial Cholsamaj.

Sam Colop, Luis Enrique. 1991. *Jub'aqtun Omay Kuchum K'aslemal: Cinco Siglos de Encubrimiento.* Guatemala: Editorial Cholsamaj.

Sanders, William, and Barbara Price. 1968. *Mesoamerica: The Evolution of a Civilization.* New York: Random House.

Sandoval, Franco. 1992. "Los Ancianos: Lección del Popol Vuh." *Rutzijol.* "Selección Quincenal de Noticias Acerca del Pueblo Maya." Chimaltenango, Guatemala: Centro Maya Saqb'e.

Sanford, Victoria D. 1999. "The Rigoberta Menchú Debate." Distributed via e-mail, February.

Schele, Linda, and David Freidel. 1990. *A Forest of Kings: The Untold Story of the Ancient Maya.* New York: Morrow.

Schele, Linda, David Freidel, and Joy Parker. 1993. *Mayan Cosmos: Three Thousand Years on the Shaman's Path.* New York: Morrow.

Schele, Linda, and Mary E. Miller. 1986. *The Blood of Kings: Dynasty and Ritual in Mayan Art.* New York and Fort Worth: George Brazillier and the Kimball Art Museum.

Schirmer, Jennifer. 1998. *The Guatemalan Military Project: A Violence Called Democracy.* Philadelphia: Univ. of Pennsylvania Press.

Smith, Carol A. 1990. "Conclusion: History and Revolution in Guatemala." In *Guatemalan Indians and the State, 1540–1988,* edited by Carol A. Smith, 258–286. Austin: Univ. of Texas Press.

———. 1991. "Mayan Nationalism." *NACLA Report on the Americas* 25(3):29–33.

———. n.d. "Maya Struggles over Time and Space: A Contribution to an Exchange on the Maya Movement in Guatemala." (unpublished manuscript).

Stephens, John L., and Frederick Catherwood. 1841. *Incidents of Travel in Central America, and the Yucatan.* 2 vols. New York: Harper and Brothers.

Stoll, David. 1999. *Rigoberta Menchú and the Story of All Poor Guatemalans.* Boulder, Colo.: Westview Press.

Sullivan, Paul. 1999. "Why Are You the Enemy?" *UC Mexus News* 36 (Winter). Berkeley: Univ. of California Institute on Mexico and the United States.

Taracena, Arturo. 1999. "Arturo Taracena rompe el silencio" (entrevista por Luis Aceituno). *El Periódico* (Guatemala), January 10.

Tedlock, Barbara. 1993. "Mayans and Mayan Studies from 2000 BC to AD 1992." *Latin American Research Review* 28(2/3):154–155.

Tedlock, Dennis. 1985. *Popol Vuh: A Mayan Book of the Dawn of Life.* New York: Simon and Schuster.

Thompson, J. Eric S. 1930. *Ethnology of the Mayans of Southern and Central British Honduras.* Anthropological Series, XVII:2. Chicago: Field Museum of Natural History.

———. 1954. *The Rise and Fall of Maya Civilization.* Norman: Univ. of Oklahoma Press.

Tierney, Patrick. 2000. *Darkness in El Dorado: How Scientists and Journalists Devastated the Amazon.* New York: Norton.

Todorov, Tzvetan. 1987. *The Conquest of America.* New York: Harper and Row.

Trask, Haunani-Kay. 1993. *From a Native Daughter: Colonialism and Sovereignty in Hawai'i.* Monroe, Maine: Common Courage Press.

Trennert, Robert A. 1975. *Alternative to Extinction: Federal Indian Policy and the Beginning of the Reservation System, 1846–1851.* Philadelphia: Temple Univ. Press.

Tzián, Leopoldo. 1994. *Kajlab'alil Mayaiib' Xuq Mu'siib' Ri Ub'antajiik Iximulew; Mayas y ladinos en cifras: El caso de Guatemala.* Guatemala: Editorial Cholsamaj.

Ujpán, Ignacio B., and James D. Sexton. 2001. *Joseño: Another Maya Voice Speaks from Guatemala.* Albuquerque: Univ. of New Mexico Press.

United Nations. 1994. "Acuerdo Sobre Identidad y Derechos de los Pueblos Indígenas." Document signed between the Guatemalan Government and the URNG, March 31, 1994. Jean Arnault, Moderator for the UN, Mexico, D.F.

Van Cott, Donna Lee. 1994. "Indigenous People and Democracy: Issues for Policymakers." In *Indigenous People and Democracy in Latin America,* Donna Lee Van Cott, ed. New York: St. Martin's Press.

Varese, Stefano. 1988. "Multiethnicity and Hegemonic Construction: Indian Plans and the Future." In *Ethnicities and Nations: Process of Interethnic Relations in Latin America, Southeast Asia, and the Pacific,* Remo Guideri, Francesco Pellizi, and Stanley J. Tambiah, eds. Austin: Rothko Chapel Books and Univ. of Texas Press.

Vickers, Scott. 1998. *Native American Identities: From Stereotype to Archetype in Art and Literature.* Albuquerque: Univ. of New Mexico Press.

Vogt, Evon Z. 1964. "The Genetic Model and Maya Cultural Development." In *Desarrollo Cultural de los Mayas,* Evon Z. Vogt and Alberto Ruz, eds., 9–48. México: Universidad Nacional Autónoma de México.

———. 1969. *Zinacantán: A Maya Community in the Highland of Chiapas.* Cambridge, Mass.: Harvard Univ. Press.

Wagley, Charles. 1949. *The Social and Religious Life of a Guatemalan Village.* Memoirs of the American Anthropological Association No. 71. Menasha, Wisc.: American Anthropological Association.

Warren, Kay B. 1993. "Interpreting *la Violencia* in Guatemala: Shapes of Kaqchikel Resistance and Silence." In *The Violence Within: Cultural and Political*

Opposition in Divided Nations, Kay B. Warren, ed. Boulder, Colo.: Westview Press.

———. 1994. "Language and the Politics of Self-Expression: Mayan Revitalization in Guatemala." *Cultural Survival Quarterly* 18(2/3):81–86.

———. 1998a. *Indigenous Movements and Their Critics: Pan-Mayan Activism in Guatemala.* Princeton, N.J.: Princeton Univ. Press.

———. 1998b. "Mayan Multiculturalism and the Violence of Memories." In *Violence and Subjectivity,* edited by Veena Das, Arthur Kleinman, Mamphela Ramphele, and Pamela Reynolds, 296–314. Berkeley and Los Angeles: Univ. of California Press.

Warren, Kay B., and Jean E. Jackson. 2002. *Indigenous Movements, Self-Representation, and the State in Latin America.* Austin: Univ. of Texas Press.

Watanabe, John. 1992. *Maya Saints and Souls in a Changing World.* Austin: Univ. of Texas Press.

Watanabe, John, and Edward F. Fischer, eds. 2004. *Maya Culture, History, and Identity in Post-Colonial Mexico and Guatemala.* Santa Fe, N.Mex.: School of American Research Press (in press).

Webster, David. 2002. *The Fall of the Ancient Maya: Solving the Mystery of the Maya Collapse.* London: Thames and Hudson.

Weiner, Tim. 1995. "Long Road to Truth on Guatemala Killings." *New York Times International,* Friday, March 24. Vol. CXLIV, No.50:010

West, Cornel. 1993. *Keeping Faith: Philosophy and Race in America.* New York: Routledge.

———. 1994. *Race Matters.* New York: Vintage Books.

Whetten, Nathan. 1965. *Guatemala: The Land and the People.* New Haven, Conn.: Yale Univ. Press.

Willey, Gordon R. 1982. "Maya Archaeology." *Science* 215:260–267.

Wilson, Edward O. 1986. *Biophilia: The Human Bond with Other Species.* Cambridge, Mass.: Harvard Univ. Press.

Wilson, Richard. 1995. *Maya Resurgence in Guatemala: Q'eqchi Experiences.* Norman: Univ. of Oklahoma Press.

Wolf, Eric. 1957. "Closed Corporate Peasant Communities in Mesoamerica and Central Java." *Southwestern Journal of Anthropology* 13(1):1–18.

———. 1982. *Europe and the People without History.* Berkeley and Los Angeles: Univ. of California Press.

Woodward, Ralph Lee. 1990. "Changes in the Nineteenth-Century Guatemalan State and Its Indian Policies." In *Guatemalan Indians and the State, 1540–1988,* Carol A. Smith, ed., 52–71. Austin: Univ. of Texas Press.

———. 1993. *Rafael Carrera and the Emergence of the Republic of Guatemala, 1821–1871.* Athens: Univ. of Georgia Press.

Worsley, Peter. 1984. *The Three Worlds: Culture and World Development.* Chicago: Univ. of Chicago Press.

Zapeta, Estuardo. 1994. "Guatemala: Maya Movement at the Political Cross-roads." *Abya Yala News: Journal of the South and Mesoamerican Indian Rights Center* (SAIIC) 8(3).

———. 1999. *Las Huellas de Balam: 1994–1996.* Guatemala: Editorial Cholsamaj.

INDEX

Page numbers in italics refer to photographs.